Women in the Civil Rights Movement

Blacks in the Diaspora

Darlene Clark Hine, John McCluskey, Jr., and David Barry Gaspar
General Editors

[Photo: *Gary Meeks*]

Women in the Civil Rights Movement

TRAILBLAZERS AND TORCHBEARERS, 1941-1965

Edited by Vicki L. Crawford
Jacqueline Anne Rouse, and Barbara Woods

Associate Editors: Broadus Butler
Marymal Dryden, and Melissa Walker

INDIANA UNIVERSITY PRESS
Bloomington and Indianapolis

The articles in this volume were originally presented at the conference *Women in the Civil Rights Movement: Trailblazers and Torchbearers, 1941-1965*, held at the Martin Luther King, Jr. Center for Nonviolent Social Change, October 12-15, 1988. The conference was organized by the Division of Continuing Education of Georgia State University and sponsored jointly by Georgia State University and the Martin Luther King, Jr. Center for Nonviolent Social Change, Inc.

Sandra B. Oldendorf's "The South Carolina Sea Island Citizenship Schools, 1957-1961" appears in an expanded form in *Education of the African American Adult: An Historical Overview*, H. G. Neufeldt and L. McGee, eds. (Greenwood Publishing Group, Inc., Westport, CT). Copyright © 1990 by Harvey G. Neufeldt and Leo McGee. Used with permission.

Charles Payne's "Men Led, But Women Organized" appears in *Women and Social Protest*, Guida West and Rhoda Lois Blumberg, eds. Copyright ©1990 by Oxford University Press, Inc. Reprinted by permission.

Library of Congress Cataloging-in-Publication Data

Women in the civil rights movement : trailblazers and torchbearers,
1941-1965 / edited by Vicki L. Crawford, Jacqueline Anne Rouse, and Barbara Woods;
associate editors, Broadus Butler, Marymal Dryden, and Melissa Walker. — 1st pbk. ed.
    p. cm. — (Blacks in the Diaspora)
  Originally published: New York : Carlson Pub., 1990, in series: Black women in United States history; v. 16.
  "Articles... originally presented at the conference Women in the Civil Rights Movement: Trailblazers and Torchbearers, 1941-1965, held at the Martin Luther King, Jr. Center for Nonviolent Social Change, October 12-15, 1988. . . organized by the Division of Continuing Education of Georgia State University and the Martin Luther King, Jr. Center for Nonviolent Social Change, Inc."—T.p. verso.
  Includes biographical references (p.   ) and index.
  ISBN 0-253-20832-7 (alk. paper)
  1. Civil rights movements—United States—History—20th century—Congresses. 2. Afro-American women—History—20th century—Congresses. 3. Afro-Americans—Civil rights—Congresses. 4. Afro-Americans—History—1877-1964—Congresses. 5. United States—Race relations—Congresses. I. Crawford, Vicki L. II. Rouse, Jacqueline Anne. III. Woods, Barbara, date- IV. Georgia State University. Division of Continuing Education. V. Martin Luther King, Jr. Center for Nonviolent Social Change. VI. Series.
(E185.61.W83 1993)
323.1'73—dc20   93-2727

5   6   7   01   00   99

To

Septima Poinsette Clark

who was scheduled to appear on the program,
but who died before this conference took place

Modjesta Monteith Simkins

who was scheduled to appear on the program,
but whose hospitalization prevented her from attending

and

Myles Horton

who attended the conference and was honored at the banquet

and to three pioneer civil rights activists
in whose spirit this conference was organized

Ella Jo Baker, Fannie Lou Hamer, and Viola Gregg Liuzzo

We came together to celebrate their lives
as well as to recognize the contributions of other women
of all racial and ethnic backgrounds in local communities
who were Trailblazers and Torchbearers
in the civil rights movement.

Contents

List of Illustrations

Acknowledgments

The seed of the conference at which these papers were originally presented, *Women in the Civil Rights Movement: Trailblazers and Torchbearers, 1941-1965*, was planted when Marymal Dryden, Unit Head for Public Service of the Division of Continuing Education at Georgia State University was viewing the television documentary, *Eyes on the Prize*, in 1987. The series inspired Mrs. Dryden to conceive a national meeting that would highlight the role of women participants in the movement, many of whom had not received the same media attention as their male counterparts. She wanted to learn more about the Trailblazers—"women whose heroic acts initiated specific events"—and Torchbearers—"those who continue to carry on the struggle for reform."

Working toward the end of developing a national conference, Mrs. Dryden approached Mrs. Coretta Scott King, President of the Martin Luther King, Jr. Center for Nonviolent Social Change, Inc., for her assistance. Mrs. Dryden also formed a planning committee composed of six individuals who spearheaded this effort to its completion: Liliane K. Baxter, Director of Nonviolence Training and Research at the King Center, Vicki Crawford, Assistant Professor of English at Morehouse College, Marymal Dryden from Georgia State, Jacqueline A. Rouse, Associate Professor of History at Morehouse College, Melissa Walker, Associate Professor and Chair, Department of English, Mercer University, and Barbara A. Woods, Assistant Professor of English at Southern College of Technology.

The Planning Committee recommended a non-traditional meeting, bringing together both activists and scholars on one program. The resulting conference both inspired participants and recognized the contributions of those activists whose hard work and dedication had not been widely acclaimed outside of their immediate circles. The conference and this book were a collective effort, but credit and particular acknowledgment for the overall success of the conference, and for the existence of this book, must be given to Mrs. Marymal Dryden of Georgia State University, whose dedication, perserverance, guidance and tenacity kept everything going, even when expected financial resources and other promised assistance were not forthcoming.

Participants came from all sections of the United States and from abroad, including Canada, Brazil, and England. Our participants from Brazil, representing the Irmadade da Boa Morte (Sisterhood of Good Death), gave a special international aspect. The original purpose of their organization was the liberation of Afro-Brazilian women from slavery, the oldest surviving such group in the New World.

The conference participants commented repeatedly in conversations and written evaluations about one particular dimension of the conference—the inclusion and centrality of the women civil rights activists themselves. Much credit for this must be given to the co-conveners of the conference, Mrs. Rosa Parks and Mrs. Coretta Scott King. Mrs. King also served a principal role in inviting movement activists to the conference as well as providing the conference with national recognition. The intergenerational representation included senior activists who are octogenarians and septuagenarians and younger activists who began as student workers in SCLC and SNCC. Among the senior activists, we were delighted to have Juanita Abernathy, Gloria Rackley Blackwell, Anne Braden, Ella Mae Brayboy, Mary Fair Burks, Melissa Smith Burkehalter, Johnnie Carr, Bertha Mae Carter, Dorothy Cotton, Victoria Way DeLee, Annie Devine, Virginia Durr, Christine King Farris, Polly Heidelberg, Dorothy Height, Winson Hudson, Dovie Hudson, Evelyn Lowery, Gloria Richardson, and Myles Horton, male stalwart, whose work at the Highlander Folk School gave great support and assistance to women activists. Myles was the only male honored at the conference banquet. Among the younger activists were Joyce Ladner, Bernice Johnson Reagon, Martha Norman, Constance Curry, and male stalwart, Worth Long. The presence of all these people gave an authenticity for those of us who study and write about the movement that would not have been possible without this hands-on, face-to-face encounter. Many scholars took advantage of the opportunity to conduct interviews with the activists. Also, to complement the historical aspects of the conference, we heard noted literary people reading from their works: Margaret Walker Alexander, Toni Cade Bambara, Rosellen Brown, and Pearl Cleage.

Special thanks must also be given to Senior Vice President and Treasurer of the King Center, Mrs. Christine King Farris, for use of the King Center as the conference site. The help of the Center's staff and use of their physical facilities added a dimension that would not have been possible if the conference site had been elsewhere. Significant archival assistance was provided by the King Center Library and Archives staff, including Broadus Butler, Louise Cook, Ralph Luker and Diane Ware. Video and audio documentation was provided by the King Center Media Services Department, in particular S. R. (Stoney) Johnson and Althea Sumpter. "Rites, Rituals and Rights," an original theatrical production sponsored by the King Center's Cultural Affairs Program, premiered during the conference. A significant highlight of the conference was the rededication ceremony for the Rosa Parks Exhibit and Conference Room. King Center staff who must be given special thanks for their assistance in all aspects of the conference include Sandi Jossie, K. Lynn Cothren, Claudia Young-Hill, Rhonda Hall and Cheryl Odeleye. The historic location on Auburn Avenue in the area comprising the "Sweet Auburn" district of Atlanta, including the Ebenezer Baptist Church, the Wheat Street Baptist Church and the headquarters of the Southern Christian Leadership Conference, was especially appropriate, for it was in these quarters that many of the important decisions of the American civil rights movement were made.

Not only was the spirit of volunteerism present among the planners, but many educational institutions and corporate sponsors gave donations to the conference. The beautiful thirty-six page program was a gift of Southern Bell. Other corporate and community sponsors included the Coca Cola Company, the National Board of the YWCA of the USA, the National Association for the Advancement of Colored People, the Legal Defense Fund, Inc., the Southern Christian Leadership Conference, the Georgia Association of Black Women Attorneys, the Peachtree Suburban Chapter of Links, Inc., the Fulton County Arts Council and the Atlanta-Fulton County Library. Area educational institutions which gave financial support were Georgia Institute of Technology, the Interdenominational Theological Center, Kennesaw State College, Mercer University (Atlanta campus), Morehouse College, Southern College of Technology and Spelman College. Without their gracious support, many aspects of the program would not have been possible. The special funding of the Georgia Humanities Council and the Division of Continuing Education at Georgia State University made possible the early planning of the conference.

Much appreciation is also expressed for the media support that we enjoyed. With the support of Virginia Durr, we received coverage on the NBC *Today* show. Other coverage was given in *USA Today*, in the Atlanta area newspapers, and in newspapers and magazines in various parts of the country, as far away as Kennebunkport, Maine, where conference participant Megan Morris lived, a twelve-year-old sixth grader who was our youngest participant. The torch, the symbol of the continuing struggle, was passed on to Megan and to other young people at the conference.

Last, but not least in any way, we wish to acknowledge the Planning and Steering Committee, the Conference Executive Committee, the Cultural Affairs Committee (chaired by Liliane K. Baxter) and the staff of the Continuing Education Division at Georgia State University. Dr. Steve Langston, Director of the Division of Continuing Education and Assistant Vice President for Public Service, Byron Leach, Eva Trussel, Judith Allen Myrick, and Blanche Tarkington worked with Marymal Dryden to make this project a reality.

We would like to give special recognition to Emory University and its programs that highlight the special contributions of African-Americans and women to American history, especially the Institute for the Liberal Arts, a graduate interdisciplinary program. Four of the editors of this volume received their Ph.D's from Emory—Vicki Crawford (1987), Jacqueline Anne Rouse (1983), Melissa Walker (1974), and Barbara A. Woods (1978). We didn't know each other as students, but our common interests attest to the lasting effect that Emory's programs have on its graduates.

The essays presented in this volume represent only a fraction of the papers and panels at the conference, which proved to be a significant event rectifying a major omission in the history of the civil rights movement. This volume should be merely a beginning account of the lives of heroic American women civil rights activists. Succeeding volumes will complete the story of the conference as future researchers evaluate the political movements and forces which altered the character of modern American life.

Editors' Introduction

African-American women have played significant roles in the ongoing struggle for freedom and equality. Beginning with the abolitionist movement, black women have championed causes which promoted equal justice for all. They have organized and led struggles for suffrage, fair housing, temperance, antilynching laws, as well as to abolish poll taxes, white primaries, Jim Crow laws, and to obtain full employment for themselves and their men, and for equal educational facilities for their children. In the early decades of the twentieth century, they led much of the interracial movement to improve race relations. Hence the civil rights movement of the fifties and sixties is merely the continuation of a long-standing tradition. Still, few published accounts of the civil rights era document the major role women played in the modern movement for social change. On October 12-15, 1988, a conference was called to focus on these women. *Women in the Civil Rights Movement, Trailblazers and Torchbearers, 1941-1965* was convened in Atlanta by Georgia State University and the Martin Luther King, Jr., Center for Nonviolent Social Change. The conference was unique in bringing together for the first time activists as well as scholars of the movement. Broadly, the goals of the conference were to identify, acknowledge, and celebrate individual and group participation by women as activists, journalists, students, entertainers, attorneys, and others who struggled for reform. In addition, we sought to continue the dialogue between scholars and activists concerning social change and methods of empowerment, and to open up new questions and possibilities for the decade ahead. Four themes were then identified as a means of organizing discussion: Women and the Church—Laying the Foundation for Nonviolent Social Change; Empowerment, Citizenship, and Community Building; Civil Rights Activism and the Intersection of Race, Class, and Gender; and Forging Our New Agenda.

The papers that were selected for this volume make clear that women had a multiplicity of roles in the civil rights movement and that not all experienced it in the same way. Taken together, these papers also reveal a very different perspective on the movement from the standpoint of the women involved, a view that has been largely neglected in accounts that focus on male leadership and experience. This volume brings together for the first time many previously unheard and marginalized voices that speak to black women's unique contributions, especially in leading and sustaining the movement in local communities throughout the South. Black women's own self-perceptions and understanding of their patterns of action resonate in each account. The relentless courage and commitment of women is evident here, as well as the enormous risks and sacrifices involved. These papers reveal the sister strength of black women in shaping the direction and outcome the movement would take.

But this is only the beginning of what promises to be a rich new field of inquiry. Scholars are in the early stages of unearthing the rich sources of women's activism. Future scholarship promises not only to reclaim these experiences, but also to analyze them critically, thereby challenging previously held assumptions about the civil rights movement.

In the leading essay in the volume, Charles Payne documents the important leadership roles of black women in one rural southern community. He explores the high proportion of women involved in the movement. In examining the work of female and male activists in and around Greenwood, Mississippi, Payne sorts out conflicting lines of argument constructed to explain the predominance of women, thereby clearing the ground for a deeper understanding of their patterns of activism.

In another study of black women's involvement in Mississippi, Vicki Crawford focuses on grassroots activists and considers factors such as age and class in shaping the level and extent of their participation in the movement. By examining the work of three organizers, she shows how women with varying skills and resources utilized their talents in mobilizing others in rural communities.

The life and exemplary work of Fannie Lou Hamer, a sharecropper who lost her job and was constantly harassed for attempting to register to vote in rural Mississippi, is the subject of several papers. While Mamie Locke is concerned with Hamer's role as one of the cofounders and co-chairs of the Mississippi Freedom Democratic Party established in 1964 to challenge the seating of Mississippi's all-white regular Democratic Party, Jacquelyn Grant explores the rich texture of Hamer's religious philosophy. In both instances, we come to understand the larger vision held by Hamer in seeking freedom for all oppressed people. These papers make clear that Fannie Lou Hamer understood and articulated the connectedness of struggles across not only race, but class and gender lines as well.

Ella Baker was another outstanding leader and nationally recognized figure whose life provided a model in grassroots activism. Carol Mueller traces the ideological thought and values adopted by the student-based movements of the 1960s and the women's movement back to the ideas and values of Baker. As Mueller shows, Baker's non-hierarchical, egalitarian leadership style formed the major framework for establishing the Student Nonviolent Coordinating Committee and other movements among grassroots people.

While the press and other popular accounts of the civil rights movement have recorded the beginnings of the Montgomery bus boycott as a result of Rosa Parks's act of rebellion against the racist bus system in that city, little is known about the groundwork laid by numerous black women in the Women's Political Council long before the bus incident. Mary Fair Burks, founder of the organization, has resurrected the work of these women and provided insight into the roles of middle-class black women in bringing about social change. She documents how women's networks such as the WPC were not only initiators of action, but sources for spiritual and intellectual empowerment as well.

The pioneering roles and contributions of Septima Clark and Modjeska Simkins in South Carolina add to the rich legacy of women's leadership in local communities. Grace McFadden reviews the life and work of Septima Clark. She documents her dismissal from the public school system as a result of attempts to establish equal pay between black and white teachers. McFadden gives us a sense of the personal loss suffered by Clark and shows how she progressively became more involved in civil rights. Clark's distinguished record in registering blacks to vote and in citizenship education form the basis for the discussion. Like her colleague and friend Septima Clark, with whom she worked while both were teachers at Booker T. Washington School in Columbia, Modjeska Simkins began her activism on a local level and extended her activities to the southern region. Barbara Woods has given a background of Simkins' early life and professional career, focusing primarily on her years as secretary of the South Carolina Conference of the NAACP. As one of the founders of this organization in 1939, Simkins played a central role in the development of major lawsuits sponsored by the NAACP in South Carolina during the 1940s and 1950s. The most significant lawsuit brought by the South Carolina body was *Briggs* v. *Elliot*, which became the first of the five cases which were merged to form the landmark *Brown* v. *Board of Education of Topeka* case which outlawed segregation in the nation's public schools.

The role of Gloria Richardson in the civil rights movement in Cambridge, Maryland, is Annette Brock's subject. She demonstrates how a family of activists supported the work of this leader. Richardson worked with her mother and sister in organizing boycotts and sit-ins in that city.

Donna Langston and Sandra Oldendorf examine the significant roles played by women in education throughout the South and point to the importance of citizenship training in empowering local people and getting them to register to vote. While Langston focuses on the Highlander Folk School and the women involved there, Oldendorf explains the role of black women such as Bernice Robinson and Septima Clark in organizing people on the South Carolina Sea Islands.

Black women participated in the civil rights movement at every level and Anne Standley's paper provides an overview of their involvement. Relying on extensive quotations from such activists as Bernice Reagon, Daisy Bates, Anne Moody and Joyce Ladner she shows that these women played not one role in the black freedom struggle, but many.

The cultural and artistic expressions of the civil rights movement were a tremendous empowering and sustaining force. The freedom songs that were sung at mass meetings, protest marches, and elsewhere were one form of self-expression black women excelled in. No one was more eloquent and moving than Fannie Lou Hamer in this regard. Activist and scholar Bernice Johnson Reagon offers a powerful portrait of Hamer and the role of black women as transmitters of culture. She tells of the significance of song as it originated in the oral tradition of African-American culture and how it propelled the freedom struggle. Reagon's analysis is informed by her own role in the movement as an activist and member of the Freedom Singers, a nationally recognized group organized by SNCC workers in the Albany Movement in 1962.

In looking further at the culture and artistic expression of the civil rights movement, Clarissa Myrick-Harris points out the cultural contributions made by black women through the Free Southern Theater, a dramatic troupe that sought to raise political consciousness through theatrical presentations. In her discussion of two members of the Free Southern Theater, Myrick-Harris shows how the experiences of these younger women in the movement were not only a source of collective action, but also a basis for self-definition and personal liberation.

Finally, papers by Allida Black, Alice Knotts, and Sharlene Cochrane focus on the early period of women's activism, beginning in the early decades of the twentieth century. Black explores Eleanor Roosevelt's commitment to racial equality. Using three examples from Roosevelt's activism—Marian Anderson's 1939 concert, Pauli Murray, and the Odell Waller case—Black illustrates her demand that democracy be practiced without any limits or qualifications. The papers by Knotts and Cochrane concentrate on the struggle for racial equality by the Methodist Church and in the Young Women's Christian Association. Knotts' review of the Methodist Church women discusses their efforts to desegregate the public schools and to end discrimination in housing. Cochrane recounts the history of black female participation in the Boston YWCA. Constant pressure from activists like Lucy Miller Mitchell sought to convert the rhetoric and ideals of the YWCA into actual practice.

All of the papers included here make a major contribution to our knowledge of the little-known individual and collective efforts among black women in the civil rights movement. They are particularly valuable because of what they reveal about the successes and achievements as well as the problems and conflicts faced by these women. We hope that this volume will stimulate additional research to identify and analyze the contributions of black women in shaping the course of American history.

Vicki Crawford
Jacqueline Rouse
Barbara Woods

Women in the Civil
Rights Movement

Men Led, but Women Organized: Movement Participation of Women in the Mississippi Delta

CHARLES PAYNE

Prior to the summer of 1964, the civil rights movement had achieved few victories, especially in the rural South. The federal government, its rhetoric notwithstanding, was vacillating in its support for civil rights workers; the repressive powers of white supremacists were extensive; most blacks in the Mississippi Delta were afraid of any form of political involvement. The decision to join the movement in that early period, then, was very different from the decision to join later. It was a chancier, much more dangerous proposition, dangerous enough that the overwhelming response of local blacks in the Delta when organizers from the Student Nonviolent Coordinating Committee or other groups first entered a town was to keep them at arms' length. The men and women who signed on in the early years were very much in the minority in their communities. Nevertheless, vigorous and sustained movements were created across the Delta. I am in the process of studying the movement in and around Greenwood, Mississippi.

One of the important questions emerging from any study of the civil rights movement is the question of the overparticipation of women. My respondents, male and female, unanimously agree with Lawrence Guyot, a member of SNCC: "It's no secret that young people and women led organizationally."[1] Women took civil rights workers into their homes, of

1

course, giving them a place to eat and sleep, but women also canvassed more than men, showed up more often at mass meetings and demonstrations, and more frequently attempted to register to vote.

This paper is a preliminary attempt to suggest explanations for the greater willingness of women to join the movement in the early 1960s, a pattern all the more interesting because the pattern of the 1950s is quite different. In that more dangerous decade, black political activism in rural Mississippi was dominated by men, most of them associated with the NAACP, the Regional Council of Negro Leadership, or both—Amzie Moore, Aaron Henry, Medgar Evers, Clyde Kennard, E. W. Steptoe, C. J. Stringer, Vernon Dahmier, T. R. W. Howard, and others. It is true that, historically, black women have always fulfilled social roles not commonly played by women in white society, but that has not always led to the kind of dominance of political activity that existed in rural Mississippi in the 1960s. This higher degree of participation by women is interesting too because the standard position among political scientists has been that, "Women all over the world are less active in politics than men."[2]

The pattern of participation seems to be age-specific. That is, among older people, there is no clear sexual imbalance. In fact, in the earliest days of the movement in Greenwood, a number of older men, men in their fifties and sixties, played important roles in getting the movement off the ground.[3] Similarly, there is no appreciable difference between teenage boys and teenage girls. The gender difference is strongest in the years inbetween, roughly thirty to fifty. In that age range, some of my respondents estimated that women were three or four times more likely than men to participate.

Although the people to whom I spoke generally agreed about the nature of the pattern, there was no consensus on the reasons. They offered a variety of conflicting, sometimes contradictory explanations, and many had no way to account for the difference. Even those who did offer explanations were not confident about them or anxious to defend them. It was also my impression that these gender differences were not something my respondents had given a lot of thought to, even though they were aware of them. Given that in 1963 gender was not as politicized a social category as it is now, this is not surprising.

One factor that should be considered is SNCC's operating style. SNCC was the most active organization in the Delta and it was relatively open to women. If anyone can be called the founder of SNCC, it is Ella Baker, and in SNCC's early years, women were always involved in the development of policy and the execution of the group's program. The group was antibureaucratic and antihierarchical, willing to work with anyone who was willing to have them, traditional considerations of status notwithstanding. They worked with sharecroppers as well as doctors, with the pool room crowd as well as the church crowd. SNCC organizers emphasized finding and developing nontraditional sources of leadership. Women obviously represented an enormous pool of untapped leadership potential. Much of SNCC's organizing activity in the Delta involved door-to-door canvassing, which meant that women were as likely as men to encounter organizers. SNCC, despite the traditional definitions of sex roles held by many of its members, was structurally open to female participation in a way that many older organizations were not. Had SNCC employed a more traditional style of organizing—working primarily through previously established leader-ship—it might not have achieved the degree of female participation it did. Still, saying that SNCC was open to the participation of women does not explain why women were responsive.

One explanation that initially seems plausible—demographics—can be rejected. The argument here goes that the massive migrations out of the South in the 1940s and 1950s drew away more men in the twenty-to-forty age range than it did women. Thus there were simply more women around in the 1960s when the movement began. It is true that the migrations, especially in the early stages, took a large number of men out of the Delta, but at least for Greenwood, even when one looks at families where both husband and wife are present, the wives were far more likely to participate.

Some of the other suggested explanations are not so easily disposed of. One idea, mentioned by several respondents, is that women were less exposed to reprisals than men. The argument goes that Southern whites were less afraid of black women and thus less likely to initiate either physical violence or economic reprisals against them. Even when economic reprisals were used, the wife's salary was likely to be less important to the family than the husband's. If anyone was going to be fired, better the woman. In short, it was safer and more cost-effective for women to participate.

I do not find the differential reprisal position plausible. If, under normal circumstances, whites were more indulgent of transgressions of racial norms when they came from black women, it does not follow that the same indulgence would extend to the highly charged, abnormal situation of 1962 and 1963. By that time, whites in the Delta clearly felt threatened, and it

3

seems likely that they would have struck back at whomever they associated with the threat, old indulgences notwithstanding.

Moreover, even if a pattern of indulgence, in fact, existed, it may not have been apparent to women who were thinking about joining the movement. Reprisals against women in the rural South were constant and highly visible. Examination of SNCC's newsletters in 1962 and 1963 suggests that some of the most violent incidents of reprisals took place against women. Women who were even rumored to be part of the movement lost their jobs. Every adult woman I interviewed got fired, except for those who quit because they expected to get fired. Women were regularly clubbed at demonstrations or beaten in jail. The homes of women activists were regularly shot into. Any woman in the Delta who contemplated joining the early movement had to be aware of all this. In such a situation, even if there were some gender-related differences in the likelihood of reprisal, the women involved may not have noticed it.

Moreover, it is misleading to think of reprisals as being directed against merely the individual who was involved. Anyone who joined the movement placed his or her whole family at risk. When one person got evicted, the entire family was evicted. True, the man pressured by his boss to get his wife out of the movement could say, "Gee, boss, I can't do anything with her, you know how women are," and hope for a sympathetic response. It was only a hope, though. The Citizen's Council in particular made it a point to put pressure on the entire family. If anyone in a family was known to be a part of the movement, every adult in that family was likely to have trouble finding work or getting credit. Similarly, the most popular forms of violence in that period—arson, drive-by shootings into homes, and bombings—were reprisals against family units, not individuals.

As the severity of reprisals eventually lessened, there was not necessarily a corresponding increase in male participation. Lawrence Guyot, drawing on his experience organizing the Mississippi Freedom Democratic Party, noted that in the mid-1960s, when repression had slacked off some, there was no sudden rush of men into political activism. Indeed, Guyot recalls telling a group of women that included Victoria Gray, Fannie Lou Hamer, and Annie Devine that the time had come for them to step back and let the men come forth (a mistake he says he would not make today).

Finally, the differential reprisal interpretation strikes me as unconvincing because no woman to whom I spoke ever suggested, even indirectly, that *her own* involvement could be explained in such terms. Nor did anyone ever

4

identify any specific woman whose participation was affected by the reprisal issue.

When explaining their own decisions to join the movement, my respondents constructed answers primarily in terms of either religious belief or preexisting social networks of kinship and friendship. For many women, both factors seem operative. Thus, Lou Emma Allen was drawn into the movement by her son, a junior college student. Though she was often afraid, she was sure the Lord would see her through. She frequently led the singing at mass meetings in Greenwood. Appropriately, the first song she ever sang was "Take Your Burdens to the Lord and Leave Them There." Belle Johnson got involved after June, her fourteen-year-old daughter, was arrested along with Fannie Lou Hamer and Annelle Ponder and beaten brutally. Laura McGhee explained that she was initially interested in the movement because of her brother, a courageous NAACP officer who had been shot a few years earlier. Susie Morgan was drawn in partly by the activity of her daughters. She prayed and prayed over the decision to join and finally she saw that it was what the Lord wanted her to do. Ethel Gray was drawn into the movement by an old friend. After she joined, people drove by and threw rattlesnakes on her porch but, "We stood up. Me and God stood up." The pattern in their histories is one of joining initially because of relatives or friends and then feeling a source of support from the Lord. (There was also a third theme, which I am not going to discuss here—the growing admiration some of them felt for the young SNCC organizers.)

The religious issue raises a series of important questions. One line of explanation for the overparticipation of women might go as follows: The movement grew out of the church. Women participate in the church more than men do. (One estimate is that across all varieties of black religious activities, women represent seventy-five to ninety percent of the participants.)[5] Therefore, women were naturally more drawn to the movement.

This argument confuses the church in the urban South with that in the rural South. In urban areas, the churches certainly were an early focal point of organizing activity.[6] It is not surprising that there was a high level of participation by women in the activities of the SCLC because many of that organization's affiliates were large urban churches populated largely by women. Their rural counterparts, however, were far less supportive of the movement. In Greenwood, as in much of the Delta, the movement grew in spite of the church. In the first six months after SNCC workers came to

5

Greenwood, only two churches were open to them and one of them was only halfheartedly supportive. One of the common themes in speeches at meetings of that period was the hypocrisy and cowardice of ministers. Nine months after the first organizers came, Greenwood was fairly well mobilized—hundreds of people were trying to register and there were marches and mass meetings on a daily basis. Only *after* the general population was aroused did thirty-one black ministers sign a statement of support for the movement. How sincere they were is open to question. Sometime after they signed the statement of support, SNCC's Bob Moses wrote a memo saying that the lack of real cooperation from ministers was still the biggest single problem facing the local movement. (Ironically, sanctified churches, which historically have allowed women wider scope than other denominations, were probably the slowest to join the movement; Methodist churches were probably the fastest to do so.)

Those in the Delta who joined the movement in the early days, then, ordinarily did so in defiance of their church leadership. Nonetheless, if the church as an organization did not lead people into the movement, the religiosity of the population may have been more important. I noted that it is important to make a distinction between the pre- and post-1964 periods. The victories that affected the daily life of the average person began in the summer of 1964 with the Public Accommodations Bill. After that we got the Voting Rights Act, bringing federal registrars to the South. The same period saw a decline in the frequency of both economic and physical reprisals and increasingly vigorous federal prosecution of those who persisted in violence.

Those who joined the movement in its early days could not have known that things would work out as they did. What they did know for certain was that those who joined were going to suffer for it. From the viewpoint of most rural black Southerners in 1962 or 1963, the overwhelming preponderance of evidence must have suggested that the movement was going to fail. Joining a movement under such circumstances may literally require an act of faith. Durkheim noted the empowering function of religion: "The believer who has communicated with his god is not merely a man who sees new truths of which the unbeliever is ignorant; he is a man who is stronger. He feels within him more force either to endure the trials of existence or to conquer them."[7] Durkheim may have gotten the gender wrong, but the analysis is right. Faith in the Lord made it easier to have faith in the possibility of social change. As the slaves of a century ago, according to Du Bois, saw the fulfillment of biblical prophecy in the coming of the Civil War, residents of the Delta may have seen the civil rights movement as a sign that God was stirring. The civil rights workers, most of them Southerners and native Mississippians in this early period, were careful to respect the religious beliefs of local communities and often held the same kinds of beliefs themselves. A constant element in their rhetoric was that God was with the movement. Such an argument would have the most impact with the most religious—women rather than men, older men rather than younger ones.

It might be helpful to know more about why women, regardless of race, age, or education, are more religious than men in the first place. Despite considerable research, there is no clear answer. But the pattern seems to hold, by any measure of religiosity, for all major Western religions other than Judaism. The difference does not appear to be related to gender differences in labor force participation[8] or to the greater role that women play in the socialization of children.[9] Another popular notion, in the tradition of some Marxist thought, is that the church serves to compensate those most deprived of "real" rewards—women, the poor, the elderly. Attempts to support that interpretation have generally failed.[10] In fact, in many populations, the most economically privileged appear more religious than the least privileged, although among blacks there seems to be no relationship between religiosity and social status.[11]

If previous research does not provide any explanation of the generally greater religiosity of women, the literature has ordinarily been interpreted to mean that strong religious feelings ought to militate against participation in a change-oriented movement. One review of the literature concludes that the values reinforced by traditional churches:

> . . . include a world view focused on the private sector of life and with such immediate social orientations as the family, ethnic group or local community. They are associated with conformity and conservatism in all attitude realms and with personal and privatistic commitments not oriented to social change. They value conformity and tradition more than individual freedom and tolerance of diversity, social conservatism more than social change, and definite moral codes more than individualized moral orientations.[12]

This interpretation, consistent with the idea of religion as opiate, obviously does not cover the situation of Southern blacks. If the pre-1950s history of the rural black church conforms to this model,[13] the history since then suggests that there is nothing inherently conservative about the church, that

7

its message can as easily be packaged in order-threatening as in order-serving ways. Similarly, it is ironic that investment in "personal and privatistic commitments" should be thought to be conservatizing. Among the women I have studied, it is just such commitments that played a large role in drawing them into the movement. A more flexible model might hold that involvement in such commitments ordinarily militates against involvement in social movements, but once any one person in the network becomes politically involved, the strength of the social ties within the network is likely to draw other members in. In the Delta, there were two populations predisposed to the message that SNCC conveyed. One consisted of mostly older men associated with the NAACP who had been active around issues of voter registration since the 1950s. Thus, when Sam Block, SNCC's first organizer in Greenwood, arrived, an older man named Cleve Jordan, a man with a local reputation as a hellraiser on the registration issue, introduced him to people around town who would be responsive. The other group that responded quickly were young people. Better educated than their parents, more knowledgeable about the broader society, many of them were easily attracted to the movement, frequently against their parents' wishes. Thus the situation that SNCC usually encountered in the Delta was that while most people were initially afraid, some were interested right away and given the tightly knit social bonds of rural communities, they were able to pull others in. Since women tend to be more deeply invested than men in networks of kin and community, it is not surprising that more women tended to be drawn in during the early stages. When teenage children were drawn in, for example, that seems to have a greater affect on their mothers and aunts than on their male relatives.

The greater investment of women in kin and communal networks should also affect the nature of their work inside the movement, an idea suggested by Karen Sacks's contemporary analysis of a union-organizing drive among black women in a Southern hospital. Sacks was particularly concerned with the differing styles of leadership exhibited by men and women. As one of the women participants put it, "Women are organizers, men are leaders." That is, "women created the organization, made people feel a part of it, as well as doing the everyday work upon which most things depended, while men made public announcements, confronted and negotiated with management." Certain women operated as network centers, mobilizing existing social networks around the organizing goals, mediating conflicts, conveying information, coordinating activity, in short, "creating and sustaining good relations and

8

solidarity among co-workers."[14] Many of these skills seemed to be rooted in the way these women operated in their families. I suspect Sacks's description of the leadership style of the women she studied would also fit very well the role played by rural women in the civil rights movement, which raises another question. All apart from the issue of why more women were drawn to the movement, there is the issue of how such high levels of female participation changed the overall tone of the movement. Drake and Cayton claimed in their study of Chicago that black women community leaders were more trusted than men, at least in part because of the perception that women could not as easily capitalize off of their activities.[15] Similarly, the preponderance of women in the movement may have helped to create an atmosphere in which it was relatively easy to establish and maintain trust. At a guess, one would think that the participation of so many women meant that relationships inside the movement would have been less competitive and more nurturing than would have been the case otherwise. These women very clearly came to see SNCC organizers and some of the other out-of-town volunteers as their children. A movement with these familistic overtones, overtones reinforced in early SNCC by its ideal of the Beloved Community, must have been a supportive and empowering political environment. At a point in the movement's history when the prospects for success seemed poor, when the stresses and tensions involved in organizing were great, such a climate may have done much to sustain the activists.

While religiosity is among the issues stressed by the people I spoke to, it may be an error to take it too literally. Alberta Barnet, a Greenwood resident who joined the movement while still in high school, said: "Round here women just go out for meetings and things more than men. Men just don't do it. They don't participate in a lot of things. The most they participate in is a trade." She suggests that much of the organizational life of black Greenwood, not just the church and the movement, was dependent on women. Ella Baker, who had decades of experience as an organizer in the South, felt much the same way and as early as the late 1950s had tried to talk SCLC into developing programs that put more emphasis on women.[16] Gilkes found that in the contemporary urban North, black women community workers are more common than men,[17] which is consistent with my own experience with community organizations. Similar patterns may sometimes exist in white communities. McCourt's study of community organizations in a working-class white ethnic Chicago community found them dominated by women.[18]

Thus, the pattern of relatively high levels of female participation among either black or working-class women seems to exist in several types of nontraditional political activities in widely differing circumstances. Even without a more precise description, it seems unlikely that religion would have the centrality in all of these circumstances that it had in the Delta.

The important element, then, may not be so much religion itself as the sense of efficacy it can engender. One way to get at this is to look at situations in which men did participate in large numbers. In the Delta, one such place was Holmes County, just south of Greenwood. According to my interviews, Holmes County was one place where the movement was dominated by men from the very beginning. Indeed, the men of Holmes County did not wait for organizers to get around to them; they went to Greenwood and invited organizers to Holmes. Holmes has a distinctive history. It has traditionally been a black-majority county, which is not unusual for the Delta, but since before World War II it has also been a county in which most of the land has been owned by blacks. It is almost certain landownership gave them a greater degree of freedom from economic reprisals, but one student of the county's history feels that the tradition of landownership and cooperative work contributed to a distinctive worldview among the men. Salamon found that compared to local sharecroppers, the landowners were more optimistic about the future, had a higher sense of personal efficacy, and were more likely to feel that they had been of help to others.[19] By every measure, landowners were far more likely to participate in the early civil rights movement. Thus it may be that landowning for men, perhaps especially when blacks own whole communities, has some of the same psychological effects as religion for women, particularly with respect to an enhanced sense of personal efficacy.

NOTES

1. Quoted in Howell Raines, *My Soul Is Rested* (New York: Putnam, 1977), p. 241.
2. Donald Matthews and James Prothro, *Negroes and the New Southern Politics* (New York: Harcourt, 1966), p. 65.
3. Joe Sinsheimer,"Never Turn Back," *Southern Exposure* (Summer 1987).
4. Sara Evans, *Personal Politics* (New York: Vintage, 1980).
5. Cheryl Gilkes, "Together and In Harness: Women's Traditions in the Sanctified Church," *Signs* (Summer 1985), p. 679.

6. Aldon Morris, *The Origins of the Civil Rights Movement* (New York: Free Press, 1984).
7. Emile Durkheim, *Elementary Forms of the Religious Life* (New York: Free Press, 1965), p. 494.
8. Holley Ulbrich and Myles Wallace, "Women's Work Force Status and Church Attendance," *Journal for the Scientific Study of Religion* (1984).
9. Dean Hoge and D. Roozen, *Understanding Church Growth and Decline* (New York: Pilgrim Press, 1979).
10. *Ibid.*
11. Leonard Beeghley, E. Van Velsor, and E.W. Block, "Correlates of Religiosity Among Black and White Americans," *Sociological Quarterly* (Summer 1981).
12. Hoge and Roozen, *Understanding Church Growth.*
13. Harry Richardson, *Dark Glory: A Picture of the Church Among Negroes in the Rural South* (New York: Friendship Press, 1947); David Cohn, *Where I Was Born and Raised* (Boston: Houghton, Mifflin, 1948), pp. 173-84; J. Edward Arbor, "Upon This Rock," *Crisis* (April 1935).
14. Karen Sacks, "Gender and Grassroots Leadership" (unpublished paper, University of California at Los Angeles, n.d.), pp. 5, 16.
15. St. Clair Drake and Horace Cayton, *Black Metropolis* (Chicago: University of Chicago Press, 1970), pp. 393-94.
16. Eugene Walker, "Interview with Ella Baker: 9/4/74," Southern Historical Collection, University of North Carolina, Chapel Hill, p. 21.
17. Cheryl Gilkes, "Building in Many Places: Multiple Commitments and Ideologies in Black Women's Community Work," in A. Bookman and S. Morgan, eds., *Women and the Politics of Empowerment* (Philadelphia: Temple University Press, 1988).
18. Kathleen McCourt, *Working Class Women and Grassroots Politics* (Bloomington: Indiana University Press, 1977), pp. 42-43.
19. Lester Salamon, "The Time Dimension in Policy Evaluation: The Case of the New Deal Land Reform Experiments," *Public Policy* (Spring 1979).

Beyond the Human Self: Grassroots Activists in the Mississippi Civil Rights Movement

VICKI CRAWFORD

Despite the major influence of black women in the civil rights movement of the 1950s and 1960s, few studies document the roles and contributions of these women to the struggle for equality and social justice in America. With few exceptions, most accounts of this period focus on male leaders and the organizations they led. Very little is known about the countless black women who were the backbone of the civil rights struggle in local communities across this nation. Not only were black women supporters—fulfilling traditional female roles of nurturing and caretaking—but also major leaders, organizers, and strategists who helped to mold and shape the direction that the movement would take. Seasoned by a society that systematically oppresses black women, civil rights activists used their knowledge and experience to challenge the racist and sexist traditions that circumscribed their lives.

In the South in general, and in Mississippi in particular, the fight for civil rights was first and foremost a day-to-day struggle for survival; it was a battle against a system of physical and economic oppression that had exploited blacks and their labor for generations. While Mississippi was not unique in its legally sanctioned oppression of blacks, it was considered the most violent, dreadful pocket of resistance in the South.[1] In 1960, Mississippi was still largely a rural state, producing the third largest cotton crop in the nation. Like every place else in the South, Mississippi was segregated. Public schools were segregated by law and only open to blacks four months out of the year; the remainder of the year was spent picking cotton in the fields. All public facilities, including restaurants, bus stations and restrooms were either reserved for whites only or segregated. Blacks were effectively barred from voting by an outrageously complex literacy test that would have them interpret the Mississippi state constitution and by a poll tax. But perhaps most oppressive of all was the sharecropping system that replaced slavery and kept blacks under the yoke of white landowners for life. Black sharecroppers were given a small plot of land on what were known as plantations to work, in addition to food, seed and credit at the local white landowner's store. At harvest time, blacks were required to settle accounts with the landowner, who inevitably kept them indebted, thus one never escaped the system. In the early sixties, the majority of Mississippi's black population lived in the Delta region of the state, where sharecropping was a way of life.[2]

By the time the civil rights movement gained momentum throughout the South in the early 1960s, the large number of Mississippi blacks were so impoverished that any efforts to organize them had to focus first on meeting the demands of everyday survival. Moreover, because resistance to civil rights was greatest in the remote, isolated areas that dominated the state, organizing there was life-threatening work. Very often the first rural blacks to engage in civil rights work found themselves and their families victims of violent threats and harassment. It is within this context that we can come to understand the courageous, relentless work of black female activists throughout the state.

Despite the hardships facing grassroots organizers, black women were intrepid, working individually and collectively to empower rural people. Their civil rights work began with community-building and self-sustaining efforts that would help to free blacks from the severe economic dependency on whites. Before blacks—who were often frightened and apathetic toward civil rights work—could be encouraged to register to vote, the basic essentials of food, clothing, and housing had to be met.

Most significant of all grassroots efforts was the establishment of rural cooperatives, which grew out of a larger effort called the Poor People's Corporation, established in 1965. Women made up the majority of the cooperative memberships and special efforts were made to find work for those who had lost their jobs as a result of civil rights participation. The cooperatives were based on the idea that if poor people could manually pick cotton most of their lives and clean white folks' homes, they could also learn to make things with their hands. This did not require the ability to read or write. The co-ops were managed by the people in them, who invested "shares" in the business and, in turn, received a portion of the company's profits. Maggie Douglass, president of the Madison County Sewing Firm, remembered that the idea for the co-op originated in a meeting of the Council of Federated Organizations (COFO):

> People was working for white people and thought that was the only thing they would do. When we realized that we could do something for ourselves, we really became involved. I really wasn't too involved in the civil rights movement before that. I really became interested in this sewing organization when I was laid off my job at the American Tent Company in Canton after I worked there for seven years. They didn't give me any reason at all.[3]

There were numerous co-ops, such as the Ruleville Sewing Co-op, the Prairie Sewing Group, the Hopedale Sewing Project, and the Shelby Group, which employed black women throughout rural Mississippi. The products from each of these were distributed and sold through the Liberty Outlet House, a retail store owned by the Poor People's Corporation in Jackson. The cooperative idea fostered a sense of pride and self-empowerment among people who had worked for whites all of their lives. Freed from the fear of losing their jobs women began to overcome some of their fears about participation in voter registration and other civil rights work: "When I went to freedom meeting as a maid, the police would stand around and watch you, and they would harass you all the time. Now things are different. Almost all the women in the factory have decided to enroll their children in white schools."[4]

Hilda C. Wilson, a staff member of the Poor People's Corporation in Mount Beulah, wrote in her diary how the co-ops not only provided skills training and a real opportunity for economic advancement, but also engendered a sense of positive self-esteem:

> The ladies of the sewing group arrived at 9:30 a.m. ready to learn and work, about ten of them. A great group. We talked about organizing a business, what has to go into it. That, and how much they were willing to sacrifice in order to make that grow. They are determined to learn cutting. They are determined to learn to sew. They set up machines; they practiced sewing

15

straight seams, cutting to save cloth's quality. A very good day . . . These ladies are fast learners; they only need the opportunity, that's all.[5]

While many black women were sharecroppers and, indeed, among the "poorest of the poor," there were others whose socioeconomic conditions were slightly better. The success of grassroots activists such as Winson Hudson of Harmony and Annie Belle Robinson Devine of Canton was due, in part, to their varying degrees of economic self-sufficiency. When outside civil rights workers entered the state in the early 1960s, both Hudson and Devine had already held long-standing positions of leadership and respect in their communities. Both housed civil rights workers in their homes and paved the way for these "outside agitators" to organize local residents. Because Hudson and Devine were able to read and write, they were often called on by others in their communities.

Harmony, Mississippi, home of Winson Hudson, is unique. It is a tiny community of black landowners dating back to the turn of the century who share a long history of resistance to white rule; its residents were known for fighting back. Blacks in Harmony were trained hunters who did not hesitate to use their weapons for self-protection. When whites attempted to take their land, residents fought long and hard to retain it. Hudson recalled, "We had our own land, our own bread and our own syrup. And that's what we lived off. We grew our own meat and made our own bread. We bought milk, flour, sugar, lard, and baking powder. There was a river swamp nearby and it had all the game you wanted. That's how I learned to shoot. I could hunt game and handle a gun just like the men."[6] Harmony residents built and staffed their own school and people came from all around Leake County to attend their school. With the 1954 *Brown v. the Board of Education* desegregation ruling, Harmony residents were threatened with losing their school. Shortly following the decision, Mississippi courts sought to centralize all school systems throughout the state. Power was then stricken from local authorities, like the Harmony trustees who helped to build the school; it was forced to close shortly thereafter. With the knowledge that the ostensible integration of schools would only further hinder blacks, Harmony residents organized to reopen the school. Hudson and her sister led the fight:

> With the building of the black schools, after the court decision, [whites] wanted to do away with the Harmony school. That's what tore this thing up. We worked to save Harmony school. This is what stirred up Leake County. I was once a student at Tougaloo, and had some education, but it was

Harmony school that prepared me. . . . Some of the whites even wanted to keep this school 'cause they felt like it was going to be a terrible thing when they messed with the people in Harmony community. But you couldn't tell that school board nothing. They built three schools and named them after blacks. And one black principal was for all this. Some blacks did a lot of damage. . . . My sister's house was bombed with her eleven children in it at the time because she wanted to save Harmony school. Them children never did get over that bomb. Her baby was a nervous wreck. . . . They had really fixed up the black schools, but they were separate. When they moved that school [Harmony school], I went crazy. I didn't care what happened, live or die. We invited Medgar Evers [state president of the NAACP] out to organize the NAACP and once upon a time we said, "We might better give this thing up," but then we said, "We ain't gonna give up nothing." When they killed Medgar, I double went crazy. After that, though, people really got afraid.[7]

Along with her sister Dovie, Winson Hudson was the plaintiff in numerous lawsuits against Mississippi authorities. As she became more openly involved in civil rights, white resistance mounted against her and her family. In one instance, Hudson's sister and her husband had borrowed money from a local bank to make some home repairs. When the bank officials discovered that the Hudsons were plaintiffs in a school desegregation suit, Dovie Hudson was and notified that the bank would be foreclosing on her home. According to her sister, "A man came out and he took as much as he saw. He got a mule, two milk cows, and a wagon. But we already hid all the rest of it. So he could only get what he saw, which was not too much. But boy were we mad. That's what [whites] do to you when you're in this stuff."

The Hudson sisters stood firm; they refused to surrender to attempts by whites to get them to back down. Winson Hudson spent the next two years struggling to register to vote.

We had to fill out an application and had to read and interpret the Mississippi constitution, section 44. You had to read and interpret it to the *t*. It was little bitty writing and you had to copy it and interpret it and I mean you couldn't leave an *i* undotted. . . . My husband was registered; I guess they thought he was white. You couldn't tell him from a white man. . . . We finally got the justice department in here and they went over to the courthouse and they asked about me and my sister and the clerk said they can register. We went back over there and filled out the application. [The registrar] gave me this same section 44 of the Mississippi constitution. When it got to the part that said interpret, I wrote that it said what it meant and it meant what it said. The clerk said, "Winson, you passed."[8]

Hudson, like other female grassroots organizers, was a personal example. Her own activism encouraged others to take the first step in challenging white authority. But she was always patient and compassionate in her efforts to organize, remembering that not everyone could overcome the fear of economic reprisal as she had:

> I could drive a car and so I could get around. See, I was like a tomboy all of my life. If my husband had been in my position, he'd have gotten killed. He wouldn't have lived six months. . . . I have been honest with my people. I don't never turn nobody down. They just call on me and worry me to death to help them with this and that and won't even give me a membership in the NAACP. But I don't never turn nobody down. . . . You know, you have a lot of people who get so proud that you got to get an appointment to talk with them. The people know me as walking the streets in Carthage. . . . I don't get dressed up to get with my folks neither. . . . You got to learn to smile when you don't want to smile, to hug when you don't want to hug, and to kiss when you can't hardly stand the odor. I just like it 'cause my father was like that. He just liked people, especially people who could not help themselves.[9]

Equally selfless and unyielding in her commitment to improving the lives of people in her community was Annie Belle Robinson Devine of nearby Canton. Like Hudson, Devine had lived all of her life in Mississippi. There was never a time when she was not aware that blacks were severely mistreated in the state. At a very young age, Devine worked briefly as a domestic in a white woman's home: "I did everything as a servant, but just would not say 'yes, sir' or 'yes, mamam.' I just wasn't going to say this." This simple act of resistance was only the beginning of a life's work spent overturning racial oppression. Also like Hudson, Devine had been fortunate; she was able to read and write and "had a little training." Early in her career, she taught elementary school in Flora, a few miles from Canton where she made $35 a week and spent summers taking courses at Tougaloo College. At this time, back in the early 1950s, black schoolteachers were not required to have degrees. An eighth-grade education was enough to qualify a willing person for the job.

Later, as an insurance sales agent for a black-owned company, Annie Devine had a great deal of contact with blacks throughout Madison County. It was in this position that she was first drawn to civil rights work. Years before the Congress of Racial Equality (CORE) formally set up in Canton, several of the old-guard "established" men in town had begun discussing ways of organizing local blacks. Devine was among this small cadre of leaders. Her position in a traditionally male-dominated occupation had put her in contact with men who came to respect her abilities.[10] Devine would later join CORE as a middle-aged, single parent. She recalled her early experiences working in the organization:

> Early in those days, I was a victim because the people who had started [CORE] were young and this didn't attract me very much. They were just there making noises, singing songs, and clapping their hands and saying that you might as well get in it because you were born in it. . . . It was rather annoying for quite a while. Then this young lady, Annie Moody came by and said, "Mrs. Devine, why don't you come to one of the meetings because you're an insurance lady and you could have a lot of influence on people."[11]

Devine reluctantly went to a meeting at the Pleasant Green Holiness Church, which was surrounded by policemen. The next day the manager of the housing project where she lived threatened her with eviction:

> When it came time to pay the rent I didn't have the money. When I went to tell the woman in the office, who was white, she said something like, "Well, it seems you have the time for everything else, so I hear." I knew she had been informed I had gone to a movement meeting. . . . I think I made a decision right there. If I was going to be harassed, be made to move just because I went to a meeting, then I was already in the movement. Either I was going to be a part of it or out of it, and I wanted to be a part of it because something had to be done.[12]

Devine quit her job selling insurance shortly after this incident and went to work for CORE as a full-time staff member. Many of her friends and church members at St. Paul's AME Zion Church questioned this decision. Even her children wondered why their mother would take this risk.

Like so many other grassroots organizers, Annie Devine brought a wealth of resources to the movement. Not only was she mature, level-headed, and a highly respected woman of the community, Devine also had concrete skills that were essential to the movement's survival. From her work in insurance she had become comfortable traveling alone by car throughout the country. In addition, she had learned to work effectively with people, which was extremely useful in mass mobilization. Devine knew how to conduct meetings, and the younger CORE activists came to depend on her as an advice-giver and stabilizing force within the organization.

> She directed us to blacks who were trustworthy in the community, told us what blacks would do and what they wouldn't, how to address them. In many ways, she acted like a go-between with black, male leaders [notably preachers] and young folks [who resisted their authority]. We were not saying to leadership, "you ought to be ashamed not to be doing this and that for our people," and Mrs. Devine was saying "you ought to do this because of what has happened." She could draw on her lived experience. She was the backbone, one of the strategists. She understood clearly how we should handle and conduct ourselves in Canton. We came in like we're here to save you folks and Mrs. Devine instructed CORE that this was the wrong approach. You can't relate to people in this community using this approach. Mrs. Devine was a country diplomat.[13]

Although Devine was employed and had never experienced the sharecropping life-style that oppressed many of the blacks living around her, she knew what it meant to be poor. She did more than just sympathize with the plight of sharecropping families; she saw herself inextricably tied to their struggle. Because of her closeness to the people in the community, Devine was able to canvass and distribute civil rights literature on visits to homes where she also explained and outlined the goals of the movement in Canton. A large part of her days was spent delivering leaflets from the Freedom House to the poor, uneducated people in the community. Rarely did she participate in marches and sit-ins, and only once did she go to jail. Her role was clearly that of strategist and policy-maker.

> I never intended to go to jail. I believed in nonviolence, but nonviolence is hard to take. I find that people who practice it, though, are much better off. I didn't see myself as a jail person. There were the young people for that. I was a part of the group that would come up with what [CORE] would do. I remember a march in Jackson where I was up in the office with Jim Forman and some other SNCC people. The rest of them were out in the street. . . . I have never really suffered any undue harassment or intimidation. One reason is because I have been careful and I've kept myself out of the way of people. I really haven't shouted at people. It's just not my nature to get out and make noise. . . . The Negro woman does not in many cases have to go through all the things that men go through. That's not true in every case, but it is true in some.[14]

Later, Annie Devine, along with Fannie Lou Hamer and Victoria Gray, was elected state representative for the radically progressive Mississippi Freedom Democratic Party (MFDP). The MFDP was an alternative to the all-white state Democratic Party that sought to challenge the Mississippi regulars at the Democratic National Convention in Atlantic City in 1964.

Another grassroots organizer who worked in the MFDP along with Devine, Hamer, and Gray was Unita Blackwell, a younger woman from Mayersville. From dirt-poor beginnings as a daughter of sharecroppers, Unita Blackwell became involved in civil rights and has since become mayor of Mayersville, the tiny town on the Mississippi River that over fifty years ago denied her the right to register to vote. As the state's first black female mayor, elected in 1977, she has continued organizing blacks. Blackwell reminisced about her role during the civil rights struggle:

> I'm sure my mother never thought that her black, barefoot child would become in a position of power; I'm not the kind of material this society whips up to make a mayor. I come out of a struggle. . . . I was not groomed to be a mayor. I didn't come out of the so-called middle-class background, the high academic so-called echelon of white America. I'm grassroots. I'm classified as a grassroots mayor. . . . I started out with some of the same goals, they haven't all been met. Freedom for myself and for my people—we're still working for it. At different times in our lives, we go after the same thing in different ways. . . . A lot of people don't understand about us in Mississippi. The same people, we had all these differences but we had to stay and work with each of them. In the North, it's more of a distant racism. Here, it's close up. . . . Folks do know one another, it's a very interesting thing. Everybody in the town, they know me. They knew me at a time when I was picking cotton and the time I was a Ford Foundation consultant and I know them. It's like an inner understanding you get as a grassroots mayor. I know everybody in the community and I know why and what and how they function. Small towns develop more strong personalities, more skills at dealing with people.[15]

Blackwell's first involvement with civil rights came in 1964 when she was a young mother in her early thirties. She was an active church worker and it was while teaching Sunday school that she first met civil rights activists who had come to the state. During the Sunday service, one worker stood up and explained the goals of voter registration and asked who would join him in going down to the courthouse the next day to register. Only eight people, as Blackwell recalled, raised their hands in a church filled to capacity. She was one of them.

> I was in Issaquena County and we were just there. It wasn't that we just went looking for the movement; the movement came to us. I was teaching some children about God and they came and asked me about registering to vote. They said, 'Well, you know they doing it over in such-and-such county.' But, some of the deacons in the church were upset at the time. They were scared of white folks. The SNCC workers had a meeting that Thursday night and

there was a lot of fear because the whites heard about it and people were doing a lot of talk about what all was going to happen to us. So we went to the courthouse and tried to register to vote and our courthouse was circled with trucks and whites came in. They had rifles in the back of trucks. I was with a SNCC staffer at the time and the sheriff called us agitators and it just made me mad. We came back and talked about it and of course, none of us got registered. You had to interpret a whole lot of stuff. But, from then on, I was involved and that was my first encounter. . . . One young woman who came to talk to us with an Afro stayed around for two or three days and I asked her, "Don't you want to have your hair fixed" and she replied, "I'll get to it." I didn't say any more about it and we went up to Greenville to a meeting and there were about five or six other women in there like that and then I discovered that this was a style. We were used to having our hair pressed. And Muriel Tillinghast was the first black woman I saw with a nappy head smiling. She would sit and talk about what it means to be black and ensured us of what it means to be somebody. She talked about people I had never even heard of before. We didn't have nothing, and we changed the world with nothing. We changed a whole outlook.[16]

Blackwell subsequently went to work for the Student Nonviolent Coordinating Committee (SNCC) as a staff worker. She became centrally involved in voter registration and literally walked up and down the streets of Mayersville, talking to people and encouraging them to register to vote.

I became an organizer. I got angry that another human being could tell me that I didn't have a right to register and was going to deny me this right. I had found it in the Bible that all men were created equal and I didn't understand that how come that this was my constitutional right and I couldn't have that. I got mad and I was determined that I wasn't gonna take no more. I realized that I was angry and that I had really felt this all of my life. . . . I didn't know what I was doing at first and [SNCC] acted like I was really doing something by talking to the people about civil rights. I didn't see the bigness of the thing at the time. But I learned that black people weren't so ignorant as people wanted us to believe. We black people were just unexposed. . . . [SNCC] told me that I had natural instincts in organizing techniques . . . I organized whole counties. You start off in one community and then you go into others. We had meetings and rallies and we would go into churches . . . . I love to read books; I'll read anything. I learned to read well and to understand. When I got into the civil rights movement, I got a new kind of education. . . . One of the things is that I was one of the people and when you're one of the folks, you can go and talk to them about yourself. And I would say, "I'm scared too and nothing from nothing leaves nothing and we don't have nothing so whatever chance we take, we may get something." I've always been with the people and so if you sit down with people and people understand this, this is how things get done. And you organize around what the needs of the people are. People needed decent housing to stay in; they needed food and this is basic. Then, you tell them that if they register to vote, then we'll have some of these things. That's how we organized the whole state, around the problems of the people.[17]

Like so many of the younger activists, Unita Blackwell's work in the movement became totally absorbing—she was in and out of jail and caught up in the day-to-day rigor of grassroots organizing. She and her husband, who was also active, would decide beforehand who would participate in demonstrations and risk going to jail each time. The burden of being arrested and having to spend time in prison posed significant problems for a young couple with a child. In Blackwell's case, family members helped out. This collective responsibility for child rearing among activist families was not at all unusual. Older children often accompanied young mothers in demonstrations and protests.

In addition to being arrested and jailed, Blackwell was a plaintiff in numerous lawsuits against the authorities in Mississippi. She and her husband were the plaintiffs in the landmark *Blackwell v. the Sharkly-Issaquena Consolidated Lines School.* In another case, Blackwell was instrumental in organizing a boycott of the all-black Henry Weathers High School when the principal suspended students who wore SNCC buttons to class in protest of racial conditions in the country.[17]

Blackwell has since been elected vice chair of the state Democratic Party and a member of the Democratic National Committee. Having barely left the Mississippi Delta until she was thirty, she has since received a master's degree from the University of Massachusetts and studied at Harvard. She has traveled to China many times as president of the U.S.-China Peoples Friendship Association, a private, nonprofit organization. Reflecting on her role within the community and her work for social change, Blackwell stated:

I have an inner peace on the inside now, I'm grateful to God for that, but that doesn't stop me from doing whatever it is that I've got to do. I'm happy, no jumping-up-yahoo-happy all the time, but I have a peace on the inside now. . . . What's important to me is to go through different stages. The movement will always be a part of my life. It's not been easy. One of the most important things to me was to become a real citizen, to become registered to vote and to understand what that means . . . To end up in the eighties as mayor with a master's degree. People say, "Why do you stay here, you can go someplace else to live." But Mayersville is my assignment. When God assigns you to something, you stick with it. It's the root of your work. I came into the movement in Mayersville, traveled all over the world, and now I've ended

23

up with all of these things I call wealth. It's not a lot of money. I am not hungry and I'm not out-of-doors. But I've lived a very fruitful life.[18]

The activism of women like Annie Devine, Winson Hudson, and Unita Blackwell is exemplary. Their commitment to the struggle for civil rights is courageous, particularly considering the overt racial terrorism of rural Mississippi. But the strength and accomplishments of these women were not without sacrifice. Their work was dangerous indeed, and often kept them alienated, ostracized, and victims of constant criticism. The grinding day-to-day rigor of civil rights organizing was not glamorous work; it posed all kinds of constraints. For many, the psychological and physical torture was overbearing, often resulting in circumstances women were unable to overcome. It interrupted careers, damaged personal relationships, and left some activists feeling lonely and withdrawn. And more than a few women suffered violent attacks. There are numerous accounts of brutal beatings, harassment, and intimidation. One of the more vicious cases is the incident that took place in Winona, involving Fannie Lou Hamer, Annelle Ponder, Rosemary Freeman, June Johnson, Evester Simpson, and others who were arrested and then beaten on their return from a voter registration workshop. Hamer suffered from a limp as a result of this beating and was sickly in later years.[19]

All these women are survivors; they represent victory and success. Their ability to lead the struggle for freedom with dignity and indominable spirit comes from a long history of black women's activism. To be sure, the culture of Southern black women broadened their perspective and opened up a range of possibilities for challenging their oppression. More specifically, black women's strategies of resistance can be traced to several factors in their lives.

First, the deep spirituality passed along generationally enabled them to maintain faith against seemingly insurmountable odds. A belief in God and in the teachings of the Bible was the anchor for many who had been brought up in the church. Second, the influence of other women, particularly older members of the community, provided role models who encouraged younger women's social consciousness. Third, some degree of individual autonomy was empowering, offering activists enough freedom in their personal lives to take risks and speak out on human injustice. Finally, black women's personal qualities of self-determination, strength, integrity, and resiliency strongly influenced their ability to assume leading roles in the struggle for civil rights.

Various stories recounting how black women first became involved in the movement attest to their intolerance of conditions that threatened their lives and the lives of their children. The realization of human injustice moved black women to action; they viewed their roles as activists as a natural extension of their fundamental rights as human beings. In this manner, these women sought to take back what they felt was rightfully theirs. Unita Blackwell stated that she became involved with the movement after she got "mad." Another woman recalled that she had been a "rebel" all of her life and felt that white oppression of blacks in Mississippi was just "wrong;" after years of struggling to survive, she "stopped hating and started understanding." That was the first step toward freedom.

None of these women worked alone. It was through the sisterhood of others and women's networks that each was able to get things done. Because black women understood that there were degrees of activism based on fear, economic dependency, and domestic and filial responsibilities, they were willing to care and nurture one another. Many of them shared in taking care of one another's children, exchanging responsibilities and offering financial support when it was needed. In their roles as wives and mothers, they had to juggle responsibilities in order to attend meetings and participate in boycotts and other organizing work, and for most of these women, domestic obligations were not allowed to prevent them from assuming their roles as activists. All in all, black women worked collectively to transform the movement. As Ella Baker said over a decade ago, "the movement of the fifties and sixties was carried largely by women. How many made a conscious decision on the basis of the larger goals, how many on the basis of habit pattern, I don't know. But it's true that the number of women who carried the movement is much larger than that of men."[20]

NOTES

1. James Silver, *Mississippi: The Closed Society.* (New York: Harcourt, 1966).
2. Sharecropping was little more than a substitution for slavery following the Civil War. By 1860, a white planter class had emerged in Mississippi's fertile Delta as a result of the profits made from the cultivation of cotton by black slaves. When Mississippi became the second state to secede from the Union and Jefferson Davis, a plantation owner from Yazoo County, was made president of the Confederacy, wealthy planters dominated the state and firmly established a system of white rule that carried into the next century. Many of the newly freed slaves did not migrate northward and by 1890, a new state constitution

was drawn up to keep these blacks politically and economically subjugated to white rule. The revised state constitution abolished the popular vote and established measures to disfranchise blacks. Mississippi politics was characterized by the one-party rule of the all-white Democrats who did everything in their power to uphold a caste system of white supremacy. For a more detailed discussion of the evils of sharecropping see Hodding Carter, *First Person Plural* (Garden City: Doubleday, 1963); James Silver, *Mississippi: The Closed Society* (New York: Harcourt, 1966); and a special edition of the journal *Freedomways* (Spring, 1965) on Mississippi.

3. Testimony of Maggie Douglass, in "In Canton: A New Business." *Vicksburg Citizens Appeal* (September 30, 1965): 3–5.
4. *Ibid.*, p. 5.
5. Hilda C. Wilson, diary entry, n.d., Hilda C. Wilson Papers, Zenobia Coleman Library, Tougaloo College, Tougaloo, Mississippi.
6. Winson Hudson, personal interview, July 14, 1986.
7. *Ibid.*
8. *Ibid.*
9. *Ibid.*
10. Scholars of the civil rights movement have documented that the movement was not monolithic and that there were schisms between leaders and unresolved organizational conflicts. In addition, local residents of Mississippi had begun organizing themselves as early as the 1950s, long before civil rights workers came into the state. Most of these efforts were "underground," due to the severity of white resistance. Many of these earlier organizers were members of the state-wide NAACP.
11. Annie Devine, personal interview, July 18, 1986. See also Anne Moody's autobiography, *Coming of Age in Mississippi* (New York: Dial Press, 1968).
12. Annie Devine, interview, 1982, Tom Dent Oral History Collection, Amistad Research Center, New Orleans.
13. Matthew Suarez, interview, 1982, Tom Dent Oral History Collection.
14. Annie Devine, personal interview, July 18, 1986.
15. Unita Blackwell, personal interview, July 25, 1986.
16. *Ibid.*
17. The lawsuit Blackwell initiated in response to these suspensions is *Blackwell* vs. *Issaquena County Board of Education* (363 F 2d 749, 1966).
18. *Ibid.*
19. Fannie Lou Hamer's testimony about this incident before the United States Advisory Committee on Mississippi can be found in the SNCC Papers, James Forman Collection, Martin Luther King, Jr. Center for Nonviolent Social Change, Atlanta.
20. Ella Baker, "Developing Community Leadership," in Gerda Lerner, ed., *Black Women in White America: A Documentary History* (New York: Vintage Books, 1972).

Is This America?
Fannie Lou Hamer
and the
Mississippi Freedom
Democratic Party

MAMIE E. LOCKE

In 1964, before the Democratic Party's Credentials Committee and millions of television viewers, Fannie Lou Hamer asked, "Is this America?" The question referred to the overall climate of near hysteria that permeated the very fiber of the United States as African-Americans battled to achieve justice and equality. "Is this America?" called to mind the constant violence being leveled against African-Americans, including Hamer herself. "Is this America" acknowledged that a vital segment of American society was being constantly and continually subjugated. In that one question, Fannie Lou Hamer, the twentieth child of a Mississippi sharecropper family, brought America face to face with itself—its racism, bigotry, intolerance, hatred, and hypocrisy.

Fannie Lou Hamer risked her life and livelihood when she registered to vote in 1962. In defying the laws and political mores of Mississippi, she was launched into a life that would remain politically active until her untimely death, at the age of fifty-nine, in 1977. One important aspect of Hamer's life is her legacy of leadership in the formation and activities of the Mississippi Freedom Democratic Party (MFDP). She captivated the American consciousness at the Democratic National convention in Atlantic City in 1964, singing "Go Tell It on the Mountain" and asking "Is this America?" At that moment she became a symbol of the movement and a role model for many.

The image of Mississippi prior to and during the civil rights movement can best be summarized as "a closed society." In the 1960s, James Silver argued that "within its own borders the closed society of Mississippi comes as near to approximating a police state as anything we have yet seen in America."[1] It is within this closed society that trailblazing women like Fannie Lou Hamer were born and struggled against multiple odds. These same women made lasting contributions to the African-American and female experiences in the United States.

During the civil rights movement, black women became the key element in the organization and mobilization of the black community around the struggle. Many of them were thrust into the limelight because of their articulation of the concerns of blacks, women, and the poor. Fannie Lou Hamer became one of those champions.

Born Fannie Lou Townsend in rural Montgomery County in 1917, she was the youngest of twenty children. When she was two years old, the family moved to Sunflower County, where she spent the remainder of her life.[2] Watching her parents struggle in a system designed to keep them subjugated, Hamer came to the realization at an early age that something was wrong in Mississippi. She grew up determined to change things, even at the expense of her own life.[3] Her entrance into the struggle was several years down the road, but she never lost the indomitable spirit of a woman with a mission.

After marrying Perry Hamer, she worked as a sharecropper and timekeeper on a Sunflower County plantation, a job she held for eighteen years. In August 1962, she went to her first mass meeting held in her hometown of Ruleville, where James Forman of the Student Nonviolent Coordinating Committee (SNCC) and James Bevel of the Southern Christian Leadership Conference (SCLC) spoke. Forman and Bevel emphasized the importance of voting. Hamer was so inspired by the speeches that she volunteered along with seventeen others to go to the county courthouse in Indianola to try to register. She subsequently became the group's leader.[4]

At the courthouse, the group was met with hostility. As the group spokesperson, Hamer indicated to the clerk their desire to register. They were told that only two persons could enter at a time, and they readily complied.

The kind of information sought (i.e., residence, employment, etc.) would be used later by organizations like the Citizens' Councils to intimidate the applicants. The applicants had to also take literacy tests by reading and interpreting sections of the Mississippi state constitution, a process that took all day for the group to complete. They were not informed if they passed or failed. After leaving the courthouse, the applicants' bus was intercepted by local authorities who ordered them back to Indianola. The driver was fined one hundred dollars for driving a bus of the wrong color. After the judge accepted a thirty-dollar fine, the group continued its journey back to Ruleville. When Hamer finally reached home, she learned that her boss was angry that she had tried to register. Because she refused to withdraw her name, Hamer was fired and ordered off the plantation. She also received word that she had failed the literacy test, but she informed the registrar that she would return every thirty days until she passed. She eventually did in January 1963. She could not vote immediately, however, because of another obstacle, the infamous poll tax.[5]

Because she stood up for her rights, Hamer and her family faced intimidation and harassment every day. Her husband and daughter were arrested and lost their jobs. She received a nine-thousand-dollar water bill for a house that did not have running water. She was shot at from a speeding car and police entered her home without a search warrant. Despite this, she became an active member of the movement, serving as a field secretary for SNCC, working with voter registration, helping develop welfare programs, and circulating petitions to secure federal commodities for needy black families. After becoming a political activist, Hamer had to deal with intermittent employment because no one would hire her.[6] The highlight of her political activism occurred when she and several others set the wheels in motion for the formation of the Mississippi Freedom Democratic Party (MFDP).

By the time John F. Kennedy was inaugurated in 1961, many Mississippians and Southern whites had excommunicated themselves from the national Democratic Party. Although many still used the label, they called themselves "state Democrats" or "true Democrats." In fact, they were any type of Democrat except a national one. Regular Mississippi Democrats resented the attack by the national party on their belief in segregation, and felt that because of such a confrontation, a strain had been placed on their Democratic identification. Since the state party was considered more conservative than the national party, Mississippians felt justified in calling themselves the true Democrats, claiming that the leaders of the national party had betrayed the underlying principles of the party.[7] Of course, their principles were designed to uphold segregation laws in the South.

As the civil rights movement gained momentum, the desire to keep blacks from becoming registered voters was heightened. The most effective device was economic pressure. A law was approved by the state legislature in 1962 that provided for the publication of the names and addresses of applicants in the newspapers.[8] This made retaliatory action by whites easier to accomplish. Further, blacks who attempted to register were threatened with the loss of their jobs, loss of credit, and other economic reprisals.

The establishment of the MFDP in 1964 was one of the most compelling actions taken as a part of the "Freedom Summer" program initiated by the Council of Federated Organizations (COFO). The goal of the organization was to dramatize to the nation the principles of the Mississippi Regulars (the state Democratic Party) which, as a matter of praxis, excluded black participation in voting. The MFDP favored the liberal principles of the national party and rejected the "old politics" of the Regulars by attempting to replace it with a system based on participatory democracy.[9] Fannie Lou Hamer was one of the party's cofounders and was eventually appointed as cochair of the delegation headed for the national convention.

Initially the Freedom Democrats attempted to participate in precinct, county, and state conventions of the traditional state party apparatus. They were either barred from meetings or limited in their rights and participation when they did get in. As a result, they decided to challenge the all-white Regulars at the national convention to be held in Atlantic City. The Regulars would be charged with the responsibility for violence and voter intimidation in the state. The Freedom Democrats hoped the regular delegation would be barred from the convention by virtue of the fact that they constantly declared themselves independent of the national party. It was the contention of the MFDP that they were the only Democratic organization in Mississippi that could be relied on to support the nominees of the national party.[10] It was apparent to the MFDP and its supporters that the Regulars did not want to be a part of the national party structure. However, the Regulars did not want any other group representing the national party in Mississippi. Therefore, the Regulars obtained a temporary restraining order forbidding the Freedom Democrats from using the word *democratic* in their name. At the same time, the Regulars adopted a platform that not only opposed civil rights but rejected the national party platform as well.[11]

Fannie Lou Hamer's televised appearance at the 1964 Democratic Convention representing the Mississippi Freedom Democratic Party thrust her into the national limelight. She continued to participate in the black freedom struggle until her untimely death in 1977 at the age of 59.
[Photo: *Schomburg Center for Research in Black Culture, NYPL*]

31

After being excluded from participation in the state party procedures, the MFDP held their own state convention and selected sixty-eight delegates to send to Atlantic City. The group established an office in Washington and began to solicit support for their challenge. The party received endorsements from several state delegations, including California, Michigan, Massachusetts, and Colorado. They also received support from twenty-five congressmen.[12] The Regulars had the support of other Southern states and, although not overtly at the time, the support of Lyndon Johnson. The Southern states threatened to walk out of the convention if Johnson did not back the Regulars. Johnson did not want anything to mar his nomination for the presidency and sought ways to prevent the upstart MFDP from stealing the headlines.[13]

As the cochair of the MFDP, Hamer spoke on behalf of the organization on the first day of the convention. In her testimony to the Credentials Committee, Hamer recounted the atrocities committed against the black citizens of Mississippi. She told of the murder of Medgar Evers, the violence associated with the enrollment of James Meredith at the University of Mississippi, and the murders of three young civil rights workers, James Chaney, Michael Schwerner, and Andrew Goodman. She also spoke of the abuse she herself had suffered at the hands of Mississippi law enforcement officers when she was beaten so badly in a Winona jail that she had no feelings left in her arms.[14] She stated: "If the Democratic Party is not seated now, I question America. . . . Is this America? The land of the free and the home of the brave? Where we have to sleep with our telephone off the hook, because our lives be threatened daily?"[15] After her dramatic testimony, Hamer wept before the committee and before the millions of Americans watching the proceedings on television. President Johnson, again trying to prevent the MFDP from stealing the show, attempted to block the live coverage of the Credentials Committee by hastily scheduling a press conference to preempt the proceedings. Although he managed to block the committee proceedings, he was unable to prevent the broadcast of Hamer's testimony on the evening news programs. This coverage led to a deluge of calls and telegrams to the Credentials Committee in support of the MFDP challenge.[16]

After all arguments had been heard, the convention adopted what it called a compromise proposal. Developed by Hubert Humphrey and Walter Mondale, the compromise stated that: (1) no Mississippian would be seated without a pledge to support the national party ticket; (2) two members (not selected by the MFDP, but by Humphrey) of the MFDP would sit in the convention, not as official representatives of Mississippi but as delegates "at large"; and (3) no future convention would seat state delegations that excluded citizens from participation by reason of race or color.[17] It was also proposed that a committee be created to help states comply with the reforms. The Regulars denounced this compromise and all but three of them walked out of the convention. The MFDP also rejected the compromise, walked out, and held a press conference stating their objections. Hamer argued that the two "at large" seats were "token rights, on the back row, the same as we got in Mississippi. We didn't come all this way for that mess again."[18] She further demonstrated the intention of the MFDP to reject any compromises by leading the delegation onto the convention floor. After borrowing passes from supportive delegates, they managed to occupy the vacant seats allocated for Mississippi before the guards escorted them out. Determined to thwart further disruptions, President Johnson ordered the removal of all except three seats (for the Regulars who had not walked out) from the Mississippi area. This did not prevent the MFDP delegation from going onto the convention floor once again and occupying the space reserved for Mississippi. Hamer led her delegation in freedom songs right on the floor.[19]

The MFDP lost its challenge, but Hamer stressed the importance of not succumbing to the compromise, for to have done so would have compromised the people of Mississippi. She and others were disillusioned by the leadership, both black and white, in Atlantic City who urged acceptance of the compromise. Since she argued so vehemently against the compromise, Hamer was barred from other meetings held to discuss the dilemma. However, she never gave up the struggle for what she felt was right, even as the defeated group headed back to Mississippi.

Under Hamer's leadership, the Freedom Democrats did not discontinue their fight against the legitimacy of the lily-white faction. The party decided to have candidates run against the regular candidates in the next congressional election. Candidates, of which Hamer was one, acquired the signatures necessary to qualify as independents, then petitioned the secretary of state to place their names on the November ballot. They were told that each name on the petition had to be certified by the local circuit court. For all practical purposes, this was rejection, for no satisfaction would be obtained from county registrars.[20]

As a candidate for Congress from the Second District, Hamer knew that her chances of winning were very slim. She argued that she was running because she wanted to show people that a black person could run for public office. Further, when confronted once by a white man who said that whites were getting tired and tense at the movement, Hamer responded: "I have been *tired* for 46 years and my parents were *tired* before me and their parents were *tired*; and I have always wanted to do something that would help some of the things I would see going on among Negroes that I didn't like and I don't like now. . . . All my life I've been sick and tired. Now I'm sick and tired of being sick and tired."[21] With iron-willed determination, she challenged the political structure of Mississippi. Although unsuccessful in gaining a seat in Congress, her struggles did not end.

The MFDP next planned to challenge the seating in the United States House of Representatives of Mississippi's five congressmen in January 1965. The challenge was based on a little-known Mississippi statute that made it possible to protest the validity of state elections. The statute in question dated back to 1870 when Mississippi had been readmitted to Congress during Reconstruction. Under the statute's provisions, the state was not to change its existing suffrage qualifications and disfranchise any citizens. Counselors for the Freedom Democrats argued that Mississippi had violated this law by enacting the poll tax and literacy tests as suffrage requirements.[22]

House Majority Leader Carl Albert of Oklahoma introduced a resolution that would have the five Mississippi congressmen sworn in. There was no full hearing on the matter; the House simply ended all discussion. However, the Freedom Democrats conducted their own hearings in the state and took over six hundred depositions filled with charges of racial bias. The material was filed with the clerk of the House. Nine months after the challenge had been filed, the House administration, after conducting three hours of closed hearings, rejected the claims of the Freedom Democrats. The rationale of the panel was that the congressional members had a prima facie right to their seats because the House had sworn them in the past January, this despite the fact that the challenge preceded the delegation being sworn in. The panel also stated that the Voting Rights Act, which had subsequently passed during the course of the nine-month wait, had rendered the question of disfranchisement obsolete.[23]

With little national support, the party continued to struggle in the state in local elections. There were some successes (the election of Robert Clark to the state legislature in 1967), but the party had to contend with efforts to discredit them, most notably by Congressman G. V. Montgomery. Before the House of Representatives he argued: "I do not believe the members of this House approve of the type of politics advocated by the militant organization which is trying to take control of the State of Mississippi. . . . In fact the Freedom Democratic Party should be recognized and branded by responsible conservatives and liberals alike as a vicious advocate of race hatred and revolution."[24]

These efforts at discrediting the MFDP had an impact as the 1968 national convention approached. Internal dissension in the ranks led to an eventual split of some from the MFDP to form a biracial coalition, the Loyalist Democrats of Mississippi. The Loyalists managed to unseat the Regulars at the violence-laden Democratic National Convention in Chicago. The MFDP then began a slow descent into obscurity, but it left its mark on national Democratic Party politics. More important, it catapulted to fame a magnificent woman who sought to expose America's hypocrisy and dispel the image of America being the land of the brave and the home of the free. She sought to transform the ideal into reality. Through the MFDP and other grass roots efforts, Fannie Lou Hamer brought America one step closer to dismantling the barriers keeping African-Americans on the periphery of political involvement. This strong, invincible woman, without benefit of formal education, showed the country that knowledge, wisdom, and organizational skills did not come with the acquisition of an academic degree. As Hamer stated, "whether you have a Ph.D., D.D., or no D., we're in this bag together. And whether you're from Morehouse of Nohouse, we're still in this bag together."[25]

Hamer believed "there will be more interest generated in politics at the grassroots level by the everyday kind of people who have lost confidence in the democratic process because of corrupt politicians and their desire to perpetuate themselves in office while causing the masses to suffer."[26] She was one of those "everyday kind of people" who stood firm in their beliefs and became role models for many. She became a symbol of the struggle for survival in a racist, hostile environment.

In reflecting on Fannie Lou Hamer's life shortly after her death, Eleanor Holmes Norton stated that Hamer "had a singular capacity to impart courage and to chase timidity. She was a mixture of strength, humor, love, and determined honesty. She did not know the meaning of self-pity."[27] Hamer had a fighting spirit that guided her life, a spirit that allowed her to serve as a model to poor black people who felt the system had left them behind. Her life is a shining example of what can be accomplished if one perseveres. And because she lived, others have been able to overcome what appear to be insurmountable odds to become active participants in the American political system.

In March 1977, Fannie Lou Hamer died somewhat as she had lived—poor, humble, and much loved. Because she dedicated her life to improving the lives of others, in every sense of the word, Fannie Lou Hamer was the consummate trailblazer.

NOTES

1. James Silver, *Mississippi: The Closed Society* (New York: Harcourt, 1964), p. 151.
2. Jerry DeMuth, "Tired of Being Sick and Tired," *The Nation*, 198 (June 1, 1964): 549.
3. Fannie Lou Hamer, "Life in Mississippi: An Interview with Fannie Lou Hamer," interview by J.H. O'Dell, *Freedomways*, 5 (Spring 1965): 232.
4. George A. Sewell, *Mississippi History Makers* (Jackson: University Press of Mississippi, 1977), pp. 348-49.
5. DeMuth, "Tired of Being Sick and Tired," p. 550; Sewell, *Mississippi History Makers*, p. 350.
6. Sewell, *Mississippi History Makers*, p. 357.
7. William Simpson, "The 'Loyalist Democrats' of Mississippi: Challenge to a White Majority, 1965-1972" (Ph.D. diss., Mississippi State University, 1974), pp. 29-32; F. Glenn Abney, "The Mississippi Voter: A Study of Voting Behavior in a One-Party Multifactional System" (Ph.D. diss., Tulane University, 1968), pp. 93, 105.
8. Mississippi *Laws* (1962), ch. 572, sec. 7.
9. Juan Williams, *Eyes on the Prize: America's Civil Rights Years, 1954-1964* (New York: Viking-Penguin, 1987), p. 232; Reese Cleghorn, "Who Speaks for Mississippi," *The Reporter*, August 13, 1964, p. 31.
10. Steven F. Lawson, *Black Ballots: Voting Rights in the South, 1944-1969* (New York: Columbia University Press, 1976), p. 301; Cleghorn, "Who Speaks for Mississippi," p. 31.
11. U.S. House of Representatives, "Brief of the Mississippi Freedom Democratic Party," *Congressional Record*, August 20, 1964, p. 20113; Williams, *Eyes on the Prize*, p. 234.
12. "Brief of the MFDP," p. 20108; Williams, *Eyes on the Prize*, p. 234.
13. Williams, *Eyes on the Prize*, p. 234.
14. *Ibid.*, pp. 241-42.
15. *Ibid.*, p. 241.
16. *Ibid.*, p. 242.

17. *Ibid.*, pp. 242-43; George B. Tindall, *The Disruption of the Solid South* (Athens: University of Georgia Press, 1972), p. 43.
18. Williams, *Eyes on the Prize*, p. 243.
19. *Ibid.*, pp. 243-44.
20. Lawson, *Black Ballots*, p. 322.
21. Hamer, "Life in Mississippi," p. 239; DeMuth, "Tired of Being Sick and Tired," p. 549.
22. Lawson, *Black Ballots*, pp. 322-23.
23. *Ibid.*, pp. 325-26.
24. U.S. House of Representatives, Extension of Remarks of Honorable G.V. Montgomery of Mississippi, "Mississippi Democratic Party," *Congressional Record*, November 3, 1967.
25. Fannie Lou Hamer, "It's In Your Hands," in Gerda Lerner, ed., *Black Women in White America: A Documentary History* (New York: Vintage, 1972), p. 613.
26. Fannie Lou Hamer, "If the Name of the Game is Survive, Survive," in Nathan Wright, ed., *What Black Politicians Are Saying* (New York: Hawthorn, 1972), p. 44.
27. Eleanor Holmes Norton, "The Woman Who Changed the South: A Memory of Fannie Lou Hamer," *MS* 6 (July 1977): 98.

Civil Rights Women: A Source for Doing Womanist Theology

JACQUELYN GRANT

Move on over or we'll move on over you. Move on over or we'll move on over you. Move on over or we'll move on over you. Cause we're movin', movin' on.

We are fighting in Mississippi for the common democracy. Men and women and children are dying. All because of liberty. Jesus died to make me holy. Let us fight to see me free. Cause we're movin', movin' on.

Move on over or we'll move on over you. Move on over or we'll move on over you. Move on over or we'll move on over you. Cause we're movin', movin' on.

Fannie Lou Hamer was noted not only for her dynamic speaking but also for her soul-stirring singing which was inspiration for activists involved in the civil rights movement. This particular song underscores the nature of the work of the women and other activists. They identified oppression—racism in particular, but also sexism and classism. Having committed themselves to the movement from an oppressive structure to a liberating and liberative one, they recognized that it might require moving over those who obstruct the process. Interestingly, in the song we find two options provided for those who hold stock in the status quo. Option one is to "move on over," to share power and resources with those who have been historically and systematically disfranchised. A second option is provided for those who decline the first—if you don't move over, "we'll move on over you." This was an affirmation of the belief that black people's day had come. God had indeed sent for such a time such women as Fannie Lou Hamer, Annie Devine, Ella Baker, Dorothy Cotton, Mae Bertha Carter, Winson Hudson, and others.

Certainly, we saw the power of God working in the prophetic voices and the activism of Martin Luther King, Jr., Ralph Abernathy, Andrew Young, John Lewis, Wyatt T. Walker, Hosea Williams, Medgar Evers and the many other brothers who walked and marched in the forefront of the movement. Works in Black or Afro-American Studies have kept these names before us to varying degrees, keeping us mindful of their significant contributions to the movement and to the black theological process.

The women who provided leadership at the local level and beyond for the most part were held in the background—their "proper" place—but the debilitating, oppressive structures of patriarchy and sexism could not hold them back.

Fannie Lou Hamer was only one, though a significant one, in the movement of women's activism in the struggle for civil rights. Hamer has been a person of fascination, for she exuded the qualities of womanism. She was courageous; she knew more than what was good for her, if the criterion of goodness was personal security. But perhaps of most significance was her audacity in speaking the truth of what she knew, risking great danger to herself and her family.

Born October 6, 1917, in Montgomery County, Mississippi, Fannie Lou Hamer was a stranger neither to racism in its most insidious and degrading forms nor to abject poverty in its most deadly form. Her life and work have implications for womanist theology.

The Mississippi Reality, the American Reality

In order to understand theological perspectives, it is important to understand the context out of which they emerge. The theology of Fannie Lou Hamer must be contextualized if we are to grasp its impact in this historical moment. The social, political, and economic location gives us a handle for making sense of religious commitments.

Fannie Lou Hamer, the twentieth child of sharecropper parents, was deprived of many of the conveniences and benefits common to twentieth-century America. When her father was finally able to work the family out of abject poverty, they were tossed back as a result of the sabotage of a racist and envious white man, who could not tolerate the economic advancement of a black man and his family. For Hamer, as for many black Americans, the firsthand experience of exploitation began at a very early age. When she was six she was seduced into the oppressive sharecropper system. She recalled her particular entrapment incident:

> One day when I was about six, I was playing beside a gravel road . . . and the landowner came and asked me could I pick cotton, I told him I didn't know. He told me if I picked 30 pounds of cotton that week that they would carry me to a commissary store . . . on the plantation[s] . . . that Saturday, and I could get Cracker Jacks and Daddy-Wide Legs . . . and cherries . . . And this was things that we had never had. I picked 30 pounds that week . . . Then the next week I was tasked to 60 because what he was really doing, was trapping me into work . . . I . . . had to pick more and more. By the time I was 13 years old, I was picking 3 and 400 [pounds]. . . . I just wondered what in the world was wrong that all of the people that didn't work—they were people that had something, that people that worked didn't have anything as still is to what's going on now.[1]

Having been purposefully designed to maintain economic imbalance in favor of white people, the sharecropper system effectively kept blacks poor and whites economically secure. Of course, even the young eyes of children were able to see that there was a radical difference between the conditions of being white and being black, especially in the deep South, so much so that it was not uncommon for blacks, particularly the young, to wish whiteness for themselves. Even Hamer asked her mother, "Why weren't we white?" The question came of her existential experience that whiteness meant plenty of good food to eat and plenty of good room to live in; blackness sometimes meant nothing but bread and water.

Anne Moody recognized that even the setting of a table for the meal illustrated the difference between blacks and whites: ". . . we never set a table because we never had but one fork or spoon each; we didn't have knives and didn't need them because we never had meat."[2]

It would be well if we could say that Hamer's experience was an exceptional one, but it was not. Blacks in the South in general and Mississippi in particular lived under the most inhumane conditions. It was not uncommon even in the 1960s for a black person to work for three dollars a day—and under horrendous conditions. The saying, "A black man has no rights that a white man had to respect," was certainly true; in Mississippi, as in other parts of the United States, "A white person could kill [a black person] without bothering to explain."[3] In Sunflower County, Hamer's home, 70 percent of the black people were disfranchised and consequently government was unrepresentative of the majority of the population. In the early 1960s, Hamer estimated the black population of Sunflower County to be fourteen thousand of which only four thousand were registered to vote, while all eight thousand whites were registered. The figures statewide were no better.

Because black life was cheap, blacks suffered many abuses. Hamer's life was no exception. Inheriting the impoverished tradition of her sharecropper family, she and her husband were caught up in the cycle of poverty. Her life took a turn in 1962 when she met workers of the Southern Christian Leadership Conference (SCLC) and the Student Nonviolent Coordinating Committee (SNCC) who began mobilizing people to fight for freedom. As a result of this empowering experience, Hamer became active in politics in Mississippi, especially Ruleville. Her work catapulted her to vice chairperson of the Mississippi Freedom Democratic Party (MFDP), under which she ran for Congress from the Second Congressional District. It was as a leader of the MFDP that she gained national attention when the MFDP challenged the lily-white Mississippi delegation to the 1964 Democratic National Convention in Atlantic City. The challenge resulted in the nation hearing her story as she testified before the credentials committee. Her story included atrocities such as her loss of employment because of attempts to register to vote; her brutal beating when trying to integrate the Winona, Mississippi, Trailways bus station; and her arrest in Indianola for trying to register.

In Fannie Lou Hamer's life we find the embodiment of black women's experience of racism in the United States.

The Making of the Human Being

When one considers the conditions under which blacks were forced to exist in Mississippi and other parts of the deep South, it is easy to conclude that in the minds of whites, blacks were less than human. In our modern history, what we find is the viewing of black life through the lens of white racist America. In so doing, then, blacks are defined not in terms of their own existence, but in terms of the needs of whites. Though slavery was no longer legal, blacks were still perceived as servants, whose only function was to facilitate the needs of whites.

Hamer constantly longed for the time when black people would dare to stand up and be counted. She longed for the dismantling of illegal slavery, and that could be done only when black people took control of and defined their humanity.

Hamer spoke about the affirmation of our humanity in three ways. First, humanity is affirmed through the struggle for political empowerment, which is achieved partially through the vote. It is always instructive to note that the victory of women's suffrage won in the 1920s in fact was no victory for black women. In actuality, Negro suffrage did not result in open freedom to vote. If Negro suffrage and women's suffrage had significantly and positively affected the lives of black women in particular and black people in general, there would have been no reason for Fannie Lou Hamer's life and work to take the direction that they did. For black people, to exercise one's political responsibility to vote was not a given even as late as the 1960s. Hamer came on the scene declaring simply: "All we want to do is to be treated as human beings and we have a chance to elect our own officials and we want people in office that's going to represent us because so far we haven't had it."[4]

The vote, then, became not only an issue of civil rights, but also an issue of human rights. What was at stake was the public dignity of black people as human beings, which is possible only when they are allowed the free and open participation in the political process.

It is important to note that Hamer's aim was not equality—as was the rhetoric of the day—but freedom. As she said: "I couldn't tell nobody with my head up I'm fighting for equal right with a white man, because I don't want it. Because if what I get, got to come through lynching, mobbing, raping, murdering, stealing, and killing, I didn't want it, because it was a shocking thing to me I couldn't hardly sit down."[5] Hamer's choice was clear. She was not interested in inclusion. She would settle for nothing less than liberation.

Humanity is also affirmed through our interconnectedness. Hamer was very clear about the ties that bind people. We shall either live together as human beings or we will die together as fools. Part of her main agenda, therefore, was to get white people to understand that they cannot destroy black people without destroying themselves.[6] Additionally, on the grass roots level the important connection was made between blacks, poor whites, and native Americans. The racial wall that divided us prevented many from seeing our commonalities.

Hamer admonished: "We have the same problems from coast to coast. The future for Black people in America is the same as the future for white people in America. Our chances are the same. If you survive, we will too. If we crumble, you are going to crumble too."[7]

Finally, humanity is affirmed by self-determination and self-definition. This was particularly illustrated in the confrontation at the 1964 Democratic National Convention. A compromise was offered: of the sixty-eight MFDP delegates, two would be given seats. This was called a "moral victory" and supported even by some of the black leaders (Roy Wilkins advised them to drop the complaint; Aaron Henry advised them to accept the compromise). Hamer's response was characteristic: "don't go telling me about anybody that ain't been in Mississippi two weeks and don't know nothing about the problem, because they're not leading us."[8] Contrarily, the leaders of SNCC argued that since they knew the Mississippi situation better than anyone else, they should make their own decision about their response. "See, we'd never been allowed to do that before. Cause you see, if we are free people as Negroes, if we are free, then I don't think you're supposed to tell me how much of my freedom I'm supposed to have. Because we're human beings too."[9]

All human beings must be allowed to participate in their own destiny. Black people in general and black Mississippians in particular have been denied this right. The convention pointed this out most sharply. It was here that Hamer discovered that politics in the United States of America was the same as politics in Mississippi.[10]

The God of Freedom and The Freedom of God

Fannie Lou Hamer's basic understanding of God and Jesus Christ was that they meant freedom.

When James Cone speaks of the meaning of Jesus he says, "we know who he is when our own lives are placed in a situation of oppression, and we then have to make a decision for or against our condition. To say no to oppression and yes to liberation is to encounter the existential significance of the Resurrected One. He is the Liberator par excellence whose very presence makes persons sell all that they have and follow him." He implies further what these words mean by locating Jesus with the poor. "He was for the poor and against the rich, for the weak and against the strong."[11]

J. D. Roberts makes a similar point. He declares that Black Theology cannot accept either the Jesus who preserves the American way of life or the Jesus of the counterculture. "Jesus must not be locked into a given cluster of political and cultural perceptions. We seek a Christ above culture who is at the same time at work in culture and history for redemptive ends—setting free the whole person, mind, soul, and body."[12]

It is safe to assume that Hamer never read E. Kaseman's book, *Jesus Means Freedom* or J. DeOtis Roberts' article, "Jesus Means Freedom." European scholarly theology was not common reading for black people in America. And for the masses of black people, Black Theology as an academic discipline was also uncommon. Certainly for Fannie Lou Hamer this was the case. With a sixth grade education she was, along with many of her contemporaries, poorly educated.

But Hamer's notions of God, Jesus and Christianity are representative of this black theological perspective. "We can't separate Christ from freedom," she argued, "and freedom from Christ. The first words of Jesus' public ministry was Luke 4:18, where freedom is the central theme." She continued: "We serve God by serving our fellow [human beings]. Kids are suffering with malnutrition. People are going to the fields hungry. If you are Christians, we are tired of being mistreated. God wants us to take a stand. We can stand by registering to vote—go to the court to register to vote.[13] Here again Hamer links empowerment, even Christian empowerment, to the exercise of the vote.

Hamer acknowledged that to be involved in freedom work is a demanding job. She often quoted Ephesians 6:11–12 to keep her in touch with the gravity of the problem. "Put on the whole armor of God, that ye may be able to stand against the wiles of the devil. For we wrestle not against flesh and blood, but against principalities, against powers, against spiritual wickedness in high places."

Hamer admitted that before 1962 she would have been afraid to speak before more than six people, but after that she spoke before thousands, and she attributed her strength to God. God gave Hamer the strength to call in the overdue check.

So we are faced with a problem that is not flesh and blood, but we are facing principalities, and powers and spiritual wickedness in high places; that's what St. Paul told us. And that's what he meant. America created this problem. And we forgive America, even though we were brought here on the slave ships from Africa. Even though the dignity was taken away from the black men, and even though the black women had to bare not only their own kids but kids for the white slave owners. We forgive America for that. But we're looking for this check now, that's long past due to let us have our share in political and economic power, so that we can have a great country, together.[14]

Freedom is of divine origin. Because of this we can speculate as to where Christ is in the freedom struggle.

The churches have got to remember how Christ dealt with the poor people, in the 4th chapter of St. Luke, and the 18th verse, when he said, "The Spirit of the Lord is upon me, because he hath anointed me to preach the gospel to the poor he hath sent me to heal the brokenhearted, to preach deliverance to the captives, and recovering of sight to the blind, to set at liberty them that are bruised." Because Jesus wasn't talking about black people, or about white people, he was talking about *people*. There's no difference in people, for in the 17th chapter of the Book of Acts, the 26th verse, Paul says, "God hath made of one blood all nations of men for to dwell on all the face of the earth." That means that whether we're white, black, red, yellow, or polka dot, we're made from the same blood.

Hamer moved forward in her specification regarding Christ:

If Christ were here today, he would be branded a radical, a militant, and would probably be branded as "red." They have even painted me as Communist, although I wouldn't know a Communist if I saw one. A few weeks ago the FBI was checking on me, and the agent was telling me all the bad things the Communists would do. I told him, "Well, that is something! We're sure got a lot of Communists right up there in Washington, don't we Ed?"[15]

The Movement as Church, the Church as Movement

James Cone has said that the Christian Church is that community of persons who "got the hint [of the gospel proclamation], and they thus refuse to be content with human pain and suffering," especially those which result from the institution of so-called law and order. The Church "is that community that participates in Christ's liberating work in history, meaning that it can never endorse law and order while people are suffering," especially since it itself causes much of the suffering.

Cone continues by explicating a threefold task of the Church: (1) it proclaims the reality of divine liberation and Christian freedom; (2) it actively shares in the liberation struggle; and (3) as a fellowship it is a visible manifestation that the gospel is a reality.[16]

J. D. Roberts holds that "the church needs to seek its own self-understanding. It needs to compare its present life with the purpose for which our Lord calls it into existence." We must constantly be engaged in testing our understanding of the church against that purpose. This is why Roberts further states: "The biblical images have been one means by which the church has sought and found self-knowledge. Our hermeneutical task is to discover the initial rootage and worldview of the images used in reference to their meaning in our present understanding."[17] This appropriation process, I would argue, enables us to move beyond the narrow confines of any imagery of the past to a progressive functional one for the present. The present context continues to be one of pain and suffering for blacks and other third world peoples. It is a cross-experience not unlike the crucifixion experience of Jesus and the persecution of the early church.

As we can compare the experience of black people in the United States with the crucifixion of Jesus, we can see the link between the Church and the Incarnate Christ. The Church becomes an extension of the incarnation.[18] As such it must be involved in the mission of saving the world. Recognizing this Roberts declares:

> The Church has a ministry of liberation and reconciliation in a world experiencing bondage and estrangement both personal and social. Its mission is to heal and disturb. Its message is at once a healing balm and a word of judgment. Jesus, who is Lord of the church, is its priest and prophet. He leads the Church onward towards God's kingly rule. The church militant moves toward the church triumphant.[19]

This threefold conception of Jesus Christ has its corollary ecclesial implications: the Church must govern, preach, and be prophetic.

But if the Church proclaims divine liberation and Christian freedom, and if it is to share in the liberation struggle, then it must be more than an institution and it certainly cannot be contained within the confines of a building (although it can be located there). Fannie Lou Hamer and her associates were indeed convinced that liberation was of divine origin and freedom the very basis of Christianity. Hamer was strong in her faith and Christian belief and, as noted, she often quoted Luke 4:18; she perceived it to be the primary focus of the gospel and consequently the central core of Christianity itself. The fellowship dimension of the Church/Christian experience *must* be more than a mere social event. Indeed, it must direct the struggle towards liberation and freedom.

The Church must be willing to risk active involvement in the struggles of oppressed peoples. This means taking a stand even when it is not expedient to do so, even when personal security is threatened. It is clear that from the beginning of Hamer's active work she recognized and accepted the risks, both collective/public and personal/private. When she and the others first attempted to register to vote they were harassed. When Hamer continued her involvement she was fired from her job and dismissed from her family on the plantation; that same night the home of the relatives to which she fled was shot up sixteen times. Her many beatings caused permanent physical damage.

Even the supposedly simple matter of telling the truth became a risk. Hamer reported:

> . . . right now if you tell the truth, you're watched like you're some kind of criminal. They put secret service men following you. . . . When you speak out somebody's there to crush you and then will say, "The land of the free and the home of the brave." And a person say well, "I don't want to fight in Vietnam, because I think it's wrong." The first thing they going to do is drag him before the House un-american activities and that ain't no lie. The House Un-American activities that's the most un-american thing that I ever heard.[20]

Even when one is dedicated to the Church, one risks racist and oppressive investigations.

Hamer and her associates were constantly in the line of fire because they stood up for justice in a context where injustice reigns supreme. Even the Church must take risks.

Womanist Reflection on the Life and Work of Hamer

Fannie Lou Hamer was a religious person, indeed a God-fearing person. Though few records exist of her church activities, her religious beliefs were continually demonstrated in her actions. The principle that governed the life and work of Hamer was freedom. All of her energies were directed toward the achievement of freedom for black people.

As a womanist, the life of Fannie Lou Hamer provides a vast resource from which womanist theologians must draw. Most notable is her ability to make the necessary human connections and interconnections in the Christian movement toward liberation. She makes real Anna Julia Cooper's notion of being broad in the concrete. When black women take God's intention for liberation seriously, they are concrete in their work and at the same time broad. In their struggle against racism and sexism they are connected with black men and with all women.

Fannie Lou Hamer was able to connect not only struggles against racism, classism, and sexism, she also connected the religious, the political, the economic and the cultural. She demonstrates that one area of struggle is inextricably related to another. She successfully resisted the tendency of others to mask critical issues by universalizing them out of existence. She is an example of black women's experience taking us to new heights and deeper depths in the theological enterprise.

All of us involved in the struggle for freedom and liberation would do well to continue in the spirit of Fannie Lou Hamer and to join her singing:

This Little Light of Mine . . .
I'm gonna let it shine . . .
Let, it shine . . . everywhere I go.

NOTES

1. Robert Wright, "Interview with Fannie Lou Hamer," August 9, 1968, pages 1-2, from the Civil Rights Documentation Project, Moorland-Spingarn Research Center, Howard University, Washington, D.C.
2. Anne Moody, *Coming of Age in Mississippi*, (New York: Dial Press, 1968), p. 45.
3. Fannie Lou Hamer "Black Voices of the South," *Ebony*, Vol. 26 (August 1971), p. 51.
4. Interview by Anne Romaine and Howard Romaine, 1966, p. 8, from the State Historical Society of Wisconsin, Madison, Wisconsin.
5. Wright interview, p. 26.
6. Fannie Lou Hamer, "Sick and Tired of Being Sick and Tired,", *Katallagete*, Fall 1968, p. 26.
7. *Ibid*.
8. Excerpt from an interview conducted by Anne Romaine in 1966, printed in *Southern Exposure*, Spring 1981, p. 47.

 9. *Ibid.*
10. Hamer, "Sick and Tired", p. 22.
11. James Cone, *A Black Theology of Liberation* (Philadelphia: Lippincott, 1970), p. 214.
12. J. Deotis Roberts, *A Black Political Theology* (Philadelphia: The Westminster Press, 1974), p. 119.
13. Hamer, "Sick and Tired", p. 25.
14. *Ibid.*
15. *Ibid.*
16. Cone, *A Black Theology*, pp. 230-232.
17. J. D. Roberts, *Black Theology in Dialogue* (Philadelphia: The Westminster Press, 1987), p. 51.
18. *Ibid.*
19. *Ibid.*
20. Romaines' interview, p. 4.

Ella Baker and the Origins of "Participatory Democracy"

CAROL MUELLER

Introduction

The sources of ideas that guide the transformation and renewal of societies are often obscured by dramatic events and charismatic leaders that fit the media's emphasis on conflict and celebrity and the public's demand for mythic leaders and heroic sacrifice. Yet the beliefs that may ultimately inspire the mobilization of thousands (and millions) have often been tested and retested in obscure and out-of-the-way places by individuals who may never write manifestos, lead demonstrations, call press conferences, or stand before TV cameras. As Ella Baker said of herself, "you didn't see me on television, you didn't see news stories about me. The kind of role that I tried to play was to pick up pieces or put together pieces out of which I hoped organization might come. My theory is, strong people don't need strong leaders."[1]

In the 1960s, a complex of ideas coalesced under the label "participatory democracy," bringing together in a new formulation the traditional appeal of democracy with an innovative tie to broader participation. The emphasis on participation had many implications, but three have been primary: (1) an appeal for grass roots involvement of people throughout society in the

51

decisions that control their lives; (2) the minimization of hierarchy and the associated emphasis on expertise and professionalism as a basis for leadership; and (3) a call for direct action as an answer to fear, alienation, and intellectual detachment. These ideas not only informed the student wing of the civil rights movement and the new left during the 1960s, but also the movements of the 1970s and 1980s that came to be called the "New Social Movements" in Western Europe and the United States.[2]

Participatory democracy legitimated an active public voice in a wide range of governmental decisions. Citizens now insisted on a voice in decisions regarding the composition of the Democratic Party—first in the challenge of the Mississippi Freedom Democratic Party in 1964 and later in the reforms of 1972; in the decisions of the government-sponsored Community Action Programs of the War on Poverty and the Model Cities Program; in the decision regarding foreign policy of the Vietnam War, the acquisition of new weapons systems such as the B-1 bomber and the MX missile as well as the later deployment of the Cruise and Pershing missile systems in Europe; and in the decisions regarding nuclear power and environmental pollution.

In addition, the ideas of participatory democracy encouraged a broader base for decision-making within social movement organizations. Experimentation with direct democracy and consensus decision-making ranged from the early voter registration projects of SNCC in Mississippi and Georgia,[3] to the ERAP projects of SDS in the slums of Northern cities in the mid-1960s,[4] to the consciousness raising groups of women's liberation in the late 1960s and early 1970s,[5] to the affinity groups associated with the antinuclear and peace movements of the late 1970s and early 1980s.[6] In many of these movements there has been a conscious effort to minimize hierarchy and professionalism.

Finally, this has been a period of unprecedented direct action.[7] Since the United States has had a long history of open resistance and rebellion (the slave revolts, the revolution against England, the Civil War, the labor movement, the Molly Maguires) and of civil disobedience (the women's suffrage movement of the World War I period, the nonviolent phase of the civil rights movement), it would be an obvious mistake to credit one particular formulation of ideas with legitimating direct intervention in the affairs of civil society or the state. Yet the ideas of participatory democracy frame the call to direct action—not as periodic response to crisis, but as part of a broader set of collective citizenship obligations.

These have been a powerful set of ideas, providing one of the major frameworks for legitimating, understanding, and stimulating the collective actions and protests of a period during which new resources combined with unprecedented political opportunity.[8] Despite the importance of these ideas, there is confusion and misunderstanding among historians regarding their origins. Particularly among some scholars studying the history of the Students for a Democratic Society (SDS), there is the assumption that participatory democracy originated with the intellectual core of students (Al Haber, Tom Hayden, Sharon Jeffrey, Bob Ross, Richard Flacks, and Steve Max) who participated most actively in drafting the Port Huron Statement of 1962.[9]

In contrast, I argue that the basic themes of participatory democracy were first articulated and given personal witness in the activism of Ella Baker. These ideas served as the basis for her decisive intervention in support of an independent student-led organization within the civil rights movement. The Student Nonviolent Coordinating Committee not only set much of the agenda for the civil rights movement during the next few years, but also served as a model for later student-led political organizations such as SDS. During those years, SNCC also served as a laboratory field station directly testing the ideas of participatory democracy in daily practice. An appreciation of the role of Ella Baker in the creation of the participatory democracy frame is important for recognizing the source of transforming ideas in a context of ongoing struggle.

Ella Baker's Participatory Democracy

As was well known within the civil rights movement but not very far outside it, Ella Baker was one of its key leaders and the most important nonstudent involved in the phase of student activism that began with the formation of the Student Nonviolent Coordinating Committee following the dramatic sit-ins of the winter and spring of 1960. In dedicating his book, *SNCC: The New Abolitionists*, to Ella Baker, Howard Zinn (political scientist, then faculty member of Spelman College, and adviser to SNCC) wrote in his acknowledgments, "And finally, there is the lady to whom this book is dedicated, who is more responsible than any other single individual for the birth of the new abolitionists as an organized group, and who remains the most tireless, the most modest, and the wisest activist I know in the struggle

53

for human rights today."[10] Writing his own history of SNCC at the close of the 1960s, James Forman, its executive director for most of that decade, begins "Book Two: A Bond of Sisters and Brothers, In a Circle of Trust" with a chapter on Ella Baker. It starts, "Ella Jo Baker, one of the key persons in the formation of SNCC, is one of those many strong black women who have devoted their lives to the liberation of their people."[11]

When this strong, black woman died in December, 1986, after fifty years of political activism, a funeral service was held in Harlem where she had lived most of her adult life. The list of pallbearers gives eloquent testimony to her central role in SNCC and the high regard in which she was held by many of its leaders. They were (listed in alphabetical order as they were on the program for the service):

Jamil Abdullah Al-Amin—formerly H. Rap Brown, elected chair of SNCC in 1967 to succeed Stokley Carmichael.

Julian Bond—for five years communications director of SNCC in the Atlanta office and later state representative in the Georgia House of Representatives.

Vincent Harding—minister and close associate of Martin Luther King.

Doug Harris

Charles McDew—chair of SNCC from October 1960 until the election of John Lewis in 1963.

Reginald Robinson—one of the first SNCC members to begin voter registration work in McComb, Mississippi, in 1961; later worked with Ella Baker in mobilizing Northern support for the challenge of the Mississippi Freedom Democratic Party.

Charles Sherrod—SNCC's first field secretary and leader of community work in southeast Georgia.

Kwame Toure—formerly Stokley Carmichael, elected chair of SNCC in 1966; gave voice to SNCC's emerging black power orientation in the mid-1960s.

Robert Zellner—the first white field secretary hired by SNCC.

Honorary pallbearers included James Forman and Bayard Rustin, one of the key figures with Ella Baker in the organization of In Freedom, the Northern support group for the Montgomery bus boycott who also worked with her in creating the Southern Christian Leadership Conference and one of her oldest political associates. The memorial service brought other civil rights leaders to pay their respects—Ralph Abernathy, cofounder of the SCLC and close associate of King; Wyatt T. Walker, who replaced Ella Baker as executive director of the SCLC in 1960; and Bernice Johnson Reagon of the Albany Movement and the SNCC Freedom Singers. The service included special tributes from Percy Sutton; Jo Ann Grant, veteran SNCC worker and

A legend in the civil rights movement, Ella Baker died in December 1986, after fifty years of political activism. This photograph was used in publicity for the documentary film *Fundi: The Story of Ella Baker*, produced by long-time SNCC activist Jo Ann Grant.
[Photo: *Schomburg Center for Research in Black Culture, NYPL*]

55

producer of *Fundi*, a documentary film of Miss Baker's life; Anne Braden, editor, with her husband, Carl, of the *Southern Patriot* newspaper published by the SCEF Education Fund, which Ella Baker served as a consultant; and Bob Moses, whose long years of organizing in the Mississippi project embodied, perhaps more than anyone else in SNCC, the philosophy of participatory democracy.

The words of Howard Zinn and James Farmer and the many who paid their respects at her funeral only begin to suggest the tributes to Miss Baker in the annals of the civil rights movement. Her lifetime of contributions to the goal of human freedom cannot be adequately chronicled here, but the major themes of her life are central to an understanding of the roots of participatory democracy as an outgrowth of active participation in the process of political struggle. The three themes of participatory democracy—grass roots involvement by people in the decisions that affect their lives; the minimization of hierarchy and professionalization in organizations working for social change; and direct action on the sources of injustice—grew out of more than twenty years of political experience that she brought to the fledgling student movement in the spring of 1960. The philosophy of social change that led her to insist on an independent student organization at the Raleigh Conference in April 1960 was the logical extension of these experiences combined with a Southern upbringing based in a strong allegiance to family and community.

Her great sense of social responsibility was based in the traditions of the small North Carolina community where she moved in 1911 at the age of eight with her family.[12] The local church was presided over by her grandfather, a former slave, who had bought the land on which he once had served, vowing to provide amply for the needs of his family and neighbors. It was a commonplace for his household to take in the local sick and needy. Regardless of their social position, Miss Baker learned at an early age to be responsible for all of them.

Her sense of community and responsibility expanded after graduating from Shaw University in Raleigh, North Carolina, in 1927. Unable to afford graduate work in sociology at the University of Chicago, she moved to New York where she could rely for support on her network of kin. Refusing to follow the traditional woman's route of schoolteaching, she at first found it impossible to find a job doing anything other than waitressing or domestic service—despite her college degree. By 1929, the Depression had struck and the problems of the poor and needy multiplied around her.

Empowerment of People at the Grass Roots

The type of solutions that Ella Baker sought in responding to the suffering of the Depression consistently reflected her belief that political action should empower people to solve their own problems. After several years of editorial work for the *American West Indian News* (1929-30) and the *Negro National News* (1932), she helped form the Young Negroes' Cooperative League, became its national director, and began organizing group buying through consumer cooperatives. Her experience as an organizer, speaker, and writer on consumer education led to her employment with the New Deal's Works Progress Administration (WPA). In the WPA, she continued to bring people together to augment their meager resources through collective buying.

Equally important, in the WPA, Ella Baker was exposed to the fermenting ideas on social change that were widely discussed in Harlem at this time. Miss Baker later said of those years, "New York was the hotbed of—let's call it radical thinking. You had every spectrum of radical thinking on the WPA. We had a lovely time! The ignorant ones, like me, we had lots of opportunity to hear and to evaluate whether or not this was the kind of thing you wanted to get into. Boy it was good, stimulating."[13]

The diversity of opinions that she characterized as "the nectar divine" apparently reinforced Ella Baker's commitment to social change through organizing people to act on their own behalf. In the late 1930s, as a young woman, she began working for the NAACP as a field organizer, traveling to cities, towns, and rural villages throughout the deep South, speaking wherever she could find a group of people who were willing to listen.

In an interview with historian Gerda Lerner, she described her work: "I used to leave New York about the 15th of February and travel through the South for four or five months. I would go to, say, Birmingham, Alabama and help to organize membership campaigns . . . You would deal with whatever the local problem was, and on the basis of the needs of the people you would try to organize them in the NAACP."[14] In the early 1940s, she was made assistant field secretary for the NAACP and in 1943 she was named the association's national director of branches.

In her many years of travel for the NAACP trying to help people organize against the pervasive racial violence of the South, she was developing her own understanding of how people can collectively fight oppression. In the early 1970s, she described what she had learned from her many years as a field organizer:

My basic sense of it has always been to get people to understand that in the long run they themselves are the only protection they have against violence or injustice. If they only had ten members in the NAACP at a given point, those ten members could be in touch with twenty-five members in the next little town, with fifty in the next and throughout the state as a result of the organization of state conferences, and they, of course, could be linked up with the national. People have to be made to understand that they cannot look for salvation anywhere but to themselves.[15]

Her belief in empowering people through their direct participation in social change assumed a new form when she took on the responsibility of raising her niece and gave up the annual six months of travel required of a field secretary. After several years of working in fund-raising for the National Urban League Service Fund, she was elected president of the New York branch of the NAACP. "We tried to bring the NAACP back, as I called it, to the people. We moved the branch out of an office building and located it where it would be more visible to the Harlem community. We started developing an active branch. It became one of the largest branches."[16]

When the Supreme Court's *Brown* decision came down in 1954, she was serving as chairman of the Education Committee of the New York branch of the NAACP. This committee began to fight segregation in the New York schools. Her view of what was successful about the work of this committee characteristically emphasized that "out of it came increased fervor on the part of the black communities to make some changes."[17]

She was critical of the national NAACP's failure to emphasize the development of self-sufficient local communities and, in 1944, initiated a series of regional leadership conferences, one attended by Rosa Parks of the Montgomery, Alabama, branch, to . . . "help local leaders develop their own leadership potential."[18]

She continued to emphasize meaningful participation and the development of the resources within individuals and institutions when she worked with the SCLC in the late 1950s. In its first project, the Crusade for Citizenship, a drive to register black voters in the South, Miss Baker worked with its first executive director, Reverend John Tilley, in local communities to try to get churches to organize social action committees, set up voter clinics, and affiliate with the SCLC. She attempted to interest its ministerial leaders in citizenship classes to teach basic reading and writing skills so that blacks could register to vote.[19] She argued that the classes could draw on the considerable resources that already existed at the local level in religious and educational groups of women. These as well as other suggestions to broaden

Ella Baker was the instigator of the conference at which SNCC was created and a constant defender of the autonomy of the organization. She is shown here (at left) at a Student Leadership Conference in Chapel Hill, North Carolina, in 1962. Others in the photograph include Carl Braden (hands on knees) beside his wife Anne Braden; Tom Hayden is at the far right.
[Photo: *State Historical Society of Wisconsin*]

the involvement of youth and women in SCLC fell on deaf ears and contributed to her dissatisfaction with its ministerial leadership.

The theme that later became a slogan, "Power to the People," served as Ella Baker's criterion for evaluating political work throughout her life. In the 1970s, when she was asked to comment on the movement for community control of schools, she saw it as part of a broad strategy:

> First, there is a prerequisite: the recognition on the part of the established powers that people have a right to participate in the decisions that affect their lives. And it doesn't matter whether those decisions have to do with schools or housing or some other aspect of their lives. There is a corollary to this prerequisite: the citizens themselves must be conscious of the fact that this is their right. Then comes the question, how do you reach people if they aren't already conscious of this right? And how do you break down resistance on the part of powers that be toward citizens becoming participants in decision making?
>
> I don't have any cut pattern, except that I believe that people, when informed about the things they are concerned with, will find a way to react. Now, whether their reactions are the most desirable at a given stage depends, to a large extent, upon whether the people who are in the controlling seat are open enough to permit people to react according to the way they see the situation. In organizing a community, you start with people where they are.[20]

Group-Centered Leadership

Ella Baker's impatience with the pretensions of hierarchy dated from her earliest childhood. Recalling her youth growing up in the South, she said:

> Where we lived *there was no sense of hierarchy*, in terms of those who have, having a right to look down upon, or to evaluate as a lesser breed, those who didn't have. Part of that could have resulted, I think, from two factors. One was the proximity of my maternal grandparents to slavery. They had known what it was to not have. Plus, my grandfather had gone into the Baptist ministry, and that was part of the quote, unquote, Christian concept of sharing with others. I went to a school that went in for Christian training. Then, there were people who "stood for something," as I call it. Your relationship to human beings was more important than your relationship to the amount of money that you made.[21]

This sense of equality contributed to her capacity to identify with people from all walks of life in her organizing work for the NAACP and later the SCLC and SNCC.

On what basis do you seek to organize people? Do you start to try to organize them on the fact of what you think, or what they are first interested in? You start where the people are. Identification with people. There's always this problem in the minority group that's escalating up the ladder in this culture, I think. Those who have gotten some training and those who have gotten some material gains, it's always the problem of their not understanding the possibility of being divorced from those who are not in their social classification. Now, there were those who felt they had made it, would be embarrassed by the fact that some people would get drunk and get in jail, and so they wouldn't be concerned too much about whether they were brutalized in jail. 'Cause he was a *drunk*! He was a so-and-so. Or she was a streetwalker. We get caught in that bag. And so you have to help break that down without alienating them at the same time. The gal who has been able to buy her minks and whose husband is a professional, they live well. You can't insult her, you never go and tell her she's a so-and-so for taking, for not identifying. You try to point out where her interest lies in identifying with that other one across the tracks who doesn't have minks.[22]

Miss Baker's antipathy to hierarchy combined with her commitment to grass roots organizing led to a particular concept of leadership that she called "group-centered leadership."[23] This pattern of leadership emphasized the role of the leader as a facilitator, as someone who brings out the potential in others, rather than a person who commands respect and a following as a result of charisma or status.

This view began in her organizing work in the South and continued as a source of tension in her many years with the NAACP. In commenting on the leadership of Walter White, she noted that, "Unfortunately, he also felt the need to impress government people. He had not learned, as many people still have not learned, that if you are involved with people and organizing them as a force, you didn't have to go and seek out the Establishment People. They would seek you out."[24]

She felt that some of this same attitude characterized the entire organization. In 1968, she told an interviewer:

Basically, I think personally, I've always felt that the Association got itself hung-up in what I call its legal success. Having had so many outstanding legal successes, it definitely seemed to have oriented its thinking in the direction that the way to achieve was through the courts. It hasn't departed too far from that yet. So, I said to you that when I came out of the Depression, I came out of it with a different point of view as to what constituted success . . . I began to feel that my greatest sense of success would be to succeed in doing with people some of the things that I thought would raise the level of masses of people, rather than the individual being accepted by the Establishment.[25]

Miss Baker remained a tough critic of professionalized leadership throughout her association with the NAACP.[26] In particular, she criticized its emphasis on membership size without creating opportunities for members to be meaningfully involved in the program. At the time of her association in the early 1940s, much of the NAACP's membership of four hundred thousand primarily provided a financial base for its professional staff of lawyers and lobbyists. Payne's research into the reports of the association's field secretaries to the National Board has found a strong preoccupation with membership size rather than activities.[27] These tensions contributed to Ella Baker's resigning as its national director of branches in 1946 (as did accepting responsibility for raising her niece).

The same issues over organizational leadership led to her eventual departure from the SCLC in 1960. Having been instrumental in the founding of the SCLC in 1957, Miss Baker agreed to go to Atlanta to set up its first office. She originally served as its only staff member. Her first responsibility was to coordinate meetings throughout the South on Lincoln's Birthday 1958 to kick off the SCLC's first program, a Crusade for Citizenship, which would seek to double the number of black voters in the South in one year.[28] With no resources and little support from the new ministerial associates of the SCLC, the fact that thirteen thousand people turned out in twenty-two cities "on the coldest night in 50 years" was miraculous.[29]

Ella Baker was the central figure in the SCLC Atlanta headquarters during the late 1950s.[30] She organized the office, carried on correspondence, and kept in touch with the local branches. With John Tilley, the executive director, she traveled throughout the South developing voter registration programs and SCLC affiliations that included a commitment to direct action.

It was not a compatible arrangement, however. Where Miss Baker had found earlier that professionalism and status concerns were an obstacle to group-centered leadership in the NAACP, she found in the SCLC that the emphasis on charismatic ministerial leadership was similarly at odds with her view of how organizations should be built to empower people to seek social change.

Despite considerably greater experience in working for social change than the ministers she worked for in the Atlanta office (she was fifty-four when she went to Atlanta), she was expected to handle administrative matters while her policy suggestions for greater emphasis on local organizing and the inclusion of women and youth were largely ignored.[31]

Ella Baker is shown here speaking at an Anti-Poverty Conference in 1965.
[Photo: *State Historical Society of Wisconsin*]

Although Tilley decided within a year to leave his post and return to his church in Baltimore, there was never any serious consideration of replacing him with Ella Baker. Instead, she was appointed acting director until an appropriate minister could be found. Reverend Wyatt Walker, who succeeded her, later told Morris, "When John Tilley left, it was within 90 days of his leaving or less [that] they knew they were going to hire me if they could get me, and Ella was just a holding action." Walker felt that Miss Baker could not fit into the preacher's organization: "It just went against the grain of the kind of person she is and was."[32]

The incompatibility between the SCLC and Ella Baker reflected their very different understandings of leadership and, thus, of programs. Miss Baker was very critical of placing great emphasis on a single leader, the organizing principle of the SCLC, focused as it was on the leadership of Martin Luther King, Jr. Thus, Miss Baker opposed not only its organizational principle, but the specific leadership of King as well. Asked in the early 1970s why she had not had a more prominent position in the civil rights movement, she stated her general philosophy of leadership:

> In government service and political life I have always felt it was a handicap for oppressed peoples to depend so largely upon a leader, because unfortunately in our culture, the charismatic leader usually becomes a leader because he has found a spot in the public limelight. It usually means he has been touted through the public media, which means that the media made him, and the media may undo him. There is also the danger in our culture that, because a person is called upon to give public statements and is acclaimed by the establishment, such a person gets to the point of believing that he *is* the movement. Such people get so involved with playing the game of being important that they exhaust themselves and their time, and they don't do the work of actually organizing people.[33]

For Ella Baker, it was more important to serve "what was a potential for all of us," than to look after her own needs for status or position. She said, "I knew from the beginning that as a woman, an older woman, in a group of ministers who are accustomed to having women largely as supporters, there was no place for me to have come into a leadership role. The competition wasn't worth it."[34]

Direct Action

The third component of the participatory democracy framework was an emphasis on opposing violence and the intransigence of bureaucratic and legalistic obstacles by collective demonstrations of the "will of the people."[35] Designed to counter apathy, fear, and resignation through an assertion of independence, as well as to exercise influence on behalf of collective goals, for Ella Baker it was always a part of an overall strategy of empowering people, never an end in itself.

In the deep South where she worked as an organizer for the NAACP, public affiliation with the organization in the 1940s and 1950s was itself an act of defiance that gave people a sense of strength through a collective effort. She said of those years:

> As assistant field secretary of the branches of the NAACP, much of my work was in the South. At that time, the NAACP was the leader on the cutting edge of social change. I remember when NAACP membership in the South was the basis for getting beaten up or even killed.
> You would go into areas where people were not yet organized in the NAACP and try to get them more involved. . . . Black people who were living in the South were constantly living with violence, part of the job was to help them to understand what that violence was and how they, in an organized fashion, could help to stem it.[36]

For years it was her job to convince people that they should take this risk.

Ella Baker saw direct action in the creation of an insurgent organization such as the Southern NAACP in the 1940s. In 1955, however, mobilization of the Montgomery Improvement Association inspired her, Bayard Rustin, and Stanley Levison of the New York support group In Friendship to believe that a new stage of public mass action had arrived.[37] Following the integration of the Montgomery buses, Miss Baker worked with Rustin, Levison, and King on seven "working papers" that the New York group hoped would serve as the basis for discussion at the meeting of January 1957 that would lead to the formation of the SCLC. Although the meetings were officially entitled the "Southern Negro Leaders Conference on Transportation and Non-violence Interpretation," the working papers called for a broad strategy.

The strategy called for two principal tactics: voting power and mass direct action. Until more blacks could vote, they argued, "we shall have to rely more and more on mass direct action as the one realistic political weapon."[38]

65

Montgomery showed that the center of gravity had shifted from the courts to community action; the only question was what kind of mass action to use. The In Friendship group considered many of the tactics later developed by SNCC under Ella Baker's tutelage, particularly mass arrests and the creation of a "small disciplined group of non-violent shock troops to lead community mass actions."[39] These working papers failed to have a significant impact on the formation of the SCLC for a variety of situational reasons. Yet commenting later on those formative days of the SCLC, Miss Baker thought there were other reasons as well: "The other, I think, factor that has to be honestly said is that Martin was not yet ready for the kind of leadership that would inspire these men to really grapple with . . . ideological differences and patterns of organization."[40] Nevertheless, the working papers indicated the direction of the thinking among the more experienced organizers from New York. Particularly, they are important in showing the ideas that Ella Baker would shortly bring to SNCC.

During her tenure with the SCLC in the late 1950s, her own efforts were still directed toward direct action in the context of empowering local people. As associate director and later as acting executive director, she went to Shreveport, Louisiana, to help with voter registration drives. There she supported an all-day stand-in at Caddo Parrish, where a strong local movement sent 250 to register but only forty-six were interviewed and only fifteen were actually allowed to complete registration. She also worked with Dr. C. O. Simpkins, a local dentist, to prepare sixty-eight witnesses who gave testimonies at a Louisiana hearing.[41] Altogether, she spent five months in Shreveport working with local leaders to counter the countless reprisals against blacks who tried to register.

Despite her efforts and those of many local leaders, Miss Baker felt that the SCLC at this time offered little support for a massive confrontation. Of her years with the SCLC's Crusade for Citizenship, she said, "It was very difficult to get it from being oriented in the direction of just big meetings; you know, having an annual conference, and a big meeting . . ."[42]

After Tilley left the position of executive director in April 1959, Ella Baker was named acting director. The following October, she wrote a memorandum expressing her frustration with the progress of the branches:

> The word Crusade connotes for me a vigorous movement, with high purpose and involving masses of people. In search for action that might help develop for SCLC more of the obvious characteristics of a crusade, a line of thinking was developed which I submit for your consideration. . . . To play a unique

role in the South, SCLC must offer, basically, a different "brand of goods" that fills unmet needs of the people. At the same time, it must provide for a sense of achievement and recognition for many people, particularly local leadership.[43]

At this time Ella Baker already knew that the SCLC had not provided the leadership in direct mass action that she, Rustin, and Levison had hoped for. She also saw it as limited by a conception of leadership that inhibited mass participation and exalted the charismatic leader. She felt that both limitations failed to organize the people for self-sufficiency.

Conclusion

When the winter of 1960 brought a massive wave of sit-ins by black college students throughout the South, it was Ella Baker who saw their potential more clearly than anyone else.[44] As conversations began within the civil rights organizations over how this new energy could be harnessed to fuel the lagging efforts of the movement, it was Ella Baker who called for an organizing conference of student sit-in leaders at her old alma mater, Shaw University. When the Raleigh meeting was held in April 1960, it was Ella Baker who insisted that the students who had created the sit-ins should decide their own future independently of the already established civil rights organizations.[45] When the Student Nonviolent Coordinating Committee was formed as a result of the Raleigh meeting, it was Ella Baker's unlabeled, but fully articulated, ideas on participatory democracy that were most compatible with the students' search for autonomous and active leadership roles in the civil rights movement.[46] As SNCC began to develop an office, a staff, and a program, it was Ella Baker who served as their chief adviser from 1960 through the challenge of the Mississippi Freedom Democratic Party in the summer of 1964. In the summer of 1960, she wrote of her hopes and dreams for the new student movements:

> By and large, this feeling that they have a destined date with freedom, was not limited to a drive for personal freedom, or even freedom for the Negro in the South. Repeatedly it was *emphasized that the movement was concerned with the moral implications of racial discrimination for the "whole world" and the "Human Race."*

67

This universality of approach was linked with a perceptive recognition that "it is important to keep the movement democratic and to avoid struggles for personal leadership."

It was further evident that desire for supportive cooperation from adult leaders and the adult community was also tempered by apprehension that adults might try to "capture" the student movement. The students showed willingness to be met on the basis of equality, but were intolerant of anything that smacked of manipulation or domination.

This inclination toward group-centered leadership, rather than toward a leader centered group pattern of organization, was refreshing indeed to those of the older group who bear the scars of the battle, the frustrations and the disillusionment that come when the prophetic leader turns out to have heavy feet of clay.[47]

When hundreds and then thousands of Northern white students supported the sit-ins or went South to view at first hand a student-led movement to end racial oppression, Ella Baker's ideas found another receptive audience and spread and spread and spread.

NOTES

1. Ellen Cantarow and Susan O'Mally, *Moving the Mountain: Women Working for Social Change* (Old Westbury: Feminist Press, 1980), p. 55.
2. Claus Offe, "New Social Movements: Challenging the Boundaries of Institutional Politics," *Social Research* 52, 4 (Winter 1975); Bert Klandermans and Sidney Tarrow, "Mobilization Into Social Movements: Synthesizing European and American Approaches," in *From Structure to Action: Comparing Movement Participation Across Cultures* (Greenwich, CT: JAI Press, 1988).
3. James Forman, *The Making of Black Revolutionaries* (Washington, D.C.: Open Hand, 1985); Clayborne Carson, *In Struggle: SNCC and the Black Awakening of the 1960s* (Cambridge: Harvard University Press, 1981).
4. James Miller, *Democracy is in the Streets* (New York: Simon and Schuster, 1977).
5. Joan Cassell, *A Group Called Women* (New York: David McKay, 1977); Jo Freeman, "The Tyranny of Structurelessness," in Jane S. Jaquette, ed., *Women in Politics* (New York: Wiley, 1974).
6. Steven E. Barkan, "Strategic, Tactical and Organizational Dilemmas of the Protest Movement Against Nuclear Power," *Social Problems* 27, 1 (October 1979).
7. See Craig Jenkins, "Interpreting the Stormy Sixties: Three Theories in Search of a Political Age," *Research in Political Sociology*, forthcoming, for a summary.
8. See John McCarthy and Mayer Zald, *The Trend of Social Movements in America: Professionalization and Resource Mobilization* (Morristown, NJ:

General Learning Press, 1973) on new resources; Craig Jenkins and Charles Perrow, "Insurgency of the Powerless," *American Sociological Review* 42 (April 1977); Doug McAdam, *Political Process and the Development of Black Insurgency* (Chicago: University of Chicago Press, 1982) on shifts in the political opportunity structure.

9. See especially James Miller, *Democracy Is In the Streets* (New York: Simon and Schuster, 1987).

10. Howard Zinn, *SNCC: The New Abolitionists* (Boston: Beacon Press, 1964), p. iii.

11. Forman, *Making of Black Revolutionaries*, p. 215.

12. Cantarow and O'Mally, *Moving the Mountain*.

13. *Ibid.*, p. 64.

14. Gerda Lerner, "Developing Community Leadership," in *Black Women in White America* (New York: Pantheon, 1972), p. 347.

15. *Ibid.*

16. *Ibid.*, p. 348.

17. *Ibid.*, p. 349.

18. Charles Payne, "'Strong People Don't Need Strong Leaders': Ella Baker and Models of Social Change," unpublished paper, Northwestern University, Department of African American Studies, 1987.

19. Aldon Morris, *The Origins of the Civil Rights Movement* (New York: Free Press, 1984), p. 114.

20. Lerner, "Developing Community Leadership," p. 20.

21. Cantarow and O'Mally, *Moving the Mountain*, p. 60.

22. *Ibid.*, p. 70.

23. See especially Payne, "'Strong People Don't Need Strong Leaders.'"

24. John Britton, Interview with Ella Baker, June 19, 1968, p. 6, Civil Rights Documentation Project, Moorland-Spingarn Research Center, Howard University.

25. *Ibid.*, p. 12.

26. Payne, "'Strong People Don't Need Strong Leaders,'" p. 5.

27. *Ibid.*, p. 36, n 4.

28. David Garrow, *Bearing the Cross* (New York: William Morrow, 1986), pp. 102-104.

29. Morris, *Origins of Civil Rights Movement*, p. 109.

30. *Ibid.*, pp. 102-108.

31. *Ibid.*

32. *Ibid.*, p. 115.

33. Lerner, "Developing Community Leadership," p. 351.

34. *Ibid.*; also Britton, Interview with Ella Baker, p. 34.

35. Miller, *Democracy Is In the Streets*.

36. Lerner, "Developing Community Leadership," pp. 346-47.

37. Garrow, *Bearing the Cross*, pp. 85-87.

38. *Ibid.*, pp. 85-86.

39. *Ibid.*, p. 86.

40. Britton, Interview with Ella Baker, p. 21.

41. *Ibid.*, p. 25.
42. *Ibid.*, p. 23.
43. Quoted in Morris, *Origins of Civil Rights Movement*, p. 112.
44. See Carson, *In Struggle*, pp. 19-30; Morris, *Origins of Civil Rights Movement*, pp. 195-223.
45. See especially Garrow, *Bearing the Cross*, pp. 131-34.
46. See Carol Mueller, "From Equal Rights to Participatory Democracy: Frame Generation in a Cycle of Protest," paper presented at American Sociological Association, August 1988.
47. Ella J. Baker, "Bigger Than a Hamburger," *The Southern Patriot* (June 1960).

Trailblazers: Women in the Montgomery Bus Boycott

MARY FAIR BURKS

W hen I was invited to participate in this conference, I was not sure of the difference between trailblazer and torchbearer; I often regard them as synonyms. So I looked them up in the Oxford English Dictionary. Briefly, trailblazer is a pioneer in a field of endeavor. Torchbearer can be used as a synonym, but it also indicates one who follows the trailblazer, imparting tested knowledge or truth provided originally by the pioneer in its rudimentary form.

Rosa Parks, Jo Ann Robinson and members of the Women's Political Council were trailblazers. Martin Luther King, Jr., was a torchbearer.

Rosa Lee McCauley Parks was a quiet, self-composed girl who did not seek to outshine anyone in the classroom but was always prepared. She was always pleasant and friendly, although I do not recall any very close friendships. She was self-sufficient, competent, and dignified, never needing to prove herself to others.

Rosa's schoolmates did not impose themselves on her. Instead, we respected her and admired her from a distance. Our teachers held her up as an example. In our day there were strict rules and regulations in school. We wore uniforms, which included lisle stockings. At recess the girls played on the south side of the campus while the boys played on the north. To be caught out of uniform wearing silk stockings or on the boys' side meant suspension. Rosa was never out of uniform, nor did she ever go on the boys' side as some of us did. She learned what was expected of her, always had a clean uniform, and never had to wear silk stockings because her lisles had not

71

dried. She planned ahead and avoided confrontations or suspensions. Her schoolmates admired her. Her teachers regarded her as a model student.

When Rosa McCauley finished her education, she went to work and later married Raymond Parks. Without fanfare she joined organizations such as the National Association for the Advancement of Colored People and devoted herself to community services and to her church.

In light of her probity, I was taken aback when I heard that Mrs. Parks had refused to give up her seat on a bus and had been arrested. Yet when the facts were verified and I reflected on what I knew about her, I decided it had not been out of character after all. No, Rosa as a rule did not defy authority, but once she had determined on a course of action, she would not retreat. She might ignore you, go around you, but never retreat.

I became convinced that she refused to give up her seat not only because she was tired, but because doing so would have violated her humanity and sense of dignity as well as her values regarding right and wrong, justice and injustice.

As for being a "plant" for the NAACP, Mrs. Parks has consistently denied this and there is no reason to doubt her. Had she been acting in behalf of the NAACP, she would have done so openly and demanded a group action on the part of the organization, since duplicity is not a part of her nature. Nor would she have gone to jail except out of principle.

Whatever her reasons for refusing to give up her seat on the bus, her arrest sparked an outburst of protest never before seen in Montgomery. Despite her self-effacing demeanor, she was highly respected by the black establishment of the city. She possessed sterling qualities, which its members were forced to admire in spite of their usual indifference.

The anger her arrest aroused is in contrast to what Martin Luther King, Jr., wrote about the black middle class of Montgomery. He commented that the community was crippled by the indifference of educated blacks, "expressed . . . in a lack of participation in any move toward better racial conditions and a sort of tacit acceptance of things as they were." In the same context he pointed out the terrible "passivity of the majority of the uneducated."[1]

But Mrs. Parks's arrest penetrated the indifference of the middle class and shook the passivity of the masses. The educated class realized that what had happened to her could happen to any one of them. Most of the passive masses did not know Rosa, but when the boycott was called, they identified with her situation. They had experienced it all too often. Their passivity, I

In 1946 Mary Fair Burks was inspired by a Vernon Johns sermon to begin the Women's Political Council, the members of which played a central role in the bus boycott in Montgomery almost ten years later.

Described by Dr. Burks as the "patron saint" of the Montgomery bus boycott, Rosa Parks had attended a workshop on school desegregation [*see* photograph on page 155] at Highlander Folk School two months before her momentous decision to refuse to give up her bus seat.
[Photo: *Schomburg Center for Research in Black Culture, NYPL*]

believe, merely covered their helplessness as well as their terrible will to survive—at any cost.

Mrs. Parks's arrest changed both the indifference and passivity. The question is why. I have tried to indicate one probable reason, but cause and effect are not easily connected, as history and the sciences prove. Perhaps the time for the boycott had come, or as Plato would have it, "mankind censure injustice fearing that they may be the victims of it." Even so, a catalyst was needed.

There is no doubt that Rosa Parks was the catalyst. Her quiet determination, her belief in principles, her sense of justice and injustice, her certainty of right and wrong, her never failing dignity, her courage in the face of adversity—all these qualities made her the inevitable catalyst.

I was in Montgomery recently and experienced a thrill when I came to Cleveland Avenue where Mrs. Parks had lived and saw a bright, new, shiny sign with Rosa Parks Avenue on it, replacing the old Cleveland Avenue sign.

She has become a legend not only in Montgomery, but throughout the nation. Schoolchildren, white and black, know the names of Rosa Parks and Martin Luther King, Jr., as surely as they know the names of George Washington and Abraham Lincoln.

Jo Ann Robinson, a name usually included in a footnote, an appendix, or at most in a paragraph, came to Montgomery in 1949 to work in the English department of Alabama State College. She was born in rural Georgia and educated in the Georgia schools and at Atlanta University. She was one of twelve children, the only one who received a college degree and did significant work in a doctoral program. This says something about her ambitions, her ideals, and her energy.

As a colleague, I liked Jo Ann instantly and in a very short time we became friends. Soon after her arrival, she became a member of Dexter Avenue Baptist Church and joined the Women's Political Council. Although Montgomery had the reputation of being cool to strangers, she was invited to join several civic and social clubs and became a much sought after dinner guest.

Jo Ann regarded everybody as a friend. Everybody, in turn, accepted her friendship. In addition, she is a dedicated and committed person, committed to friends, committed to work, committed to causes. She also is a woman of great faith.

When Jo Ann joined the Women's Political Council in 1950, she was a welcome addition. She did the work of ten women. I had organized the council in 1946 and had served as its president since its founding. The position was demanding and I had been in office longer than I intended. Fortunately, at the end of the year Jo Ann agreed to accept the presidency.

Contrary to Giddings,[2] she did not reorganize the council. However, it was under her presidency that we concentrated our efforts on bus abuses, confronted the City Commission, and precipitated the bus boycott.

Whether the boycott was solely Jo Ann's idea, as she claimed,[3] is debatable. What is important is that the boycott occurred. And once it was underway, nobody worked more diligently than she did as a member of the board of the Montgomery Improvement Association and as a representative of the Women's Political Council. Although others had contemplated a boycott, it was due in large part to Jo Ann's unswerving belief that it *could* be accomplished, and her never-failing optimism that it *would* be accomplished, and her selflessness and unbounded energy that it *was* accomplished.

Jo Ann's book on the boycott documents in detail what she and other unchronicled women contributed. It gives the most valid account of her own role as well as that of other women. The description by her publisher states her contribution with eloquence and objectivity:

> Histories of the Montgomery Bus Boycott of 1955-56 typically focus on Rosa Parks, who refused to yield her bus seat to a white man and a youthful Martin Luther King, Jr., who became the spokesman for the black community organization set up to pursue a boycott of Montgomery's segregated city buses. In an important revision of the traditional account, this extraordinary personal memoir reveals for the first time the earlier and more important role played by a group of middle-class black Montgomery women in creating the boycott. . . .
> With the publication of this book, the boycott becomes a milestone in the history of American women as well.[4]

Coretta Scott King also emphasized the book's importance:

> This valuable first hand account of the historic Montgomery Bus Boycott, written by an important behind the scenes organizer, evokes the emotional intensity of the civil rights struggle. It ought to be required reading for all Americans who value their freedom and the contribution of black women to our history.[5]

Conclusions about Jo Ann's contributions can also be judged by the fact that she—as well as I—was among the seventeen professors fired from

Alabama State College following the boycott. Jo Ann Robinson was the Joan of Arc of the Montgomery Bus Boycott and Rosa Parks was its patron saint.

I would like to add the name of Johnnie Carr to the roster of women of the boycott who should be more than a footnote. From Jo Ann's account, Carr was very active in the Montgomery Improvement Association and became its president when the major players dispersed and went their separate ways to begin new projects. She deserves Jo Ann's accolades.

The Women's Political Council was the outgrowth of scars I suffered as a result of racism as well as my desire to arouse black middle-class women to do something about the things they could change in segregated Montgomery.

Everyone remembers a painful incident that introduced him or her to racism. Mine occurred when my brother, on being called "nigger," rushed into the house to get his BB gun so he could kill the offending whites. Until then I had never heard the word "nigger," nor was I aware of differences in skin color. I was devastated when my mother explained these facts of life. I also remember being abruptly jerked from the front seat of a bus by my mother who, fiercely gripping my hand, took me to the back, where we stood. I knew it had to do with being a "nigger." I finally learned about segregated water fountains, rest rooms, buses, taxis, trains, restaurants, parks—the gamut.

The more I learned, the more bitter I became. So I angrily started my own private guerilla warfare. I told no one and fortunately I knew nothing about *Plessy* v. *Ferguson*, which legalized "separate but equal."

I went into rest rooms with signs FOR WHITE LADIES ONLY. Often I had no choice since there were neither other facilities for Negroes nor nearby bushes. I frequently ignored signs on elevators saying FOR WHITES ONLY. I became a sprinter by getting to doors before whites had a chance to slam them in my face. I was nearly arrested for walking through the segregated park with its sign on the gates FOR WHITES ONLY.

My capers ended when at eighteen I was accepted in the graduate school of the University of Michigan. Ann Arbor was almost Eden. For the first time since I had learned about segregation, I knew what it meant to feel and live like a whole human being. However, the Ann Arbor experience made it that much more difficult to accept the segregated South. When I came back to Montgomery, I was even more embittered by its unrelenting racism.

Jo Ann Gibson Robinson's memoir *The Montgomery Bus Boycott and the Women Who Started It* [edited, with a foreword by, David J. Garrow, University of Tennessee Press, 1987] made many people aware for the first time of the role members of the Women's Political Council played in the protest. Mary Fair Burks describes her as the "Joan of Arc" of the boycott.

On my return I was hired to teach in the English Department of Alabama State Laboratory High School. My new job was demanding, and since I was only nineteen, I was only two or three years older than most of my students. Soon afterward I married the principal and my former professor.

I put outside problems on hold until I was finally arrested. My arrest was ironic, since this time I had broken no law. I was in my car just behind a bus when the traffic light turned green. As I started to accelerate, I saw a white woman attempting to get to the curb. The short of it was that after the woman stopped cursing me, I was arrested.

When the woman was located and pressured into making charges, I tried to explain that it was she, not I, using profanity, but I was stopped by a policeman's billy club. Before being thrown into a cell I insisted on my right to a telephone call. (I had learned such legalities in Michigan.) My husband came to the jail accompanied by a family friend and a white lawyer who read the charge, tore it up, and demanded my release. There were no black lawyers at the time, but even if there had been, only a white lawyer could have torn up that charge and secured my release. It was after this truly traumatic experience that I resolved to do something more about segregation besides waging my own personal war. My arrest convinced me that my defiance alone would do little or nothing to remedy such situations. Only organized effort could do that. But where to start?

I had no idea until Vernon Johns, pastor of Dexter Avenue Baptist Church, mounted one of his scathing attacks on the complacency of his affluent membership. I looked around and all I could see were either masks of indifference or scorn. Johns's attacks, his patched pants, and his Thoreauvian philosophy of plain living and high thinking did not endear him to his congregation. I was a feminist before I really knew what the word meant and so I dismissed the hard-faced men, but I felt that I could appeal to some of the women. I played bridge with them, but more important, I knew that they must suffer from the racial abuse and the indignity accorded all blacks, even though they were somewhat insulated from it. Their outward indifference was a mask to protect both their psyche and their sanity. I believed that I could get enough such women together to address some of the glaring racial problems. Thus the idea of the Women's Political Council was born on that Sunday morning following my arrest.

During the next week I contacted fifty women, sounding them out about the idea of an organization of women to deal with some of the city's racial problems. To my surprise, forty of them attended the organizational meeting held in the early fall of 1946. *Brown v. the Board of Education* was just an idea being discussed by lawyers of the NAACP. *Plessy v. Ferguson* remained unchallenged in the deep South. Yet these forty women were willing try to improve conditions for blacks.

In this initial meeting nearly every woman recalled an incident similar to mine. They were mortified over the circumstances of my arrest. No, we did not consider overthrowing *Plessy*. Only a miracle could do that. What we could do was to seek political leverage as we protested racial abuses.

We finally agreed on a three-tier approach: first, political action, including voter registration and interviewing candidates for office; second, protest about abuses on city buses and use of taxpayers' money to operate segregated parks (we assumed that segregated schools and housing would be with us forever, and they still are); and third, education, which involved teaching young high school students about democracy and how it was intended to operate as well as teaching adults to read and write well enough to fulfill the literacy requirements for voting.

The name of the organization was more divisive than the program. The majority were in favor of a vague title that included the phrase human relations. I was vehemently opposed. Our goal was political leverage and I wanted a title that made this unequivocally clear. We voted on two titles—The Women's Political Council and the Women's Human Relations Council. The former won by a narrow margin.

At the time we did not know we were making history and would become trailblazers of the civil rights movement. More than thirty women pioneered the organization and their names should not go unchronicled. Among them were Cynthia Alexander, Elizabeth Arrington, Sadie Brooks, Albertine Campbell, Mary Cross, Faustine Dunn, Thelma Glass, Frizette Lee, Jewel Clayton Lewis, Thelma Morris, Geraldine Nesbitt, Ivy Pettus, Zoeline Pierce, Louise Streety, Cleonia Taylor, Portia Trenholm, Ruth Vines, Irene West, and Bertha Williams. There were others whose names have escaped me. Later, Jo Ann Robinson and Uretta Adair joined our ranks. They both became members of the board of the Montgomery Improvement Association.

To my dismay, I was chosen as president of the WPC. It was not unexpected, however. Present an idea or a program and almost without exception you will be elected to carry it out. Perhaps there is some kind of fairness in such a situation. If you cannot carry out your ideas, keep them to yourself.

Our first undertaking was to become registered voters ourselves. That we all were not voters may seem strange in light of our goals, but that was why one of our purposes was to break down the barriers that kept Negroes such as ourselves from becoming registered voters—literacy tests, accumulated poll taxes, intimidation. The literacy test alone had prevented many of the group from becoming registered. Even Ph.D.s failed the test, since Negroes could never be sure of minor details such as their precinct number, which was changed arbitrarily without notification. Our first order of business was to take the test as often as necessary to become qualified. All finally qualified.

Meanwhile, WPC began its citywide registration schools. These were set up in various churches with the cooperation of the ministers. They met weekly to teach people how to fill out registration forms as well as how to write, if necessary. When applicants were ready, we took them to the courthouse where they filled out the forms. We even accompanied them when they returned to the courthouse to check on the results of the applications (which should have been mailed to them). This last strategy, we believe, increased the success rate.

As for voting, members of the WPC enlisted the aid of the League of Women Voters to have white candidates appear before the group and state the issues and their policies. (Unable to join the Montgomery League of Women Voters—a segregated group to which black women were denied membership—we invited the members of the League to our meetings to help keep us informed about who the political candidates were and how they *really* stood on various issues.) Other black organizations, such as the Progressive Democrats and the Citizens Steering Committee, also had candidates appear before them. We combined our information and came up with candidates whom we recommended for bloc voting. As chairman of the Political Action Committee of the Dexter Avenue Baptist Church—a committee formed by Dr. King—following church services I would read the names of the candidates whom we had decided were the least objectionable, considering the fact that we would be voting under the slogan "White Supremacy." Other churches initiated similar practices. To our dismay, white friends in the Montgomery Council of Human Relations, a branch of the Alabama Council, objected to this practice, but survival made pragmatists of the most idealistic of us. By bloc voting in very close races our votes often could decide the outcome. So we voted in a bloc, despite the disapproval of the Human Relations Council.

Youth City was another success story of the WPC. It was modeled after Youth City sponsored for white high school students attending the million-dollar Sidney Lanier High School. Successful candidates were rewarded by becoming governor, state legislators, mayor, and commissioners for a day. Of course Negroes were not included.

The WPC, knowing the value of such training, developed a plan for a Negro Youth City. There were only two black high schools, Alabama State Laboratory and Booker T. Washington. To their credit, the principals of both schools cooperated, despite the serious consequences if our real purpose were known. They excused all seniors for one day, Friday, which enabled us to use Saturday and thus have a two-day program.

In addition to electing counterparts to government officials, we also taught Negro students what democracy could and should mean. On the surface we were merely imitating, but in reality we were using subversive tactics to serve our own ends.

Later we felt justified when we saw students who had participated in Youth City become political leaders. They registered at twenty-one and quickly became active in politics. Some of them today are lawyers, judges, and state legislators.

The bus boycott was still several years away. So our next target was opening up the public parks to Negroes.

As we walked through the park on our way to the office of the commission, I remembered my almost disastrous walk several years earlier. This time there were no policemen to confront us.

We met the commission and pointed out that blacks paid taxes for the segregated park. The commissioners countered that most Negroes rented. We argued that their white landlords made sure that any taxes owed were paid by the Negro renters. We also made the case that there were other indirect taxes paid by all but borne disproportionately by blacks who earned so much less than the average white worker.

We held several meetings with the commission but made little headway, mainly I think because separate facilities were allowed under *Plessy*. The only concession we received was to let Negroes walk through the park on their way to work for the whites. The age of the swim-ins and sit-ins unfortunately had not yet arrived. However, we paved the way for them.

Meanwhile we had been working on abuses on the buses. In light of *Plessy*, we were not fighting segregation as much as the abuses of Negroes who constituted the buses' major patrons.

We took our complaints to City Hall. In our early meetings the City Commission feigned surprise over what they called "alleged" abuses, despite the fact that bus conductors legally carried guns. Members of the WPC appeared before the commission at least six or seven times before the Colvin case. To my knowledge, the council was the only group to do so. True, we succeeded only in annoying the commission, but this was better than nothing.

It was not until Claudette Colvin, a young high school girl, was arrested that all of the Negro organizations came together and met the commission with a united front. Dr. King was present, along with other members of the Ministerial Association. Rufus Lewis, president of the Citizens Steering Committee, and E. D. Nixon, president of the Progressive Democrats, also were there. Representing the Women's Political Council were Jo Ann Robinson, Irene West, Uretta Adair, and I.

It was at this heated meeting that a boycott was mentioned. At that point we had neither discussed a boycott as a group nor did we have any strategies for carrying out such an action. We did discuss a boycott later, but it was abandoned when it was learned that Colvin was pregnant and that the charge had been changed to resisting arrest.

Meanwhile, several other cases occurred, but it was not until Rosa Parks was arrested that resistance coalesced. The rest of the story is history.

Let me add a footnote about the distribution of leaflets announcing the boycott. The announcement distributed on Saturday was composed on Friday night after the official boycott vote by representatives of the Women's Political Council in the basement of the Dexter Avenue Baptist Church (the men were on the other side of the room planning strategy). In addition to Jo Ann Robinson and me, Irene West and Uretta Adair participated. After our formulation had been approved by everyone present, it was typed by Jo Ann and mimeographed.

The distribution of these leaflets on Saturday provides some insight into the attitudes of many middle-class black women in Montgomery. Jo Ann Robinson and I had accepted invitations weeks before to attend a large bridge party that evening. Once such an invitation was accepted the only valid reason for not attending was death—your own. Our solution to the dilemma of distributing the leaflets and attending the bridge party was to get an early start on Saturday morning—six o'clock to be precise.

Despite our early start, progress was slow. Often we not only had to take time to explain the leaflet, but also first to read it to those unable to do so.

It was my first encounter with masses of the truly poor and disenfranchised. I remember thinking that not even a successful boycott would solve the problems of poverty and illiteracy which I saw that day.

As a result of these delays, we were an hour late for the bridge party. Our partners were irate, despite our explanations. My partner was not only irate, but also prophetic. She said "I hope you will have a job on Monday." We were not fired on Monday, but later, fired we were—just as she had prophesied. And so about one hundred black women played bridge a scant thirty-six hours before the boycott began, much like Nero had played his fiddle while Rome burned. That was the black middle class before the boycott.

My remarks about the Women's Political Council have centered around Robinson, West, and Adair, but I do not mean to diminish the contributions of the other women of the council. They gave us their moral support, supplied funds, drove in the car pool. Without the participation of all the women in the council there would have been no voter registration schools or Youth City, and certainly the women who represented the council on the board of the Montgomery Improvement Association would have had less authoritative voices.

I have concentrated on the women who were trailblazers in the Montgomery Bus Boycott—Rosa Parks, Jo Ann Robinson, Johnnie Carr, and members of the Women's Political Council, but I also pay tribute to the nameless cooks and maids who walked endless miles for a year to bring about the breach in the walls of segregation.

NOTES

1. Martin Luther King, Jr., *Stride Toward Freedom* (New York: Harper & Row, 1958), pp. 20,21.
2. Paula Giddings, *When and Where I Enter: The Impact of Black Women on Race and Sex in America* (New York: William Morrow, 1984).
3. David J. Garrow, editor, *The Montgomery Bus Boycott and the Women Who Started It: The Memoir of Jo Ann Gibson Robinson* (Knoxville: University of Tennessee Press, 1987), p. 45.
4. *Ibid.*, jacket copy.
5. *Ibid.*

Septima P. Clark and the Struggle for Human Rights

GRACE JORDAN McFADDEN

Septima Poinsette Clark's death on December 15, 1987, ended her struggle for human rights for her people within the framework of the United States' political, social, and economic system. Referred to as the "Mother of the Movement," by Martin Luther King, Jr., she had been at the vanguard of the human rights quest.[1]

A native of Charleston, South Carolina, she was born on May 3, 1898. Her father, Peter Poinsette, was born a slave on the Joel Poinsette farm between the Waccamaw River and Georgetown. Her mother, Victoria Warren Anderson Poinsette, was born in Charleston and was taken to Haiti by her uncle in 1864, along with her two sisters, Martha and Maseline.[2]

> My father was very gentle and my mother was very haughty. The English did a better job in Haiti teaching them to read and write, so she [Victoria Poinsette] boasted of being a free issue. She often said, "I never gave a white woman a drink of water." My father was such a gentle, very wonderful guy. It was good for those two to be together because my mother, with her haughtiness, and my father, with his gentleness, I felt that I stood on a platform that was built by both. And when I went to Mississippi and Texas and places like that, I had a feeling that his nonviolence helped me to work with the people there and her haughtiness helped me to stay. . . . I got into many places where we had a lot of harassment from the Ku Klux Klan and the White Citizen's Council in Tuscaloosa, Alabama, and Grenada, Mississippi, and Natchez, Mississippi. I stood on a platform built by my mother and father.[3]

Septima Poinsette's father worked as a caterer following the Civil War. Her mother took in laundry. Since teaching was one of the few professions available to black women at the beginning of the twentieth century, Septima took the state examination in 1916 after having completed twelfth grade at Avery Normal Institute in Charleston, South Carolina.[4] Teaching would enable her to have a career and help her family financially.

> I had to take an examination of eleven subjects in order to teach. . . . I received the licientiate of instruction and went over to John's Island to teach in a two-teacher school there. In that two-teacher school we had 132 children and a building that was creosoted black. We were all black together. Across the road from where I worked was a white schoolhouse that was whitewashed and three children attending that with one teacher. That teacher received $85 a month for her teaching and living. And the rest of us, the two teachers who taught across the street—I was the teaching principal so I got $35 and the assistant $25. Both of us made $60 to the one teacher who made $85 for three children. And there we were working for $60 a month with 132 children.[5]

Poinsette remained on John's Island for three years, during which time she became a crusader for the equalization of teachers' salaries as well as an active proponent for black teachers being allowed to teach in Charleston's public schools and becoming public school principals. In 1919, she returned to Charleston to teach sixth grade at Avery Normal Institute. It was then that her civil rights work commenced. She attended NAACP meetings in Charleston and heard Edwin Halston, a prominent artist and civil rights advocate, discuss the conditions facing black people during that historic epoch. She was inspired by Halston as well as by Thomas Ezekiel Miller, who had served as a congressman from South Carolina during Reconstruction and later became president of South Carolina State College. Miller and Halston addressed mass meetings in order to generate support for black teachers to teach in the public schools of Charleston. Poinsette began her civil rights work by going door-to-door, asking people to sign petitions.

> Now, a lot of people in downtown Charleston said that only the mulattoes wanted their daughters to work in the schools, but that the chauffeurs and cooks didn't mind whatsoever. They were satisfied for their daughters to come to us as they had. And that's when we put on the door-to-door campaign. Some people wrote their names on pieces of paper bags to say that they wanted their daughters to work in the public schools as well. I was teaching at Avery then. I was teaching the sixth grade. So I took my class one day, with the permission of the principal, and we walked the streets from one door

to another and received those signatures. And those signatures Mr. Halston gave to Tom E. Miller who was at State College in Orangeburg. And Tom E. Miller wanted 10,000 signatures. We put them in a croaker sack and he took them up to the legislature to let them know that there were blacks who were cooks and maids and chauffeurs who wanted their children to teach black children in the public schools of Charleston. And in 1920, well, the end of 1919, when the legislature closed, that thing became a law.[6]

And the following year we had Negro principals. We had been victorious in this my first effort to establish for Negro citizens what I sincerely believed to be their God given right.[7]

As a youngster she enhanced her social and racial consciousness while watching ships from Marcus Garvey's Black Star Shipping Line dock at Charleston Harbor and passengers embark and disembark. This venture filled here with racial pride and dignity. Marcus Garvey, a Jamaican immigrant, had founded the Universal Negro Improvement Association in 1916. The UNIA was a worldwide racial and economic program among people of African descent. Later, as a student at Atlanta University in 1937, Clark would take a course from Dr. W. E. B. Du Bois whom she described as "an aloof professor" but a thorough scholar. Du Bois , an eminent scholar and author, founder of the Niagara Movement, co-founder of the NAACP and editor of its *Crisis* magazine, would influence Clark's documentation of events as well as her commitment to writing.

Septima Poinsette married seaman Nerie Clark in May 1920. Two children were born to the marriage, a daughter who died a month after her birth and a son, Nerie Clark, Jr. Nerie Clark was at sea during the early years of the marriage. Following his discharge from the navy, the family moved to Dayton, Ohio. The marriage was short-lived, however. Nerie died of kidney ailment in December 1925 shortly before his thirty-sixth birthday. Having to support her young son, Septima Clark lived with her husband's relatives in Dayton and Hickory, North Carolina, before finally settling in Columbia, South Carolina, in 1929, where she remained until 1947. During her time in Columbia she received her B.A. from Benedict College and her M.A. from Hampton Institute. In 1935, she sent her son back to Hickory to live with his paternal grandparents. Nerie, Jr. remained there through high school. Clark explained that the move was necessary because she didn't earn enough money to support her son and most boarding houses would not allow children.[8] A benefit of this separation from her child was that Clark now had the freedom necessary for social and political action.

The move to Columbia had increased her consciousness.

I hadn't been in Columbia long, in fact, before I discovered that upcountry Columbia, in the center of the state, was different from my native low country Charleston. In Charleston, both white and Negro were rooted in tradition. Columbia was more democratic. . . . In Columbia everyone mixed, and the schoolteachers were considered rather high up in the social ladder and the doctor's wife and the schoolteacher and the woman working as a domestic sat down at the bridge table. In fact, when Negro doctors in Columbia had their meetings, they would invite not only their wives and their more elite friends to the social functions but also their patients. They left no one out.[9]

During her years in Columbia, South Carolina, Clark began her work in citizenship education. Wil Lou Gray, head of the South Carolina Adult Education Program in 1935, had been asked by the army to establish a program to help educate black illiterate soldiers stationed at Camp Jackson (now Fort Jackson) following World War I. Approximately 50 percent of South Carolina's men who sought military service were not accepted because of illiteracy.[10] This introduction to citizenship education trained soldiers to sign their names to pay slips, read bus routes and learn to count. The Camp Jackson program later became the basis for the citizenship schools Septima Clark designed at Highlander Folk School and SCLC. Clark's ability to link social reform with educational advancement began with her teaching on John's Island in 1916. It would continue throughout her life as a proponent of citizenship education.

It was in Columbia that Septima Poinsette Clark became actively involved in the teachers' salary equalization campaign. She worked with Booker T. Washington High School principal J. Andrew Simmons; NAACP lawyer Thurgood Marshall, South Carolina' civil rights lawyer Harold R. Boulware, and others in preparing a court case. Proclaimed Clark: "My participation in this fight to force equalization of white and Negro teachers' salaries on the basis of certification, of course, was what might be described by some no doubt, as my first radical job. I, however, would call it my first effort in a social action, challenging the status quo. It was the first time I had worked against people directing a system for which I was working."[11] The hearings were held in the South Carolina State House. The black people who attended were not allowed to sit on the main floor. Clark recalls:

When we were having the hearings for the teachers' salaries equalization, we had to sit in the balcony. We couldn't sit on the main floor. Segregation was still in '35 and '36. But, I went and stayed from around 3:00 p.m. in the afternoon until around nine o'clock at night. And, I was hearing this thing through. And, finally they decided that we would have to take an examination. . . . I took the examination and made an A on it. Immediately my salary tripled. I thought I was wealthy then. . . . Now the principal who worked on the equalization, J. A. Simmons, he resigned after we met because he felt they were going to dismiss him. But, I worked on until 1947, from '36 until '47, when my mother took sick and she had a stroke and then I came home because I wanted to be with her. I had been in Columbia for eighteen years. Following that court decision my salary had advanced to almost $4,000 a year.[12]

In 1945 Federal District Judge J. Waties Waring of South Carolina, who later became a friend of Septima Clark, ruled in Viola Duvall's class action suit on behalf of Charleston, South Carolina's black teachers that teachers with equal education should receive equal pay.[13]

Clark worked in the Charleston public schools from 1947 to 1956. During this time, she was active with the YWCA, attended workshops on desegregation at Highlander Folk School in Tennessee, and supported civil rights efforts. She was also a member of the Charleston NAACP, serving as its membership chairperson. On April 19, 1956, the South Carolina legislature passed a law stipulating that no city or state employee could be affiliated with any civil rights organization. But Clark refused to conceal her membership: "I couldn't refuse them, and I was dismissed." Clark's political action was well grounded by now. She had signed her name to 726 letters that were sent to black teachers requesting that they protest the law. Only 26 answered, and when Clark urged them to talk to the superintendent of schools, only 11 agreed to go and only 5 actually showed up. (The superintendent told them that they were years ahead of their time.) Shortly thereafter, Clark was fired. She was 58 years old and had been teaching for forty years. She not only lost her job, but also her state retirement benefits. In 1976 Governor James Edwards, the first Republican governor of South Carolina, wrote Clark to acknowledge that she had been unjustly terminated and thus was entitled to her pension.[14]

Once again Clark turned adversity to her advantage. She now had more time for social activism, and Myles Horton, director of Highlander Folk School in Monteagle, Tennessee, recruited her as director of workshops. Highlander was an authentic proponent of social change: the school advocated human brotherhood; sought to eliminate stereotypes, break down racial barriers, and develop leaders. Beneficiaries of its programs spanned a wide gulf, from Esau Jenkins of John's Island who gained social welfare skills to aid his fellow islanders to Rosa Parks who gained knowledge of civil disobedience and, as a consequence, sparked the Montgomery bus boycott.

[Rosa Parks] came to Highlander Folk School while I was directing the education program in 1955. She was working with a youth group in Montgomery and she said, "I want to come and see if I can do something for my people." So she came. We sent money and gave her a scholarship. And when she went home, she had gained enough courage, enough strength to feel that she could stand firm and decide not to move when that man asked for her seat.[15]

Highlander Folk School prepared Clark for her subsequent work with the Southern Christian Leadership Conference (SCLC).

Highlander workshops were planned and conducted to emphasize a cooperative rather than a competitive use of learning. They hoped through the teaching of leaders to advance a community, rather than individuals, though the advancement of the community always advanced the individuals in it. People came to Highlander to seek enlightenment on issues whose proper solution, followed by adequate social action, would promote the advancement of all. Highlander Folk School's workshops included persons of all races and levels of economic and education success.[16]

Clark sought the assistance of many outstanding black leaders to assist her at Highlander. In July 1960 she wrote to Ella Baker: "We are attempting to help these people [the young people in the sit-in movement] by bringing them to the school for a workshop on the tactics and techniques of follow-through in school desegregation, voter registration, leadership education. Won't you come to this workshop and show your experiences in the current problems?"[17] Baker came to Highlander in 1960 and worked with Clark training young people for leadership roles and responsibilities in the civil rights movement.

In the spring of 1961, Septima Clark departed from her position at Highlander Folk School, though she remained on the staff as an educational consultant. She was recruited by Martin Luther King, Jr. and joined the staff of SCLC as director of education and teaching. This affiliation paralleled her work at Highlander, focusing on citizenship training, voting, and literacy. At the age of sixty-three, Clark traveled throughout the Southern states directing workshops for SCLC. She instilled in the minds of her workshop participants that they must become cognizant of "the non-partisan basis of the American system. They are taught their constitutional rights and how to organize to obtain the political power to get streetlights or better roads and schools in their part of town. The right to peaceful assembly and to petition for redress of grievances is related to how they can organize their own

The Citizenship Schools which Septima Clark created, first under the auspices of Highlander Folk School and later under the sponsorship of the Southern Christian Leadership Conference were described by Andrew Young as the base upon which the whole civil rights movement was built. She is shown here (center) at Highlander Folk School with Rosa Parks (left).
[Photo: *Highlander Folk School*]

community for change."[18] She was the first woman elected to the Executive Board of SCLC.

Clark's involvement with SCLC fully tested the qualities of patience, endurance, and strength of mind that had been instilled in her by her parents. Of her years with SCLC, she stated:

> I went to SCLC and worked with Dr. King as director of education and director of teaching. And there traveled from place to place getting people to realize that they wanted to eliminate illiteracy. We had to eliminate illiteracy first! And then after eliminating illiteracy, then we went into registration and voting and getting them to want to register and vote. And of course, you know we had a terrible struggle because thirty or more persons were killed in the registration and voting drive. But we didn't stop! We went on! And in '64 we got the Civil Rights Bill and they couldn't harass us as we worked in the lines.[19]
>
> I first started holding workshops in a place called Liberty County, Georgia. People in Liberty learned how to write their names and read and write under trees, in beauty parlors. Then we would go down with them to the registration office. The people were eager to go there. A man in Liberty County, Georgia said to me, "It's a dangerous thing to do. Why do you live dangerous?" And I replied, "It's something that I have to do!" And it was. We were often harassed by the White Citizen's Council. Following one of our meetings in Grenada, Mississippi, just about five minutes after we got out of the church, it was set afire. I don't know how they got in to put those things around the church.[20]

Clark's work with SCLC required that she travel throughout the Southeastern United States directing workshops in citizenship, education, and voting. In southern Georgia, she conducted workshops on how to make out a bank check.

> We brought in a banker from a little town outside of Savannah. McRae, I think it was, and he put the whole form up on the board and showed them how to write this thing out and how to put your date and how to write it out. He told them, "Don't leave a space to the end of the check. Someone else could write your number in there and you'd get out more than you expected, and then when you finish putting down the amount, take a line and carry it all the way to that dollar, to the thing that says dollar."[21]

The white citizens started to harass black people who were learning proper banking methods.

The Black people had been in the habit of having them make out the check for them, and they'd just sign with a "X." One fellow said though, that he went to the bank and the White man said to him, "Just bring it over here, and I'll fix it for you." The Black man said, "No, I can write my name." The White man said, "Oh, God, these niggers done learned to write their names."[22]

The goal of the Citizenship Schools was to provide full citizenship through education. Clark sought to place non-traditional teachers at her schools. Communities which sought her teachers desired individuals who by their backgrounds would make good teachers, such as beauticians, farmers, tradesmen, etc. Clark wanted those who offered "a 'folk' approach to learning rather than a classical one."[23]

Septima Clark's recollections of SCLC provide insight into the role of women in the organization as well as the reluctance of some black ministers to have their parishioners involved in her program.

I found Dr. King to be a very, very nonviolent man. He proved to us all that nonviolence would work. He also made black people aware of their blackness and not ashamed of being black. The thing that I think stands out a whole lot was the fact that women could never be accorded their rightful place even in the southern Christian Leadership Conference. I can't ever forget Reverend Abernathy saying, "Why is Mrs. Clark on the Executive Board?" And Dr. King saying, "Why, she designed a whole program." "Well, I just can't see why you got to have her on the Board!" They just didn't feel as if a woman, you know, had any sense. See, Mrs. King has come into her own since Dr. King's death. Because most of them felt that a woman couldn't say much or do much. I don't know if you know Ella Baker who lives in New York now. She had a brilliant mind in the beginning of the Southern Christian Leadership Conference. But the men never would feel, you know, she had a rightful place there. I think that up to the time that Dr. King was nearing the end that he really felt that black women had a place in the movement and in the whole world. The men didn't, though! The men who worked with him didn't have that kind of idea.[24]

According to Clark, Rosa Parks never managed to achieve her rightful place in the civil rights movement.

If you notice the movie, *From Montgomery to Memphis*, not even Rosa Parks was accorded her rightful place in the whole movie. We talked about it, she and I. She gave Dr. King the right to practice his nonviolence. Because by refusing to get up out of that seat was the real fact that he could organize the boycott and work with people all through. And it went into many countries.

People from China sent money for station wagons and from India and other places. And it was Rosa Parks who started the whole thing.[25]

Septima Clark, too, has been an outspoken advocate of nonviolence. Her Christmas message in December 1967 articulated her convictions.

The way I see it, the test is on us now, those who believe in nonviolence and brotherhood. Things which I hear labeled out-of-date and unrealistic, we must make it work. We must build a foundation throughout the long hot summers and long cold winters. This foundation, whether rooted in Christianity or single person-to-person contact must achieve what has not been done before, and it must be solidly rooted in truth and love. This must be done more quickly than ever before, because time is running out and may have already run out.[26]

As a social activist, Clark was committed to leadership training and follow-through. In December 1963, she wrote Martin Luther King, Jr., concerning her frustrations with those who she felt were more interested in glamour of the movement than the daily work with the people.

Many states are losing their citizenship schools because there is no one to do follow-up work. I have done as much as I could. In fact, I'm the only paid staff worker doing field visitation. I think that the staff of the SCLC working with me in the Citizenship Education Program feels that the work is not dramatic enough to warrant their time. Direct action is so glamorous and packed with emotion that most young people prefer demonstration over genuine education.

It seems to me as if Citizenship Education is all mine, except when it comes time to pick up the checks.[27]

Reflecting on her years with SCLC, Clark believed that training in citizenship education helped women to realize their worth in society. Of course, she stressed that this was not a goal of the training schools. However, Clark contended that women who participated in citizenship education became aroused citizens and assumed positive roles in the quest for civil as well as women's rights. Their gaining the right to vote freed the individual as well as the group.

Women, ninety-one, eighty-one years of age, we could teach them in twenty minutes and we had cars outside waiting to take them right to the courthouse. They signed their names and they got a number that said that they could register and vote in August [1965]. Well, I stayed there from May until August and by the time we left, 7,002 of them had signed their names and had received a number. That's why we have a large number of our people in Alabama voting today.[28]

The SCLC Citizenship Education Program that Clark directed went into eleven deep South states. Her efforts resulted in black people achieving the right to vote and, thus, becoming active participants in the body politic.

After her departure from SCLC, Clark still remained a social activist. She conducted workshops for the American Field Service, helped raise scholarships for deserving young people, organized day-care facilities, and remained an advocate for civil rights. In 1975 she was elected a member of the Charleston, South Carolina, School Board. The College of Charleston awarded her an Honorary Doctorate of Humane Letters in 1978. (The home where she was born is now owned by the college.) In February 1979, President Jimmy Carter recognized her work by presenting her with a Living the Legacy Award. Since then, a section of the Charleston Highway has been named in her honor.

Clark maintained that her greatest honor was serving humanity. From collecting signatures in a croaker sack to her productive citizenship education program, she never wavered in her conviction that if you put forth the effort, change would eventually come.

> The only reason why I thought the Citizenship School Program was right was because when they went down to register and vote, they were able to register and vote. They received their registration certificate. Then I knew that what I did must have been right. . . . It was an experiment that I was trying. When I went into communities and talked to people, I couldn't say that I was saying the right thing. But as I see people work in these communities and decide that they were going to attempt to do some of the things that were recommended and after attempting to do some of the things that were recommended they were able to be successful, like housing, and being able to get checks signed at banks, getting able to be recognized in the community among their own people and in their churches, then I knew that that experiment had worked out. But I couldn't be sure that the experiment was going to work. I don't think anybody can be sure. You just try and see if it's coming.[29]

Clark's Christmas message in 1965, "A Look to the Future," articulated the essence of her political and social philosophy.

> The greatest evil in our country today is not racism but ignorance. . . . This is great challenge to black and white leadership. Our basic philosophy is clear. We do not need a new one. We are committed to an integrated

society—for a truly democratic society, there can be no freedom without integration. Our task then is to nurture and strengthen the newly developing political strength among both young Blacks and young Whites, who have already made a magnificent contribution to the struggle for a more humane and just society. But further, we must try harder than ever to reach the great mass of the uninformed, whose basic interests are no different from our own—if they but knew it.[30]

Clark nurtured her social and political philosophy with her strong beliefs. One had a moral obligation, she asserted, to serve God via his or her service to humanity. In 1971, she proclaimed:

> We are young at heart when we have a tremendous faith in God and in the future, when we have a sense of exaltation in the sweeping movements of a rapidly changing society and world.
> We are old when we rise against our times, when we resist all change.
> We are young as our dreams, our hopes and our enthusiasm.
> We are as old as our fears, our frustrations, our doubts.
> We need to feel wanted and to find the joy that grows out of service to others if the last of life for which the first was made is to be a time of happiness for those of us who are growing older.[31]

On the occasion of Dr. Martin Luther King, Jr.'s death in 1968, Clark proclaimed, "His was no middle-class write-in campaign for Civil Rights, it was a movement that took the people into the streets to confront clubs, hoses, horses, and dogs; to face the oppressors while armed only with the almighty power of love; to turn the cheek not to avoid the present pain, but to see the true nation and new order of the future that God was already making. His peace was not in a cozy rally, but in a reordering of our national priorities from military power to that of human empowerment."[32] Her tribute to King could easily be extended to her. The depth of her commitment, the magnitude of her faith, her power of endurance, and her unrelenting crusade for justice allowed her to put into operation a program of citizen participation that transformed American society. Myles Horton, who died in January 1990, gave Clark the framework at Highlander Folk School to develop her program of citizenship education. Clark, he proclaimed, was a committed public servant and dedicated advocate of social change.[33]

NOTES

1. *State Newspaper*, Columbia, South Carolina, December 15, 1987.
2. Grace Jordan McFadden, *Oral Recollections of Septima Poinsette Clark* (Columbia: USC Instructional Services Center, 1980).
3. *Ibid.*
4. Septima P. Clark, personal interview, February 1, 1975.
5. *Ibid.*
6. *Ibid.*
7. Septima Clark, *Echo in My Soul* (New York: E.P. Dutton, 1962), p. 61.
8. Clark, interview, February 20, 1987.
9. Clark, *Echo in My Soul*, p. 80.
10. DaMaris E. Ayres, *Let My People Go, The Biography of Wil Lou Gray* (South Carolina: The Attic Press, 1988), p. 76.
11. Clark, *Echo My Soul*, p. 82.
12. McFadden, *Oral Recollections of Septima P. Clark*.
13. Tinsley E. Yarbrough, *A Passion for Justice: J. Waties Waring and Civil Rights* (New York: Oxford University Press, 1987), pp. 44-46.
14. James E. Edwards to Septima P. Clark, Septima P. Clark Collection, Robert Scott Small Library.
15. Clark interview, February 1, 1975.
16. Clark, *Echo in My Soul*, p. 178.
17. Septima Clark to Ella Baker, July 11, 1960, Septima P. Clark Collection.
18. Septima P. Clark, *Nature of the Citizenship Education Program*, private collection of Septima P. Clark, Charleston, SC.
19. McFadden, *Oral Recollections of Septima P. Clark*.
20. Clark, interviews, 1975 and 1980.
21. Septima P. Clark with Cynthia S. Brown, *Ready Within: The Story of Septima P. Clark*, p. 75, private collection of Septima P. Clark.
22. *Ibid.*, p. 76.
23. Clark, *Echo in My Soul*, p. 466.
24. McFadden, *Oral Recollections of Septima P. Clark*.
25. *Ibid.*
26. Septima P. Clark, *Christmas Message 1967*, Robert Scott Small Library.
27. Septima P. Clark to Martin L. King, Jr., December 1963, Septima P. Clark Collection.
28. Clark, interviews 1975 and 1980.
29. Clark, *Ready Within*, p. 101.
30. Septima P. Clark, *Christmas Message 1965*, Robert Scott Small Library.
31. Septima P. Clark, *Christmas Message 1971*, Robert Scott Small Library.
32. Septima P. Clark, *The Occasion—Martin Luther King, Jr.*, private collection of Septima Poinsette Clark.
33. Grace Jordan McFadden, conversation with Myles Horton, October 17, 1988, Atlanta, Georgia.

Modjeska Simkins and the South Carolina Conference of the NAACP, 1939-1957

BARBARA A. WOODS

Mary Modjeska Monteith Simkins, a black woman activist of Columbia, South Carolina, is an outstanding figure with rare dedication and singleness of purpose. Born on December 5, 1899, her career of political and civic involvement has spanned more than half a century. Simkins is a member of a generation which sought to carry the load for self-improvement, to help the younger generation, to carve a path out of a seeming wilderness. This generation felt obligated to provide leadership and uplift and to function as a "talented tenth" for the black race in America. Operating in this continuum, Simkins has been 1) a woman ahead of her times, 2) a leader of men and women in both political and social arenas, 3) a politician who is astute in her assessment of current trends and political affairs and 4) a leader who will not be swayed from her course by bribes or offers of political favors (office or employment). Being financially independent, she does not have to rely upon resources which can be easily threatened by the power structure. During the 1940s and 1950s, she was a significant force in black South Carolina's major political activities, which revolved around the South Carolina Conference of the National Association for the Advancement of Colored People (NAACP).

The period into which Modjeska Monteith was born represents a nadir in race relations and fair treatment of black Americans. Within South Carolina, during the last three decades of the nineteenth century, the Democratic Party wrested political control from the state's Republicans and established its dominance. Both during the process of change and after the fact of Democratic control, organized resistance against the Party was carried out by black South Carolinians until the mid-twentieth century, when the Party was forced to abandon its racist platform. The final abdication of black civil rights came in 1895, with the establishment of the so-called White Codes, "a complex of laws, ordinances, and social customs which constituted the ground rules of segregation and white supremacy," and in 1896, with the establishment of the white Democratic primary.[1] The Democratic Party's takeover was fraught with rampant violence, intimidation, fraud, and devices implemented by the party's state conventions.

South Carolina had remained a predominantly black state since 1820 and the Democratic Party was fully aware of the potential political power of blacks. White political demagogues courted the favor of the white population by denying the vote to blacks and appealing to the whites' fear of black leadership, which those in power viewed as domination by blacks.

Columbia, the state capital and home town of the Monteith family, had been predominantly black for a few decades after slavery ended.[2] Unlike the majority of the state's black population, which lived in the rural areas, the Monteiths had the advantages of city life and ethno-density. Columbia's black community was enterprising and progressive. Several blacks owned small businesses, while many of them were employed as skilled tradesmen, although often in occupations considered too subservient or physically demanding for whites. There were several black churches. Two private colleges, which were open to everyone, had predominantly black enrollments: Benedict College and Allen University. Howard Free School, the first South Carolina public school to offer secondary education to blacks, was begun in Columbia in 1867. It provided quality education.[3]

Mary Modjeska was the first child of Henry Clarence and Rachel Evelyn Hull Monteith. This young, intelligent, and progressive black couple, with a strong religious orientation and a commitment to the Protestant work ethic, provided a positive model for their five daughters and three sons. Henry was an artisan who worked as foreman of brickmasonry at several industrial sites throughout the South. Rachel, a high school graduate, was an elementary school teacher who stayed at home to rear her children until the youngest was old enough to attend school. She kept a tight rein on family finances just as she held a firm hand in the training of her children. A strict disciplinarian, Rachel used corporal punishment to mold her children. Both parents believed that their offspring should be taught responsibility by working on the family farm and being held accountable for their assigned chores. Other values instilled in the children were thrift, independence, pride of race, and a sense of individual worth. As the oldest child, Modjeska was expected to set an example for her siblings. While her mother was recuperating from childbirth and her father was working out of town, Modjeska often was responsible for the family. She also went into town alone to take care of business matters, and she was the first child allowed to drive the family's wagon, and later, buggy. Youngest sister Emma has described Modjeska as her mother's "cherub" and the oldest brother Henry maintains that she was the "boss" whom his mother placed in charge of the children.[4]

Rachel Hull had graduated from Howard Free School, but she chose to send her children to a private black institution. Mary Modjeska entered first grade at Benedict College's elementary school in 1905 and remained there until she received an A.B. degree in 1921. (In primary school, she dropped the use of her first name.) After graduation, she followed the path of her mother and maternal aunts, Rebecca Hull Walton and Mary Ellen Hull Dunmore, and taught in the public school system.

What, then, were the major factors equipping Modjeska for leadership? Throughout her childhood and adolescence, Modjeska Monteith led a secure life, being trained in the tradition of racial pride, Christian mission, community service and respect for education that was part and parcel of black life in Columbia. Racial pride was important in the Monteith household, for Henry Monteith, the mulatto offspring of prosperous white attorney Walter Monteith, and his domestic servant Mary Dobbins, a former slave, did not want his children to feel the pain that he felt as a youth. Henry chose to have his family decorate the walls of their home with pictures of outstanding black people, such as Booker T. Washington and Paul Laurence Dunbar. These pictures were important for Modjeska, and even today, on the bookshelf next to her bed, she has an old print depicting a black angel and black children. In the first half of the twentieth century, such pictures were hard to get, not being sold in most stores, but the Monteiths managed to get these positive images of blacks from traveling salesmen. This was not insignificant since the images of blacks being sold in the South were of a servile or a comical nature, conforming to stereotypes that white paternalism favored: mammies, slaves, cooks, field hands, watermelon-holding, grinning caricatures and such. Also the family supported black businesses, father Henry having a share in a black-owned grocery store and in 1921, an account in the black-owned Victory Savings Bank, after it opened. In particular, both parents stressed the importance of their race becoming financially independent. As a model of independence, the family raised most of the foodstuffs and meats that they consumed, and at times sold the excess products, along with bread baked by Rachel, from their wagon parked by the side of a road.

In the tradition of Christian mission work, Modjeska's family felt a moral obligation to assist their neighbors, especially the poorest. Their economic status was well above the norm of the average black family. It was a regular practice for them to visit and care for the sick and the distressed after church. The black church has been the womb of the black community, especially for the masses, and it is a well-known fact that many of the leaders of the modern civil rights movement in the southern states were ministers or persons of high standing in the church. Also, even in the poorest back communities, control of the church has been under black leadership. In Modjeska's family, there is a tradition of church leadership which can be traced back to slavery. Frank Dobbins, one of her paternal ancestors, was instrumental in founding black churches in Columbia; Second Calvary Baptist Church of Columbia was founded in the home of her maternal grandparents, George and Sarah Green Hull. Even though she now rejects organized religion, Modjeska was reared in the church, was a strong church member as a young woman, and is a student of the Bible, having been well-trained in its teachings both at home and at Benedict College, where she matriculated for sixteen years, from elementary school through college. She feels that the church is no longer activist-oriented, and the narrow, fundamentalist interpretations of the Bible have alienated her, for she has read widely on the subject of religion.

In terms of community service, which is also interwoven with racial pride and a sense of Christian mission, the continuum within the black community gives honor to activism. There were established institutions such as the fraternal orders and their female counterparts and civic improvement groups in which her forebearers were active, for example, the Masons and the Columbia branch of the National Association for the Advancement of Colored People. As the woman holding the highest post, Grand Royal Matron, in the state's Order of Eastern Stars, the sisters of the Masons, Aunt

Rebecca Hull Walton worked along with the Masons and her sisters in setting up the first black-sponsored facility for treatment of tubercular patients in South Carolina. Correspondingly, Rachel held membership in the Niagara Movement, a forerunner of the NAACP, and had joined the national office of the NAACP before a branch in Columbia was established in 1917. Accompanying her mother and aunts, Modjeska attended meetings of the Columbia branch in her late teens. She remembers her mother reading to the children from publications put out by the Niagara movement and from *Crisis*, the official journal of the NAACP. The cruel realities of life, such as the lynchings, beatings and murders of blacks in America, throughout the world, and especially in the African countries, were some of the stories that Modjeska heard as a child; even today, at age ninety, she remembers vividly the oppressive conditions of the black African men working in the gold mines. The Hull and Monteith families' contributions have been recognized in a short history of the Columbia branch:

> Then there was Rachel E. Monteith, who years earlier had espoused the Niagara Movement which was the forerunner of the National Association. In the race of life, she passed the torch on to H. D., Rebecca and Modjeska, her children. There was Rebecca Walton, sister of Rachel Monteith and the aunt of our contemporary Monteiths, who was the fearless and outspoken matriarch of the Columbia branch in her day.[5]

The family, the community, and her birth order—being the oldest child of eight children and being required by her parents to be responsible for the younger ones and to *set an example* for them—were important, early-life, formative experiences. She had strong, strict parents and a secure childhood in the sense that she was free from want, that she knew her parents owned their home and their land and were both gainfully employed with notable social standing in the black community, and that as a light-skinned women with attractive facial features, she could be at an advantage in matchmaking. In the black community of Columbia, and other parts of the South, possessing light skin has been considered an advantage for black women, and during the time in which Modjeska was reared, community expectations were such that women valued highly the role of "wife and mother." The legacy of preferring lighter skin is a byproduct of European enslavement of Africans, for often the offspring of relations between white men and their black slave/servants were given privileges that the full-blooded or dark-skinned African-Americans did not have, such as freedom, money, and education. In

Modjeska's family, a favorite story is told about the slave woman, Sarah Hull, a mulatto, who ran away from the Seals' plantation in Sumter when she was whipped in the nude for breaking plantation rules by visiting her dark-skinned mother who was a field slave. On that plantation, fraternization between the light-skinned and the dark-skinned slaves was either prohibited or severely restricted. Preference was also given to the light-skinned slaves for often they were members of the owner's family or the offspring of his relatives. Thus, all of these factors, these advantages taken together, gave Modjeska a good sense of self and equipped her for leadership in the family, which blossomed into leadership in the community, the state, and in the South.

Modjeska remained employed at Booker T. Washington school in Columbia until 1929, when she married Andrew Whitfield Simkins; she had to resign because married women were not allowed to teach in the city's school system. Andrew Simkins, a prosperous black businessman who owned real estate and was the proprietor of a gasoline service station in Columbia, embodied the business acumen that Modjeska admired. Her marriage strengthened her business skill and fostered her leadership ability. She was fortunate in choosing a husband who was supportive of his wife's career and thus, did not expect that she would stay home, "keep house", and rear children. This was Andrew's third marriage. He had been widowed twice and had five children. After all of the children came to live with them, an elderly relative, Mrs. Mary Artope, came along to help with the rearing of his children and they employed a housekeeper, so Modjeska did not have to provide the primary care for his children, nor was she overburdened by domestic concerns.

Her next job put Modjeska firmly on the platform of public service in South Carolina. In 1931, she became Director of Negro Work for the South Carolina Tuberculosis Association; her role was to raise funds and assist in health education. Raising money from the most impoverished segment of one of the poorest states in the nation during the depression was a challenge indeed. This work proved important in the development of her political consciousness, for she was exposed to the dire poverty and utter deprivation in the rural areas of the state. The majority of the black population at the time were tenant farmers; their lives were characterized by hard work, drudgery, poverty, and powerlessness. The word of the landlord was law, and many of the tenants were not much better off than their ancestors had been

Modjeska Simkins was one of the central figures in the activities of the South Carolina Conference of the NAACP in the 1940s and 1950s, especially their lawsuit challenging segregation in public schools. She is show here in 1940 when she was Director of Negro Work for the South Carolina Tuberculosis Association.

under slavery. A bleak situation became more desperate as cotton sales dropped to a frighteningly low point during the country's Depression.[6]

Simkins sought to reach every stratum of the black community, from the gambling houses to the churches. Genuine hospitality remained a common feature in the rural communities, where she stayed with residents as she carried out her work. Her clinics for tuberculosis testing were held at churches, at schools, at the mills on company time, and sometimes in the fields where the blacks were working. She also worked with black teachers at summer schools and in training institutes. In order to facilitate her work, she wrote and published a newsletter, organized a state conference of black leaders, and held annual meetings.[7] During these years with the Tuberculosis Association, 1931-1942, Simkins was making crucial contributions to the physical and political well-being of black South Carolinians.

In the spring of 1939, three members of the Cheraw, South Carolina branch of NAACP came to Columbia to meet with members of the executive board of the Columbia branch, hoping to forge an alliance that would result in the formation of a state body. The Cheraw delegation was headed by Levi G. Byrd, a black plumber with a zeal for bringing about first class citizenship for blacks; Byrd had conceived his plan of action and had met with Walter White of the national office of NAACP regarding the feasibility of the undertaking. As a chairperson of the program committee, and thus, a member of the Columbia branch's executive committee, Modjeska attended this initial meeting and the organizing meeting held on October 15, 1939, at the Benedict College library.[8] The major officers elected were the three Cheraw representatives: The Reverend Alonzo W. Wright, president; Maggie B. Robinson, secretary; and Levi G. Byrd, head of the Finance Committee. In the state organization, Simkins held the same position as she had with the local branch, chairperson of the Program committee, and thus, was a member of the state's Executive Board, the only woman member. While a large percentage of the persons participating in the October meeting were women, Simkins and Robinson were the only women officers, and each of them held roles typically given to women working in male-dominated organizations. Very soon after the State Conference got underway, Simkins was elected to the Speakers' Bureau in February 1941, and she served as corresponding secretary at least as early as the spring of 1941. When elections were held in June 1941, new officers gained seats in important positions: James M. Hinton as state president and Modjeska M. Simkins as state secretary. The transition was smooth; both were asked outside of official meetings to assume these posts, the former president and secretary feeling that they were too far from Columbia, the state's centrally located capital, to continue their effectiveness. At this time, all of the offices were volunteer positions. By 1942, Simkins had taken over as head of the Publicity committee in addition to her secretarial role.[9]

Also by 1942, the tradition-bound, white supremacist administrators at the South Carolina Tuberculosis Association regarded her political work on behalf of black equality as subversive and pressured her to sever ties with the NAACP. This pressure served only to increase her commitment and thus, the organization found a "tactful way" to dismiss its Director of Negro Work, putting the blame on an insufficient budget. Simkins has described her departure:

> I couldn't divorce my interest in civil rights from my dedication to trying to solve these health problems. My boss sensed it, and she said that I would have to leave off some of these activities. And my answer was I'd rather see a person die and go to hell with tuberculosis than to be treated how some of my people were treated. Although I was not fired, my position became untenable and we parted ways.[10]

Her break with the Tuberculosis Association served as a catalyst for Simkins to come into her own as spokesperson and agitator for civil rights. Her work with the association was a good training ground for a productive full-time public service career. She had become skilled in publicity and propaganda, public speaking, journalism, and letter writing; furthermore, she had met and worked with black leadership on a state level.

From its inception in 1939 to the mid-1950s, Modjeska Simkins was in the forefront of the major projects undertaken by the South Carolina Conference of the NAACP, most of which were equal rights lawsuits. Their first lawsuit, a fight for equalization of teachers' salaries, was won by the black teachers of Charleston in 1944; in 1945 the Columbia teachers won a similar case. Simkins was active with the Columbia teachers as they worked to establish their case. She wrote letters, published articles in the black newspapers, and helped to arrange meetings of black teachers to discuss the inequities of the salary scale and to take action against it. When the campaign for teachers' salaries was begun in 1943, Modjeska was the only woman on a committee of four appointed to raise funds for the lawsuit. After the Teachers' Defense Fund was established, she served as its secretary.[11]

Because state employees were being threatened with the loss of their jobs if they contributed to cases being prepared by the NAACP, the State Conference formed a companion organization to which money could be donated and routed to the NAACP. The new organization, the South Carolina Citizens Committee, had the same officers as the state chapter and local branches of the NAACP. Simkins, elected reporter, was the only woman officer; she was asked to write the charter of the new organization.[12]

After the teachers' salary cases were won, full attention was directed to dismantling the white primary, the major project around which the founding members of the State Conference had rallied. (The salary cases had been given priority by the national office of the NAACP, and the State Conference had reluctantly deferred.) In the voting cases, Simkins was actively involved in planning court proceedings, and she attended the courtroom sessions both in Columbia and in Washington, D.C. at the Supreme Court. The attorney from the national office of the NAACP, Thurgood Marshall, a personal friend of Simkins, suggested that she pay special attention in court so that she could advise the NAACP lawyers of any points they might have missed, since she was very familiar with the details of the South Carolina case.[13] Her moral and emotional support were supplemented by her financial support to George Elmore, the plaintiff in the first voting rights case.[14] Although the *Elmore* v. *Rice* case was won in 1947, the South Carolina Democratic Party formulated devices to circumvent the ruling. For example, the new entrants whom they described as nonmembers could participate in the party only if they took an oath stating that they believed in the separation of the races, the principle of states' rights, and that they opposed the Fair Employment Practices Commission of the federal government. Thus the NAACP had to develop a second case, *Brown* v. *Baskins*, in order to obtain full voting rights. The second case was won in July 1948.

But the most important South Carolina case in terms of national significance was one that came out of Clarendon County in the 1950s. Begun in 1947 as an attempt to secure bus transportation for black students, the case was changed in 1949 to a petition for equalization of educational opportunities. By 1950 it had progressed to a "frontal attack" on segregation in the county's public schools. On behalf of Levi Pearson, a Clarendon County farmer, the State Conference of the NAACP in June 1948 initiated a case to provide equal bus transportation. The lawsuit was thrown out before the hearing on the grounds that Pearson lived in overlapping districts on which the jurisdiction was not clear.[15] At a meeting in March 1949 of NAACP officials and Clarendon County representatives, the State Conference decided to pursue a case requesting not only buses for blacks, but equal educational opportunities as well. The national office of the NAACP was willing to sponsor such major test cases; twenty plaintiffs would be required. The South Carolina Conference of the NAACP agreed to prepare a case.[16]

Getting twenty black persons in poverty-stricken Clarendon County who were willing to suffer the inevitable intimidation and economic sacrifice of plaintiffs in an NAACP-sponsored case was not an easy assignment. Levi Pearson found that his credit had been cut off by "every white-owned store and bank in the county."[17] He was thrown into deep financial distress as he tried to make a living from his farm. Modjeska Simkins was instrumental in assisting him in getting funds to continue his operation.[18]

Simkins cooperated on the many stages of the formation of the case. The Reverend Joseph A. DeLaine, a local leader and president of one of the branches of the NAACP in Clarendon County, traveled to the Simkins's home in Columbia, and together they wrote the declaration that appeared in the Clarendon lawsuit. Simkins has described their joint project:

> He came up and talked to me as secretary about what might be done. I remember we sat together near the heater, [in her living room] it was as cold as the dickens that day, as I remember, and wrote out this statement. I mimeographed it.[19]

As soon as the petitions were signed by the blacks in Clarendon County, economic reprisals began. Both DeLaine and Harry Briggs, the man whose name appeared at the head of the petition, were fired from their jobs, and later Briggs's wife was fired. In addition:

> The Briggses were not the only petitioners who suffered. Bo Stukes was let go at his garage, and James Brown was fired as a driver-salesman for Esso, though his boss commended him for never having come up a penny short in ten years on the job. Teachers got fired, Negroes had great trouble getting their cotton ginned that harvest season, and Mrs. Maisie Solomon not only got thrown out of her job at the motel but also tossed off the land her family rented and had to take rapid refuge with other blacks.[20]

Nonetheless, the *Briggs* v. *Elliot* case was filed in the federal District Court on May 16, 1950. Before the proceedings could begin, Judge J. Waties Waring privately let it be known that he wanted to try a case that attacked "frontally" the entire "separate but equal" doctrine.[21] The NAACP took advantage of the opportunity. Modjeska remembers Thurgood Marshall, who always stayed at the Simkins' home while he was working in Columbia, relating Waring's determination: "Thurgood told me . . . [that] Waring said, 'I *will not* try another separate but equal case. When you get ready to make a frontal attack on segregation in the schools, then I'll be ready to try the case.' "[22] John McCray, editor of the black Columbia newspaper, *The Lighthouse and Informer,* which functioned as the fighting journal for the South Carolina conference of NAACP during the period of the 40s and 50s, explained that the decision to change to a lawsuit challenging segregation frontally was actually a secret agreement between Walter White of the National Office of NAACP and Judge J. Waties Waring:

> Judge and his wife had also by now become good friends of NAACP's Walter White and his wife the former Poppy Cannon. The two visited the other occasionally in New York City, or that area, and of course the two now quite powerful men (and the women) worked over the best courses to be taken to establish equal rights for Negroes, especially in South Carolina. It was commonly known within our circles that Mr. Waring wanted all the cases possible on the subject brought before his court—that of a "friendly" judge. . . . Mr. Waring hammered on the futility of pursuing longer the *Plessy vs. Ferguson* [sic] (separate but equal) doctrine for Negro equal rights and Walter White assuredly welcomed the point of view. Accordingly, with Mr. White's knowledge and approval, Mr. Waring called Thurgood Marshall, told him Walter had agreed off the record and the issue in the Clarendon petition was being changed from *Plessy vs. Ferguson* to a head-on collision/attack on racial segregation per se. Mr. Marshall was told to have the amended complaint filed in Mr. Waring's court within a given number of days.[23]

This agreement between White and Waring brought about a major change in the NAACP's legal strategy:

> In July 1950, a conference of NAACP lawyers held in New York recommended that the Association handle no education cases in the future for the purpose of 'equalization' only. This recommendation was approved by the National Board of Directors of the NAACP at its October 1950, meeting. Accordingly, when attorneys in the case appeared before United States District Judge J. Waties Waring for a pre-trial hearing in November, 1950, it was indicated that the objective of the suit was abolition of segregation.[24]

Ruby Hurley, southeastern regional director of the NAACP, recounted that all of the education test cases were "redone" so that they attacked segregation.[25]

The Clarendon County case was of special significance to the NAACP because it came out of the deep South and because it was an extreme example of separate and unequal.

> This was the key case in the NAACP's nationwide campaign to break down racial segregation in public schools. Negro leaders purposely singled out Clarendon County because it presented racially segregated schools in the worst possible light. . . . The suit represented the first all-out attack in the Deep South on the system of racial segregation on the public school level.[26]

The initial hearing was held in May 1951, in a special three-judge court, which included Waring. A judgement was made against the black petitioners, in favor of the county school district; Waring dissented from the opinion offered by the other judges that the separate-but-equal doctrine was not violated. The decision was appealed to the Supreme Court by the NAACP, and almost two years passed before it was heard. The South Carolina State Conference's lawsuit in which Harry Briggs, Jr., and sixty-three other young black students sued School Board 22 "charging that Clarendon County's [black] schools were far inferior to its schools for white children" became the first of the NAACP's five desegregation cases to reach the Supreme Court.[27] In June 1952, the Supreme Court agreed to combine *Brown* and *Briggs*, and according to Supreme Court Justice Tom Clark, in order to make it clear that it was not just a Southern decision, *Brown* was put before *Briggs*. The other three cases grouped together with *Brown* and *Briggs* were *Davis* v. *County School Board of Prince Edward County* [Virginia], *Gebhart* v. *Bolton* [Delaware], and *Bolling* v. *Sharpe* [Washington, D. C.].[28]

The pioneering role of the black Clarendon plaintiffs was not overlooked or forgiven by the white establishment of South Carolina, who had always been bitter opponents of desegregation. The fear of losing control of political, social, and economic life led to extreme measures. By 1951, leading stories in South Carolina newspapers spread the general alarm felt by the officials who ruled the state.

> The South's explosive issue of racial segregation in public schools was heading in South Carolina yesterday for a showdown which may be decided by the U.S. Supreme Court this year. A federal tribunal in May will test one of the strongest legal attacks yet made upon the 75-year-old principle of segregation

in public schools in a case that ultimately may affect 17 southern states. The suit pits Gov. James F. Byrnes, former U.S. Supreme Court justice, against the National Association for the Advancement of Colored People, which is using its top legal advisor, Thurgood Marshall. Byrnes, in the background, is marshalling every resource of the state. Responsible South Carolinians are aware of the stakes and know 'this is it' as far as public school segregation is concerned.[29]

This Associated Press dispatch went farther, acknowledging that South Carolina was calling on its best and brightest to defend their holy institution of segregation: "Many persons believe this is the reason Byrnes came out of retirement to become governor at 71, after serving as U.S. senator, secretary of state, assistant to President Roosevelt and Supreme Court justice."[30]

The reaction to the *Brown* decision among the leaders of white South Carolina was to fight against the "law of the land"; their attacks on NAACP members intensified.[31] Following the lead of Mississippi, a new race organization of white supremacists who opposed integration, the Citizens Council, was formed at Elloree in Orangeburg County in early August 1955, immediately following a petition by blacks for school integration.[32] The seventeen black parents who had signed the petitions were castigated by the white power structure. Some lost jobs, others were evicted from property—the reprisals were so extensive that fourteen of the petitioners felt compelled to ask that their names be removed because they "did not fully understand the meaning of the language." The white power structure maintained its control by withholding credit and by denying home mortgages, installment loans, and rental housing.

At their 1955 annual meeting, the largest ever, the State Conference of the NAACP held discussions on: "The Economic Squeeze," "Cooperatives and Cooperative Buying," "Farmers Unions," "False Charges and Pending Legal Attacks Against NAACP," and "Implementing Recent United States Supreme Court Decisions."

Modjeska Simkins assisted in relief work in Elloree and Clarendon counties. Along with her brother, Henry Dobbins Monteith, president of the black-owned and operated Victory Savings Bank of Columbia, Simkins helped the victims secure badly-needed financial support. Under the auspices of the South Carolina State Conference, Simkins sent letters to "Heads of all State Organizations," both black and white, requesting that they "make as large a deposit as possible in the SAVINGS ACCOUNT of the Victory Savings Bank (where it will draw interest at 2 percent) to help relieve the victims of economic pressure through loans—only to persons with proper security— as is required by banking laws."[33]

Simkins was also instrumental in getting donations from sources outside of South Carolina. An appeal made by the South Carolina State Conference in *Jet* magazine, on October 20, 1955, brought contributions from across the United States and from abroad. Money and tons of food and clothing were sent in care of Simkins, as secretary of the State Conference.[34] Responses varied. A farmer in Quito, Ecuador, sent a financial contribution. Citizens of Youngstown, Ohio, through their mayor's office, proclaimed December 18, 1955, "Supplies to Aid Negroes in Dixie Day." Their proclamation stated that "local religious, fraternal, civic, and social groups, as well as the Press, have banded together in an effort to collect supplies to aid those in the Southland who face an austere winter."[35] Simkins accepted an invitation from the Young Women's Civic League of the Abyssinian Baptist Church in Harlem to appear at a rally "to raise funds and food for Negro people in South Carolina and in Mississippi." Simkins accepted and the rally was an overwhelming success. The Mem-O-Beth Social Benevolent Club of Brooklyn sent fifty dollars. The Sojourners for Truth and Justice, a community club in New York City, "adopted Columbia, South Carolina to throw . . . support economically and morally in the struggle against the White Citizens Council." This group invited Simkins to speak at one of their meetings and offered to pay all of her expenses.[36]

Simkins played an important and special role in Elloree, an area where the blacks were mainly tenant farmers whose livelihood was directly dependent on the white landowners and the white power structure. She and Lee Alonzo Blackman, president of the Elloree branch of the NAACP, worked together to provide relief for families in the area. Blackman, a courageous, outspoken stalwart himself, suffered along with his neighbors.

> Blackman has been president of the Elloree area NAACP for the past six years. The 250 families, mostly rural farmers, have looked to him for material aid in their distress. He has never failed them, although it has cost him the loss of his $25,000 building contracting business to remain loyal to his principles.[37]

At an NAACP convention in San Francisco in 1956, Blackman made an appeal for the oppressed families of Elloree:

> He asks aid for 250 courageous Negro families in the Elloree area who are victims of economic reprisal and intimidation simply because they support the

113

NAACP and demand civil rights. Blackman, who has been a member of the NAACP since 1924, is directing relief for his area. He bought 100 pairs of shoes for children, for instance, but more are needed. He is asking for clothing, shoes, canned food and money. But the outstanding need of the moment is for a chemical to spray the crops. "If the crops can be saved," said Blackman, "my people can get through the winter,"[38]

Simkins brought donated goods from Columbia to Elloree in a trailer hooked to the back of her car; Blackman stored the commodities in a building in his backyard and distributed the items to the needy families.

Simkins's involvement in the distribution of food and clothing to the needy black families caused her to be regarded as a "mother-benefactress" by them. Oftentimes she found resources to make a way "out of no way" for the people. Several letters written to her by black residents of these areas provide evidence of her role. No request was too small to warrant her attention. For example, a parent in Santee, South Carolina, wrote requesting a suit of clothing for her child: "I am asking you if you please can get me a little suit for my little boy by May first for May Day . . . if you have one size 14. Mr. Blackman said he don't have any and if you have any boys' shoes from size 5 on up please send them to me."[39]

In 1956 she had accepted a position as public relations director for the Victory Savings Bank in Columbia and the role of mother-benefactress also extended to her official capacity at the bank. Several of the black victims were not used to doing business with banks and did not know the procedure for securing loans. Therefore, they simply wrote to Simkins. Levi Pearson, the black farmer who was the plaintiff in the bus transportation case wrote: "I am starting off with my farm for 1957. And I want to know weather [sic] I can get enough money to run it. I want $1,000. And if I can't get it please let me know right away."[40] A man in Orangeburg who failed to keep up payments on a loan he received from the Victory Savings Bank sought assistance:

> This is to let you know that I have written the bank some time ago explaining my troubles, also asked them to give you the letter so you would know the condition I was in at that time. These are the reasons why I couldn't keep up those payments as I should have. My father died and because of signing that petition and loosing [sic] my outside jobs, I had to drop some of my insurance, therefore, I didn't have enougt [sic] insurance to take care of the burial. . . . The reason I wanted you to know, because you told me if anything happens that I couldn't make these payments, to let you know and you would have them flag the NAACP Relief Account.[41]

In addition to her direct involvement in relief, Simkins's work in assisting the victims included reporting eyewitness accounts of the situation. She regularly sent reports to individuals and groups across the country. She had gained notoriety and popularity because of her work with social uplift projects and became personally identified with progressive social reform. In turn, she used this recognition and influence to raise funds and bring support to the movement and to disseminate information.[42]

In November 1957, at the annual meeting of the South Carolina Conference of the NAACP, for the first time in sixteen years, Modjeska Simkins's name was not put forth by the Nominations Committee as a candidate for secretary. Eugene Montgomery, field secretary at the time, and other NAACP officials have suggested that her association with leaders of the American Communist Party and organizations which had been blacklisted by the House Un-American Activities Committee (HUAC) was the reason she lost her post.[43] This explanation is certainly plausible.

After the *Brown* decision, the NAACP was being hounded all across the South by officeholders who bitterly resented the Supreme Court's legal sanction of integration in Southern public schools. The tactic of charging that NAACP members were Communists or fellow travelers was being used to purge the NAACP of some of its most effective leaders. Simkins was a friend and supporter of many leaders of the American Communist Party.[44] And, she had worked with organizations that were often under the scrutiny of HUAC. She had served on the National Adult Advisory Board of the Southern Negro Youth Congress (SNYC) and had arranged a conference of the congress in Columbia in 1946. She had also worked actively with the Southern Conference for Human Welfare (SCHW) in the 1940s and its offspring, the Southern Conference Educational Fund (SCEF). In 1947, she attempted, unsuccessfully, to establish a branch of SCHW in South Carolina. In 1952, she chaired the local committee for a SCEF-sponsored conference in Columbia; in December of that year she was elected vice president of SCEF, the first woman to hold such a high office in the organization. While neither the SNYC or SCEF was formally tied to the Communist Party, both organizations had been branded as Communist "fronts" and several prominent Communists spearheaded activities in SNYC. A source of concern for NAACP officials was press notice of Simkins appearing with Paul Robeson at a rally for convicted black Communist leader Benjamin J. Davis, a long-time friend of hers.[45] At least as early as 1953, the state's newspapers had publicized her listing as a fellow traveler by the House Un-American Activities Committee.[46] Obviously, these attacks had been of great concern to NAACP officials in their National Office. In February, 1956, Simkins wrote to Roy Wilkins of the National Office of NAACP explaining that she would not attend a controversial meeting in New York because she did not want the NAACP to be attacked because of her participation. In the letter, she told Wilkins that the NAACP did not have the only answer to the problem of discrimination against blacks.[47]

After 1957, Modjeska Simkins transferred her leadership to activities on the local level in Columbia. She was fifty-seven years old, a full-time employee of a bank who had not held paid employment from 1942 to 1956. Those fourteen years had been spent busily involved in voluntary public service. She had been secretary, reporter, writer, adviser, editor, relief worker, strategist, and benefactress. She had worked not only with progressive, outspoken, dynamic leadership on a local and state level, but also regionally and nationally. Her interaction with many persons in the midst of political ferment led her to support both reform and radical organizations. Through it all, she maintained her independence and open-mindedness.

The pioneering work by Simkins and her colleagues in the 1940s and 1950s laid the foundation for radical changes in the political machinery operating the state. It seems only fitting that the first legal case making a frontal attack on segregated education which led to the disbanding of all dual systems of education in the nation, came from South Carolina, the state with one of the worst records in educating blacks. In 1930 South Carolina black public education suffered more, in financial terms, than anywhere else in the South, for the state was spending "ten times as much on the education of every white child as it was on every Negro child," flagrantly violating the law.[48] Clearly, those who ran the educational system were upholding the tenets of favorite son John C. Calhoun, who wanted blacks to remain in perpetual bondage to whites, no matter the extent of breaking the national law. Black communities were forced, in their own desperate circumstances of poverty and illiteracy, to raise money and donate essential items such as chalk, heating fuel, books, and sometimes, teachers' salaries to maintain formal public education. But the 1960s, 1970s and 1980s brought changes which made the black electorate a significant factor in state politics, put black politicians in office and forced the reigning political demagogues in elected office to give up their mainstay of power, race-baiting. The South Carolina Conference of NAACP had written a new chapter in the state's history. Their lawsuits had brought about equalization for teachers' salaries, the disbanding of the white primary, and the outlawing of racial segregation in the nations' public schools. Modjeska Simkins had been an important leader in this struggle. All the better for all concerned, paving the way for the next generation, making America live up to the democratic ideals that it had exported to the world.

NOTES

1. George Brown Tindall, *South Carolina Negroes, 1877-1900* (Columbia: University of South Carolina Press, 1952), pp. 8-11, 69-91. For other studies of devices used to abolish the black vote in South Carolina, see Idus A. Newby, *Black Carolinians: A History of Blacks in South Carolina From 1895-1968* (Columbia: University of South Carolina Press, 1973), pp. 27-50; August Meier, *Negro Thought in America, 1880-1915, Racial Ideologies in the Age of Booker T. Washington* (Ann Arbor: University of Michigan Press, 1963), pp. 39-40.
2. Tindall, *South Carolina Negroes*, p. 2. A comprehensive study of the black population in South Carolina during colonial times is Peter H. Wood, *Black Majority, Negroes in Colonial South Carolina from 1670 through the Stono Rebellion* (New York: W. W. Norton, 1974). See also Alretheus Ambush Taylor, *The Negro in South Carolina During the Reconstruction* (Washington, D.C.: Association for the Study of Negro Life and History, 1924).
3. Taylor, *Negro in South Carolina*, p. 68; C. G. Garrett, *Reminiscences* (1933), quoted in Helen Kohn Henning, ed., *Columbia, Capital City of South Carolina, 1786-1936* (Columbia: R. L. Bryan Company, 1936), p. 310; Tindall, *South Carolina Negroes*, p. 2.
4. Tape done by Emma Monteith Wheeler, Ann Arbor, Michigan, December 1981; interview with Henry and Martha Monteith and Frank and Susie Monteith, Columbia, South Carolina, November 7, 1981; interview with Frank and Susie Monteith, Columbia, March 14, 1977; interview with Modjeska Simkins, September 13, 1975.
5. I. DeQuincey Newman, "Historical Sketch, Columbia Branch, NAACP," personal files of Modjeska Simkins.
6. Theodore Hemingway, "Beneath the Yoke of Bondage: A History of Black Folks in South Carolina, 1900-1940," Ph.D. dissertation, University of South Carolina, 1976, p. 197; John Hope Franklin, *From Slavery to Freedom: A History of Negro Americans*, 3rd ed. (New York: Knopf, 1967), pp. 495-497.
7. See *Newsreel*, a mimeographed newsletter put out by Modjeska Simkins for the South Carolina Tuberculosis Association, personal files of Modjeska Simkins, Columbia. See also annual reports of the South Carolina Tuberculosis Association, files of the South Carolina Lung Association Papers, Columbia.

8. South Carolina State Conference of NAACP, "First Annual Meeting," Columbia, South Carolina, May 17, 1940; "1939—Ten Years of Progress—1949," *The Lighthouse and the Informer* (Columbia, South Carolina), October 15, 1949. Levi G. Byrd to Walter White, June 18, 1941, NAACP Papers, Library of Congress, Washington, D.C. Interview with Levi G. Byrd and Modjeska Simkins, Cheraw, South Carolina, July 23, 1977.

9. Simkins interview, July 31, 1977; interview with Levi G. Byrd and Modjeska Simkins, Cheraw, South Carolina, July 23, 1977; South Carolina State Conference of the NAACP, "Minutes of Meetings of the Board of Directors, 1941-1944," personal files of Modjeska Simkins; membership report forms, NAACP, Columbia, South Carolina Branch, January 24 and March 17, 1939; list of officers and members of the Executive Committee, NAACP, Columbia, South Carolina Branch, 1939-40, NAACP Papers, Library of Congress, Washington, D.C.

10. Simkins interview, September 13, 1975."Twenty-Fifth Annual Report, 1941-1942" and "Minutes of the Board of Directors, 1939-1949," South Carolina Tuberculosis Association Papers, Columbia.

11. Simkins interviews, September 13 and November 18, 1975, September 17, 1977; Modjeska Simkins, "Negro Teachers Called to Arms" (n.p., n.d. [1943?]); South Carolina State Conference of NAACP, "Minutes of Meetings of the Executive Committee, 1941-1944," meeting of February 28, 1943; mimeographed copy of a circular from the Teachers' Defense Fund, personal files of Modjeska Simkins. Thurgood Marshall, "The Legal Battle," in the *NAACP Bulletin*, Vol. III, no. 7, (July 1943), p. 2.

12. Simkins interview, July 20, 1977; "Negro Citizens Committee of South Carolina Organized," *The Palmetto Leader*, Columbia, South Carolina, 1942, personal files of Modjeska Simkins.

13. Interview with Modjeska Simkins, Columbia, South Carolina, July 28-31, 1976, conducted by Jacquelyn Hall of the Southern Oral History Program, University of North Carolina, Chapel Hill.

14. Interview with Reverend I. DeQuincey Newman, Columbia, South Carolina, January 26, 1977; Simkins interview, July 20, 1977.

15. Richard Kluger, *Simple Justice: The History of Brown v. Board of Education and Black America's Struggle for Equality* (New York: Random House, 1975), pp. 14-17; Howard Quint, *Profile in Black and White: A Frank Portrait of South Carolina* (Washington, D.C.: Public Affairs Press, 1958), pp. 12-20.

16. Kluger, *Simple Justice*, p. 18.

17. *Ibid*.

18. Interview with Billie S. Fleming, Manning, South Carolina, November 1989, conducted by Beryl Dakers of South Carolina Educational Television.

19. Interview with Modjeska Simkins, Columbia, South Carolina, October 22, 1977; interview with Levi G. Byrd and Modjeska Simkins, Cheraw, South Carolina, July 23, 1977.

20. Kluger, *Simple Justice*, p. 24.

21. Byrd and Simkins interview, July 22, 1977; interview with Septima Clark, Charleston, South Carolina, March 26, 1977; Hurley interview, March 1, 1977;

Robert Lewis Terry, "J. Waties Waring: Spokesman for Racial Justice in the New South," Ph.D. dissertation, University of Utah, 1970; Tinsley E. Yarbrough, *Passion for Justice: J. Waties Waring and Civil Rights* (New York: Oxford Books, 1987), pp. 172-212. Simkins and other major figures in the South Carolina Conference of the NAACP recalled that the national office was promoting lawsuits to force equal treatment of blacks in the public educational systems as a means to bring about integration. Judge Waring expressed to Thurgood Marshall his view that the basic concept of segregation had to be challenged directly if serious changes were to be made in the schools.

22. Interview with Modjeska Simkins, Columbia, South Carolina, October 29, 1977.

23. Correspondence, John McCray to Barbara Woods Aba-Mecha, July 15, 1978.

24. South Carolina State Conference of the NAACP, "Testimonial Honoring Parent Plaintiffs and Their Children in the Clarendon County Case Against School Segregation," Liberty Hill AME Church, Summerton, South Carolina, June 17, 1951; Byrd and Simkins interview, July 23, 1977.

25. Interview with Ruby Hurley, southern regional director of NAACP, Atlanta, Georgia, March 1, 1977.

26. Quint, *Profile in Black and White*, pp. 12-13; Kluger, *Simple Justice*, pp. 13-26, 543-581, 700-747; Newby, *Black Carolinians*, pp. 274, 305-309.

27. Loren Miller, *The Petitioners: The Story of the Supreme Court of the United States and the Negro* (New York: Pantheon, 1966), p. 342.

28. Juan Williams, *Eyes on the Prize: America's Civil Rights Years, 1954-1965* (New York: Viking, 1987), pp. 21, 27, 31.

29. United Press dispatch by William M. Bates, March 1951, files of Modjeska Simkins. See also Augusta, Georgia *Chronicle*, March 12, 1951.

30. *Ibid.*

31. A good discussion of Southern resistance to the reform efforts of the NAACP is found in Numan V. Bartley, *The Rise of Massive Resistance: Race and Politics in the South During the 1950s* (Baton Rouge: Louisiana State University Press, 1969), pp. 82-107 and 190-236.

32. Quint, *Profile in Black and White*, pp. 27, 51.

33. "To Heads of all State Organizations," sent out over the name of James M. Hinton, open letter, n.d., personal files of Modjeska Simkins.

34. Simkins interview, December 11, 1976; interview with Ruby Hurley, Atlanta, Georgia, March 1, 1977; interview with I. DeQuincey Newman, Columbia, S.C., January 26, 1977.

35. Modjeska Simkins to Carlos Alvarado, February 16, 1956; proclamation from Frank X. Kryzan, mayor of Youngstown, Ohio, Simkins files.

36. Mrs. L. Yittens to Mrs. [Modjeska] Simkins, n.d., Simkins files. Ramona Garrett to Modjeska Simkins, February 22, 1956, Simkins files.

37. L. Baynard Whitney, "Militant Integrity Marks Career, Ancestry of Carolina's Blackman," *San Francisco Independent*, July 19, 1956, Simkins files.

38. *Ibid.* Simkins's files contain correspondence between her and Blackman, which give details of the situation in Elloree.

39. Sara Felder to Modjeska Simkins, April 25, 1957, Simkins files.

40. Levi Pearson to Modjeska Simkins, January 11, 1957, Simkins files
41. Bennie Brown to Modjeska Simkins, January 9, 1957, Simkins files.
42. "The Orangeburg-Elloree Story," undated mimeographed thank-you letter signed by Modjeska Simkins on the stationery of the South Carolina Conference of the NAACP; "Economic Freeze Families Visited. Rigid Resistance and Devotion to Ideals Vividly Portrayed by Victims. Current Needs Outlined," mimeographed, May 24, 1956; "Lend a Hand," undated letter sent from 2025 Marion Street and signed by Modjeska Simkins.
43. Simkins interview, November 18, 1975; interview with Eugene Montgomery, Orangeburg, South Carolina, October 3, 1977; interview with John McCray, Talladega, Alabama, June 8, 1978; interview with Ruby Hurley, Atlanta, Georgia, March 1, 1977.
44. Simkins maintained close working and personal relationships with James and Esther Jackson, William and Louise Patterson, Herbert Aptheker, Benjamin Davis, and other well-known members of the Communist Party. See interview with James and Esther Jackson, Brooklyn, New York, December 11, 1977; Simkins interview, June 3, 1978; "Information from the Files of the Committee on Un-American Activities, U.S. House of Representatives: Subject—Modjeska Simkins (Mrs. Andrew Simkins)," printed information sheet, July 13, 1965.
45. "Friend of Communist," Charleston, S.C. *News and Courier*, August 6, 1954.
46. *Ibid*. Notwithstanding these associations, Modjeska Simkins believed that she was not returned to office in 1957 because of a deal made between the power structure of the state and the president of the South Carolina NAACP Conference, James M. Hinton. She cites the fact that soon after her ouster, Hinton stepped down from his own post, which he had held as long as Simkins had held hers. (No other official I interviewed corroborated this idea.)
47. Modjeska Simkins to Roy Wilkins, February 6, 1956.
48. Kluger, *Simple Justice*, p. 134.

Gloria Richardson
and the
Cambridge Movement

ANNETTE K. BROCK

One century after the insidious, incongruous institution of slavery had been halted by the sanguinary conflict of this nation, the Civil War, waves of protest convulsed this nation into a new internecine debate that would evoke the many horrible shades of violence before providing the national catharsis necessary to begin to right old wrongs and correct present ills. The civil rights movement, dated from the Rosa Parks bus incident in 1955, would cause the nation to tremble in its resistance to black folk struggling for liberation from economic, political, and educational suppression. The waves of protest forged new black leadership, new organizations, and new tactics. The South was the mirror in which the nation saw reflected the horrors of racism, the virulence of poverty, the degradation of disfranchisement, and centuries of pain being polished anew. Yet the South was not the only region experiencing societal ills, nor was it the only region to respond and produce new leaders.

Cambridge, Maryland, the seat of Dorchester County, located on the Chesapeake side of the Eastern Shore, was catapulted into national prominence during the 1960s as a result of the energetic leadership of Gloria H. Richardson. Richardson became the clarion caller who beckoned the state and nation to do what was right in Cambridge. Seen by many as an unlikely rebel, she galvanized the Second Ward into a *force de resistance* that challenged the status of poverty and unemployment among blacks, and segregated housing and schools.

121

Born in Baltimore in 1922, Richardson was a member of one of the most well off families in Cambridge, the St. Clairs. Richardson crossed the line from elite to grass roots with an alacrity that underscored a depth of concern for, and identification with, all suppressed peoples. "Regardless of my background, I experienced the same kinds of things that all other Blacks did in Cambridge. My father died because he could not go to the hospital most of the time. Most people had to travel to Johns Hopkins segregated clinic. I was not able to get a job of any kind since I didn't want to teach. I could not go into the restaurants if I wanted to. So I was a victim as well as the rest of the Blacks in Cambridge."[1] Richardson was reared in Cambridge. She was educated at Howard University, where she was inspired by Rayford Logan, Highland Lewis, E. Franklin Frazier, Howard Thurman, Sterling Brown, and Mordecai Johnson. She learned from them how to analyze racism, the dynamics of social action, and the necessity of introspection. Her education at Howard was preparation for her future role in the Cambridge movement.

Harriet Tubman and Frederick Douglass, champions of pre-Civil War abolition movements, had been born nearby. Cambridge experienced a decrease in slavery from the 1700s to the Civil War, to a large extent because cotton was not profitable in the area. Even so, Cambridge had the fourth largest number of slaves in Maryland. Cambridge became a major slave trading center for the Eastern Shore, with the slave market in front of the county courthouse. Side by side with this bustling slave market there existed approximately five thousand free Negroes who were treated as a separate class. Throughout the county there are many large estates that were once a part of the peculiar institution of slavery. In 1912, H. Maynadier St. Clair, Richardson's grandfather, became the second Negro to serve on the council in the city of Cambridge. (Nehemiah Henry is frequently cited as the first black leader because of his name on a 1906 cornerstone along with names of other members of the council.)[2]

H. M. St. Clair served until 1946. Throughout his tenure, though popular, he was tainted by accusations of collusion with the Phillips Packing Company, the company that controlled the town from the 1920s through World War II. In 1946, his son Herbert failed to get elected to his father's seat. Charles Cornish became the Second Ward representative. Critics were few and expectations of Cornish were many. He was perceived as the alternative to the nonproductive hegemony of Maynadier St. Clair, and improvement for the Negro was expected. By 1953, Cornish was the subject of restless criticism, and by 1962, the Richardson era, he was the target of direct criticism.[3]

At the beginning of the Cambridge movement, Cambridge had an established pattern of discrimination and segregation, like all Southern towns. As in all Negro communities, Cambridge was faced with an impoverished black population. Unemployment was up to fifty percent, the highest in the state, with the percentage in the Second Ward, the black community, three times that of Cambridge's white community and six times that of the national figure. Seven and one-half times more blacks than whites earned less than $3,000 a year.[4] Most blacks were employed in food processing, sawmills, maintenance, negro commerce, municipal maintenance, and industrial jobs in Baltimore. Women were highly represented in seasonal and service jobs.[5]

Politically, blacks in Cambridge were underrepresented as a result of gerrymandering. The Second Ward provided what political power existed, contributing to the victory and defeat of both white and Negro candidates. After successfully providing the swing vote for key officials in the local government, the officials acknowledged the role of the black vote in their election but pleaded their inability to do anything for that constituency.[6] Seeing that voting failed to effect change, Richardson would embrace direct action instead.

There were two ward officials when the Cambridge movement began: Charles Cornish, representative to City Council (Cornish owned a bus company that the Board of Education hired to transport blacks to segregated schools), and Helen Waters, representative on the Board of Education. Waters operated a beauty parlor for whites only and was openly hostile to the Cambridge Nonviolent Action Committee.[7]

Cambridge had the outside assistance of other civil rights movements. The Northern Student Movement played a big role in the beginning of the Cambridge movement. Students from Brown, Harvard, Morgan State, Howard, Maryland State, and Swarthmore were involved in initial demonstrations and canvassing. SNCC maintained close contact. This outside involvement did not persist throughout the entire sequence of occurrences in Cambridge, however.

As in many movements, the local leadership was a small but dedicated nucleus. Led by Gloria Richardson, the leadership was comprised of a community-based constituency. Richardson said, "The one thing we did was to emphasize that while you should be educated, that education, degrees, college degrees were not essential [here]. If you could articulate the need, if you knew what the need was, if you were aware of the kinds of games that white folk play, *that was the real thing.*"[8]

In some ways, Cambridge was unique. It was the first grass roots movement outside of the deep South; it was one of the first campaigns to focus on economic conditions rather than just civil rights; the Kennedy administration intervened on a broader scale than ever before (the actual signing of an "Accords" took place); nonviolence was questioned as a tactic; and it was the first major movement of which a woman was the leader.[9] The movement had far greater access to national publicity than most Northern movements. Cambridge was seventy-five miles from both Washington, D.C., and Baltimore, and fifty miles from Annapolis. Also, the Cambridge movement was more secular than other movements. The clergy as a whole did not strongly support the CNAC. Frequently, ministerial resistance was checked by anxious members who were actively involved in the demonstrations.

A unique aspect of Cambridge's economic situation was its history as a company town. During the 1920s until the end of World War II, the Phillips Packing Company was the controlling industry in Dorchester County. In the late 1940s, competition from frozen food companies and losses due to strikes and unionization forced the company into decline.[10] State Senator Frederick Malkus of Dorchester County, the most powerful person in the local political structure and a staunch opponent of civil rights legislation, headed a faction that opposed entry of industry in order to keep wages low and unions from being successful. Malkus became a constant target of Richardson and the CNAC. Because of his opposition to oyster leasing and soft clamming, blacks were driven out of work as the industry suffered.

Two features distinguished Cambridge's black political activity from the movement in the South: Cambridge was a two-party town, and blacks had never been denied the vote since attaining it in 1869. Some blacks even voted as early as 1800. Until the Depression, however, blacks voted eighty-five percent Republican.[11] Before the 1960s, the Negro population was politically ineffectual. Blacks were outside of the decision making process and law agencies maintained the status quo.

Although Cambridge's much publicized activities occurred in 1963, the beginning of the Cambridge movement can be traced to December 1961. William Hansen and Reginald Robinson were field secretaries of SNCC. Along with the Civic Interest Group headed by Clarence Logan of

Baltimore, they began exploratory investigations of conditions in the area. Demonstrations were directed against segregation in public accommodations.

William Hansen was an early casualty in Dorchester County. He was thrown out of the Choptank Inn on January 20, 1962, as two other persons were arrested in Cambridge during violent confrontations.[12] In February, students came to Cambridge and attempted a sit-in.[13] During this period Richardson's daughter, Donna, was instrumental in getting young people to act as guides for the demonstrators[14] and Herbert St. Clair opened his home to them. The black leadership (city councilman and black ministers) backed down before any of the young people's demands were addressed, so nothing changed. But parents who had acted as observers during the student phase decided to carry on. They wrote to SNCC, asking how they could become affiliated. Gloria Richardson and Freddie Sinclair's wife, Yolanda, were sent to Atlanta to a SNCC conference.[15]

Helping to spur Gloria Richardson to action was a visit by a young crew of freedom riders from New York City and Baltimore early in 1962. "There was something direct, something real about the way the kids waged nonviolent war. This was the first time I saw a vehicle I could work with. With SNCC, there's not all this red tape—you just get it done.[16] Through support for their children, the adults took the lead; after some months, the children came back into the movement.[17]

In March 1962, CNAC (pronounced Cee-nack) was formed around the St. Clair family.[18] Freddie Sinclair was the CNAC's first cochairman, along with Inez Grub. SNCC was available for help and sent field secretaries in at various times, but the CNAC was a local, autonomous group and became the vehicle for organizing protest and articulating goals for blacks in Cambridge throughout the next years. In June 1962, Gloria Richardson replaced Freddie Sinclair as cochair of the CNAC and became the virtual leader of the black community in Cambridge.

The CNAC charged no fees or dues for membership. If there was no crisis, meetings were held once a week, in the building that had once housed Richardson's father's pharmacy. During weekend demonstrations, food was supplied by people in the community. The economic resources of the CNAC varied. Dances were held, families put up property for bail, canvassing was conducted in the streets and various groups made contributions. Mass meetings were held to inform residents of news, to inspire them to greater action and commitment, and to accumulate large crowds. Bethel AME Church was frequently used; the smaller Mt. Sinai Church housed meetings early in the movement when the major churches opposed the demonstrations.

Richardson saw the fundamental problems facing blacks in Cambridge as a lack of adequate housing, discrimination in the educational process, lack of equal job opportunity, and poor health care.[19] Originally the basic push was to integrate public accommodations. After a survey of the total black community, fifteen demands were made in the areas of employment, housing, and health care.[20] The attack was on the entire system of segregation—demands for equal treatment on all scores, including employment, police protection, and schools. Then, in addition to segregation itself, the economic and social systems that segregation defended were attacked—housing, employment, working conditions, and education.[21]

The summer of 1962 was devoted to Project Eastern Shore. The CNAC was assisted by the Northern Student Movement to improve voter registration and recreation. The voter registration drive continued through the fall. At an August rally, Richardson announced that there would be a block vote effort to defeat State Senator Frederick C. Malkus in the upcoming election. One thousand three hundred black registered Republicans and five hundred black Democrats were cited as seeking a Malkus defeat. The members of the Maryland House of Delegates from Dorchester County were also targets for unseating. They, along with Malkus, opposed the Public Accommodations Law and Senate Bill 19 concerning unemployment benefits.[22] The Maryland legislature passed the Public Accommodations Law in the spring of 1963, but Malkus, who was not unseated by the Richardson effort, used "exemption" to prevent its application to Dorchester County. Eight out of nine Eastern Shore counties were exempted.[23]

Events in the spring of 1963 rose to a boiling point. In March, the Dorset Theater, Cambridge's only movie house, decided to confine blacks to the back half of the balcony (as opposed to the entire balcony). Patience short, Richardson and the CNAC simultaneously appealed to the City Council to hear its demands and organized outside support for possible demonstrations. Richardson and Inez Grub met with leaders from the Civic Interest Group of Baltimore, Ms. Penny from Fellowship House in Philadelphia (who was said to have designed the Peace Corps for Kennedy), and students from Swarthmore, Brown, Harvard, Morgan State and Maryland State colleges. Swarthmore students and CNAC leaders planned demonstrations for April and early May.

On March 25, 1963, Richardson, Grub, and Mrs. Garrison appeared before a meeting of the Cambridge city commissioners to inform Mayor

Gloria Richardson, head of the Cambridge Nonviolent Action Committee, was the spokesperson for anti-segregation protests in Cambridge, Maryland in 1963. Blacks there had been voting since they gained the franchise in 1869, but most aspects of their lives continued to be segregated.
[Photo: *UPI/Bettmann Newsphotos*]

127

Calvin Mowbray that Negroes wanted integration immediately. The meeting turned into a shouting match. The commissioners, including Cornish, insulted the group; Mowbray called Richardson and her followers "Freedom raiders."[24] Several days later, Richardson and her followers began picketing and sit-ins. The Dorset Theater and the Rescue Fire Company's Arena (the skating rink) were the first sites of demonstrations. The next seven weeks saw demonstrations at City Hall, the county courthouse, and the jail as well. In all, eighty protestors, including Richardson, were arrested.[25]

In early May, Judge W. Laird Henry presided over the much publicized "Penny Trials," a mass trial of eighty activists. In spite of Richardson's eloquent, comprehensive assessment of the relationship of Cambridge to its black community, the judge fined each a penny and suspended the sentence. Richardson was subjected to a condescending lecture about the disgrace she brought to the family name. This was perceived as an attempt to degrade the demonstrators and convince them to go home.[26]

Judge Henry misread the situation. Demonstrations and arrests continued, only now without outside help. The CNAC had vowed to fill the Cambridge jail by conducting sit-ins every day until the downtown facilities were desegregated. On May 14, 1963, Donna Richardson was among fourteen arrested at the Dorset Theater for sitting in protest in the lobby.[27] Gloria Richardson and her mother, Mabel St. Clair Booth, were arrested the same day at the Dizzyland Restaurant. Later that evening, marchers demonstrated around the jail. Before the night ended, sixty-two persons had been arrested on charges of disorderly conduct. Fifteen state police and several K-9 dogs arrived to assist local police.[28]

On May 18, Judge Henry announced that there would be an honest attempt to accommodate the integrationists. Influenced by the tenacity of the demonstrators, Henry engineered the attempts at accommodations. (Henry was a descendant of an old established Eastern Shore family. His ancestor, John Henry, was Maryland's first governor.) He said he would free the blacks incarcerated during the week, and set up a committee of whites to seek to negotiate a settlement of the dispute. Henry and his committee subsequently agreed that the following demands should be met:

1. Complete desegregation of public places.
2. Complete desegregation of public schools, with Negro students assigned to schools nearest them.

3. Creation of equal employment opportunities in industries and stores, beginning with an initial minimum goal of ten percent hiring of Negroes in each place.
4. Building of a public housing project for Negroes and a study of sewer and sidewalk needs.
5. An end to all forms of police brutality and appointment of a Negro deputy sheriff.[29]

By May 20, the prisoners had been released and the Committee on Interracial Understanding had been formalized (CIU). For the next three weeks, only token picketing occurred. On May 19, *The Washington Post* analyzed the situation as one in which Richardson had filled what many considered a gap in the Negro leadership of Cambridge. Charles Cornish had been viewed as ineffective. Further, the peaceful nature of the demonstrations was attributed to Richardson's leadership. No outside lawmen had been sent in at this point. Reginald Robinson, field representative of SNCC, who directed activities while Richardson was in jail, was the only outsider directly involved.[30]

The tenuous peace was shattered on May 25, 1963, when twelve juveniles were arrested for creating a disturbance while picketing the Board of Education office. The students were released in the custody of their parents until their appearance in Juvenile Court that next week. In the meantime they were expelled by the superintendent for leaving Maces' Lane High School without permission.

Picketing, as well as a general economic boycott, continued in Cambridge. When the Colonial Store agreed to hire two more blacks, Richardson announced that the boycott there would end.

The CIU announced that peaceful negotiations were impossible. The governor invited the Maryland Interracial Commission to discuss the problems of racial peace with the CIU.[31]

On May 31, 1963, Richardson appealed to Attorney General Robert F. Kennedy for a federal investigation of violations of constitutional rights in Cambridge. Asserting that tempers were growing short, she cited the case of Dinez White, a fifteen-year-old girl held without bond after her arrest while kneeling in prayer outside a segregated bowling alley. Richardson announced that [if the girl was not released] "they will have to pack the jail with us. They won't hold her in there alone."[32] White was released from county jail on June 3 on a writ of habeas corpus. Circuit Judge E. McMaster Duer

129

issued instructions that she was to "go home and stay there" until a Juvenile Court hearing on her case was held later in the week.[33]

Compounding the restlessness in Cambridge was action on the state level by segregationist groups to block the June 2, 1963 application of the Public Accommodations Law by securing petitions to put the statute to a referendum vote in 1964. The law, barring discrimination against Negroes and other minority groups, had already been exempted in eleven of Maryland's twenty-three counties, including Dorchester. The effect of this action was to postpone the operation of the law pending the outcome of a referendum, wherein the judgment of the voters is final. (Only in Berkeley, California had civil rights been subjected to the popular will. There a referendum on a local fair housing ordinance on April 2, 1962 was defeated.) The validity of the petitions would be determined by the courts.[34] After failure of the CIU to get action on the integration demands, the CNAC approved demonstrations.[35] On June 10, 1963, Dinez White and Dwight Cromwell, both fifteen, were sentenced to indeterminate terms in correction schools on open charges of juvenile delinquency for their participation in demonstrations. This precipitated immediate, all-out demonstrations.[36] Throughout the movement, these two children would serve as a symbol of the injustice of whites in Cambridge.

Simultaneously, Rabbi Israel Goldman of Baltimore, chair of the Maryland Commission on Interracial Problems and Relations, announced that he "must report failure in each attempt to arrange voluntary desegregation in schools and restaurants." He said the commission would recommend to Governor J. Millard Tawes the enactment of a new public accommodations law from which no county would be exempt.[37] The situation in Cambridge deteriorated, and on June 10, violence broke out. Two white men were struck in the chests by shotgun blasts, three fires broke out in white business establishments. State police armed with riot sticks and dogs were rushed in to quell fighting. Incendiary bombs were found. The night before, twenty-one blacks had been arrested. Marchers to the courthouse were followed by a crowd of whites into the black section. Gloria Richardson issued the call for further demonstrations from the front porch of her home the next day. Urging a nonviolent approach, she again appealed to Robert Kennedy for federal aid.[38]

On June 13, state troopers blocked all approaches to the Negro district after a chanting mob of approximately 350 white men and women pursued an equal number of blacks who had just staged the largest demonstration to date.

The next day, June 14, Governor Tawes called in Gloria Richardson, Reginald Robinson, Phillip Savage, and Stanley Branche of the NAACP. He also summoned Mayor Mowbray, city councilmen, other officials, and a number of leading businessmen. In all, about twenty people gathered at the gubernatorial offices in Annapolis. Tawes announced he was sending in the national guard "to create a climate for a peaceful settlement." Blacks listed their demands for jobs, housing, education, and equal accommodations legislation. The mayor and city councilmen offered to integrate the schools, see that a Negro was hired in the state employment office, make application for a federal loan for a Negro housing project, pass a public accommodations ordinance, and name a biracial commission to work on the other problems that could not be solved immediately by legislation. In return, the city officials wanted a year's moratorium on demonstrations. The CNAC would not agree to the moratorium.[39]

On June 14, 1963, the State Adjutant General and guard commander Milton Reckford broadcast the directive that martial law was imposed on Cambridge. Gloria Richardson and Reginald Robinson were still in Annapolis with Governor Tawes. Earlier, Governor Tawes had ordered 100 National Guardsmen to be in Cambridge on the 14th, and 400 more were to report the next day. General Reckford's directive ordered civilians and military to comply with a 4 P.M. curfew for liquor stores, a 9 P.M. curfew for all other stores, and a 10 P.M. curfew for persons, as well as cessation of demonstrations and marches. The next day about 500 Maryland National Guard troops—the entire Eastern Shore battalion—and about 235 troopers of the Maryland State Police force were either on patrol or on call in the bivouacs in the Cambridge Armory, the American Legion Hall, and in nearby motels. Negro leaders said that they approved of the presence of the troops because they had assurances that the guardsmen would "not be used to maintain the status quo."[40]

The next day Gloria Richardson announced that one hundred demonstrators scheduled to arrive in Cambridge from Baltimore and New York had been detoured to other destinations. Though demonstrations were banned, people appeared on the streets wearing paper badges that read "no Dignity—no Dollars." Phil Savage, the area secretary of the NAACP, addressed a rally at Bethel AME Church: "we want the National Guard removed, but it should not be removed as long as our rights are denied . . . If there is no satisfactory progress [with a biracial committee started the night before] by next Friday, thousands of people will be mobilized in Cambridge."[41]

On June 16 the white leaders sent a telegram to Governor Tawes, saying that due to a "breach of faith and the threats of the Negro representatives you invited to met with you and with us last Friday, further negotiations with these people are impossible." The telegram urged the indefinite presence of the National Guard.

It was reported that the Negroes had flatly rejected demands that all demonstrations be halted for at least a year in exchange for lowering racial barriers in restaurants, hotels, motels, and recreational facilities. It was understood that Negro leaders were demanding full school desegregation and equal hiring practices, as well as the opening of places of public accommodation, before making any promises regarding further demonstrations. On June 20, Mayor Mowbray tried to persuade the five-man City Council to adopt a public accommodations ordinance, the Negroes' chief demand. The other demands—integration of public schools and improved employment rights—were certain to follow quickly.

On July 1, the Cambridge City Council approved a public accommodations provision. The provision was an amendment to the city charter, requiring owners of hotels, motels, and restaurants within the city limits to give equal service to all persons. It would go into effect August 20. Negro leaders rejected the amendment, saying that it was loosely drawn and contained weak provisions.

Simultaneously, a dozen demonstrators continued a hunger strike at the State House in Annapolis. The strike was to last until Governor Tawes signed an executive order banning all forms of discrimination in public places.[42] On July 3, the attorney general ruled that the governor had no power to issue such an executive order and the sit-in ended. The next day, after council action, Governor Tawes ordered the Maryland National Guard to end its three weeks of modified martial law at noon on July 7. Money was considered the major factor in his decision; since June 14, an average of five hundred troops had been on duty at a cost of twenty thousand dollars a week.[43]

Black leaders said mass demonstrations might resume after troops pulled out. The CNAC would "wait and see" how the situation developed.

Meanwhile, a caravan of freedom riders from New York planned to conduct widespread sit-in demonstrations in the Cambridge area on July 3.

The expedition had been organized by the Campus Americans for Democratic Action and CORE.[44] Announcements were made by General Gelston of the National Guard that demonstrations planned in Cambridge would be barred to outsiders.[45] On noon of July 8, troops pulled out of Cambridge. The same day, students tried to enter Dizzyland Restaurant. In a much publicized confrontation, the owner, Robert Fehsenfeld, crushed an egg on the head and neck of Edward Dickerson, a white demonstrator, as the group sang while kneeling. Later Fehsenfeld poured water on Dickerson's head. At one point, Fehsenfeld yelled at city policemen, "Get these people out of here, I know my rights." That night a peaceful freedom walk from Bethel AME Church to Dorchester county courthouse (about two blocks) occurred.[46] The next day, July 9, racial violence flared up when three whites were arrested. One had punched a young white demonstrator outside the Cambridge Hotel Bar and Grille. This was precipitated as Negro marchers began to walk from the courthouse back to Bethel AME Church. Blacks were forced to detour to a grassy area beside the courthouse because whites blocked the courthouse steps where the demonstrators usually knelt.

On July 10, Gloria Richardson and other civil rights leaders met with Maceo Hubbard, a seventeen-year veteran of the Justice Department and civil rights lawyer sent to calm Cambridge. This was hours after Dizzyland Restaurant was again a headliner when three Negroes and a white girl were dragged from the restaurant. This time Fehsenfeld did not press charges and they were released.[47] That night, 300 whites surrounded 250 demonstrators who paraded to the courthouse.[48] This was the third day of racial disturbances after the National Guard pulled out. July 11 was a day of nonstop violence and protest. Early in the day a melee at Dizzyland occurred when six white and black demonstrators were beaten up inside by white patrons. Upon a signal from Stanley Branche, some picketers slipped inside before owner Fehsenfeld locked the door. Police who were watching made no attempt to enter the restaurant until blacks rushed across the street and tried to break down the door.[49] Dwight Campbell and Lester Green were beaten unconscious.[50] The *Baltimore Sun* reported that the police beat vainly on the door to get someone to open it. The National Guard arrived back in Cambridge around 5:30 P.M., and General Gelston declared himself in charge of the town. His new bans were more restrictive: curfew at 9 P.M. instead of 10, stores closed at 2 instead of 9, a ban on firearms, and automobiles subject to search.

That evening around 8 P.M. about 250 blacks staged a "freedom walk" to the Dorchester county courthouse. Shortly after the demonstrators had completed a prayer at the courthouse shooting started. The demonstrators were jeered and pelted with eggs by a crowd of about 200 whites. State police kept the two groups at bay. Two carloads of whites drove through the black section of town, exchanging gunfire with blacks. Around 10:15, five whites, including two National Guardsmen and a twelve-year-old boy, were wounded. State police using tear gas and guns entered the Negro district to disperse mobs.[51] George Collins, *Afro* staff writer, reported: "The long smoldering powder-keg finally exploded and unchained violence swept the streets of Cambridge . . . Only an act of God could have stayed the hand of death during the long night when bullets literally rained on the county seat of Dorchester County."[52] An hour-long battle on Pine Street, which reportedly shook the ground, was precipitated by two carloads of white men that sped down the street at intervals with guns blazing from the windows. Retaliation occurred from blacks crouched behind cars, in buildings, and on rooftops.

On July 15, Gloria Richardson, along with Stanley Branche and others, was arrested on the street. She had returned earlier from Annapolis, where she attended a conference on racial problems chaired by Governor Tawes. That night Reginald Robinson and Phillip Savage led blacks assembled at a rally at Bethel AME Church. They demanded the release of the blacks from jail by 8:30 P.M. Otherwise, they vowed, "We shall march." Gelston in the meantime had ordered the release of those in jail. Tawes had announced that the National Guard must stay indefinitely.[53]

On July 16, a biracial commission with two whites and four blacks was appointed. Black leaders announced a twenty-four-hour moratorium on demonstrations to allow the commission to demonstrate its good faith. That night at a mass meeting, a prayer for General Gelston's mother, who had just died, was held.[54] That the CNAC and the protestors would show concern for Gelston can be attributed to a perception of him in the black community as fair-minded.

President Kennedy, in a speech on July 17, asserted that, "Cambridge . . . lost sight of what demonstrations are about because of violence."[55] Gloria Richardson immediately sent a letter of protest.

In the meantime, it was announced that the Bar Association of Maryland had appointed a Race Relations Committee that would go to Cambridge. This prompted Richardson to declare a suspension of demonstrations to give the association a fair chance to deliberate and make recommendations. She thought the moratorium might last through the next week.[56] The next day, Attorney General Finon now admitted that he had erroneously announced that the Bar Association had agreed to mediate the dispute. Richardson, frustrated because "Governor Tawes had done nothing but make excuses for white authorities," issued an ultimatum that if commissioners were not there by 7 P.M. the next night, demonstrations would resume.[57] Gelston, in the meantime, continued to come under fire from the white community, who asserted, "We do not feel that the National Guard should have to plead with Negroes to obey the law after the Guardsmen have enforced it against white people." Richardson, at a rally at Bethel AME Church, warned that President Kennedy might have to visit Cambridge to avert a civil war. "Unless something is achieved soon in Cambridge, then no one is going to be able to control these people who have been provoked by generations of segregation, by countless indignities—and now by uncontrollable white mobs in the streets . . . Instead of progress, we have anarchy. The white men who have power—the men who can act sit in their comfortable houses, undisturbed by events until it is too late. We live in a town where a man might be killed tomorrow, where civil war might break out next week. It cannot get better while the white people fail to understand the mood of the Negro community and to realize that unless they grant the means of progress, their houses and ours may fly apart."[58]

On July 22, at the invitation of Assistant Attorney General Burke Marshall who was in charge of the Civil Rights Division, a conference was convened in Washington. The government representatives were State Attorney General Thomas B. Finon; his deputy, Robert C. Murphy; Brigadier General George M. Gelston; and Governor Tawes's top aide, Edmund C. Mester. The civil rights leaders included Gloria Richardson, John Lewis, Reginald Robinson, and Stanley Branche. The sessions included Attorney General Robert F. Kennedy and Robert Weaver, head of the Housing and Home Finance Agency. The sessions lasted from 3 P.M. to midnight. Playing it safe, Marshall left city officials off the invitation list for fear of creating a charged atmosphere that had stifled past negotiations.[59] A prime issue in the Cambridge situation was the construction of a million dollar housing project in the Negro section of the city (twice postponed by white authorities).[60] On the morning of July 23, 1963, the mayor and other city officials arrived and with Kennedy and Marshall as witnesses, the five-point Treaty of

Cambridge was signed by blacks and city officials in Attorney General Robert Kennedy's office.

The points of the agreement called for:

1. Complete and immediate desegregation of the public schools (with integrated busing) and hospitals in the county.
2. Construction of 200 units of low-rent public housing for Negroes.
3. Employment of a Negro in the Cambridge office of the Maryland Department of Employment Security and in the Post Office.
4. Appointment of a Human Relations Commission.
5. Adoption of a Charter Amendment which provided for desegregation of places of public accommodation.[61]

On the last point, although the Charter Amendment could be subjected to a referendum as provided by law, the hope of those signing the agreement was that such a referendum vote would not be necessary and that the amendment would become effective on August 20, 1963. All present expressed the belief that it was in the best interest of Cambridge that the Charter not be petitioned to referendum. However, more that 25% of the voters signed referendum petitions, which forced the amendment to be brought to an October vote (20% were required), rather than the desired implementation.

Why did Gloria Richardson agree to the accords? Many reasons have been suggested, but the overwhelming view was that she believed failure to achieve a truce would lead to bloodshed. Richardson later stated that the possibility of violence was not one of her concerns. She wanted to prove that the moral suasion of the federal government would not make local leaders keep the promises they made, as Washington thought.

In August, division occurred between Richardson and the local NAACP over the public accommodation amendment that was scheduled for an October vote. The Cambridge First Committee, which had been set up by the city administration to get support for the amendment the previous week, sought to help Richardson get out the black vote. Richardson reiterated her stand that the CNAC would not press the community's black voters to support the amendment. Reverend T. N. Murray, chairman of the local NAACP, and at least two other ministers remained firm in urging Negroes to vote for the amendment. Richardson's oft-stated position was that it was a moral issue—blacks already had these constitutional rights and they should

The "Treaty of Cambridge" which all hoped would end racial conflict in Cambridge, Maryland was signed in Attorney General Robert Kennedy's office. Shown here, left to right, are Gloria Richardson, Kennedy, and Cambridge Mayor Calvin Mowbray. [Photo: *UPI/Bettmann Newsphotos*]

137

not be subjected to a vote. This position was embraced by Representative Adam Clayton Powell at a mass meeting in Cambridge held at the Elks Home. Powell asserted, "It is divinely right for the people of Cambridge to break the law until they help in making the law. Final judgment rests with God, not with the head of the National Guard, the mayor, or the police."[62]

On September 2, Richardson resigned as leader of the CNAC. The next day she withdrew her resignation, stating that it "would be detrimental to the civil rights movement in Cambridge and across the country."[63]

Phil Savage, back in Philadelphia, said that Gloria Richardson had not won the support of the community in advocating not voting for the charter amendment. He planned to return to Cambridge to encourage blacks to vote on October 1. Richardson viewed passage of the charter amendment by a black majority and white minority as no solution to white resistance.[64] Public accommodations, according to Richardson, are a right that cannot be given or taken away by a vote. The blacks who pushed for the charter amendment's passage argued that public accommodations are a key provision in proposed federal civil rights legislation. Reverend Murray said he would have preferred a city public accommodations ordinance that would not have been subject to a referendum, but the referendum should be supported if the objective of public accommodations could be obtained. Commissioner Cornish, who supported the referendum, said "it would be a reflection on our intelligence if we do not exercise our right of franchise at all times." The theory had been that if 35 percent of Cambridge's white voters were practical and principled enough to support the amendment along with the black voters, it would pass. The whites returned a little more than the favorable 35 percent of the vote yet half of the black voters abstained. The referendum lost by 274 votes. The summer had not changed a single custom.[65]

The defeat of the referendum was laid squarely at Gloria Richardson's feet. She was accused of boycotting the polls to perpetuate civil strife and thus maintain her power as civil rights activist. She was accused of being a Communist. Richardson braved this as she had braved pressure before, even from the likes of Martin Luther King, Jr. At a rally before the referendum was held, she had occasion to share a box with King. King questioned Richardson's stance; people in the South were fighting to vote, after all. As always, Richardson pointed out that blacks had been voting in Cambridge since the 1800s, and it had not improved their lives. King and Richardson would not join hands in the Cambridge struggle.

The remainder of 1963 and the first half of 1964 saw Cambridge continue under the eyes of the National Guard. The demonstrations continued intermittently. Some successes were achieved, but many were not.

The noteworthy achievements of Richardson's unbending quest for civil and economic justice began earlier, in September when school started.

In 1955, the Dorchester County School Board had adopted a desegregation plan. Beginning with grade twelve in 1956, one additional grade would be desegregated each year. The county, although ostensibly integrated, had actually maintained two separate school systems. The practice in this case was different than the law, which was not unusual in such situations.

During the summer of 1963, the CNAC Summer Study Program was in operation. Staffed by summer workers, some one hundred young people were tutored in math and English. When school began, twenty-eight black children entered previously all-white schools.[66]

The second success was the decision rendered by the Maryland Court of Appeals on October 8, 1963. The court unanimously reversed the sentences of Dinez White and Dwight Cromwell. It stated that Judge E. M. McMaster Duer had erred not only in assigning the indeterminate commitments, but also in failing to observe ordinary rules of evidence and procedure.[67]

Richardson was to see additional support of her posture in January, 1964. Demonstrations resumed just one day before the United States Civil Rights Commission released a forty-nine-page report prepared by the commission's Maryland Advisory Committee. This report underscored the findings of the CNAC in Cambridge. Specific criticism included:

1. The state administration of Governor J. Millard Tawes.
2. Private industry, for failing to employ blacks.
3. Economic conditions regarding blacks—more unemployment, less education, worse housing, lowest income of any Maryland city; in only ten to fifteen percent of black homes did one person have a steady job.
4. Russell Davis, state personnel commissioner, who expressed ignorance of the 1961 antibias legislation prohibiting discrimination in state employment.[68]

In early March, after weeks of demands, demonstrations, and meetings with national and state officials, state officials announced that the Maryland Guard would begin distribution of federal surplus food parcels. This announcement forestalled a planned CNAC demonstration and followed on the heels of the arrest of eighteen persons who were picketing the welfare office. Cambridge city officials were bitter about the decision. The city commissioners demanded Gelston's resignation for his role in facilitating the program. The first phase of food distribution started on March 6, 1964, amid demands from the Cambridge Board of Commissioners for a congressional investigation of who initiated the program over the objection of the local government.[69]

In June, Secretary of Labor Willard Wirtz and Attorney General Robert Kennedy announced an on-the-job training program for two hundred employed Negroes in Cambridge. Designed by the Urban League under the Manpower Development Act, the program would be administered by Morgan State College. This was a long-sought goal of Richardson, who presaged the War on Poverty view that economic oppression was just as violent as civil injustice.

Daily strife continued in Cambridge, however. John Kennedy's death signaled a suspension of mass demonstrations. Richardson, departing from SNCC sentiment, which was for continued protest, canceled all mass demonstrations on November 29. This moratorium was to coincide with the national period of mourning, which was to run through December 22, 1963. This, she said, was not in recognition of any great progress on the part of local citizens to resolve the tension in Cambridge, but in recognition of the sense of bereavement for a young president who had tried his utmost, in the face of strong resistance from Congress, to make American democracy more than an ideal. Although National Guardsmen were under orders to prevent public gatherings, and despite interracial meetings designed to ease the crisis, plans had been made to demonstrate prior to the assassination.[70]

Communications did not improve between state officials and the CNAC. On January 30, 1964, Senator Daniel B. Brewster staged a conference of officials from Cambridge and state and federal agencies that had economic aid programs in the Chesapeake Bay community. The purpose was to ease the racial deadlock in Cambridge. Richardson was not an official participant, but sat in the audience. She referred to the meeting as "hogwash," asserting that the conferees were defending themselves for what they had and had not done. The senator announced that the conference was a success. Gloria Richardson said it was a sham.[71]

New obstacles were created. On February 12, Richard Matthews, Democratic member of the House of Delegates from Cambridge, introduced bills to control newspaper, radio, and television coverage of Cambridge.

Perhaps the most disheartening episode, prior to Richardson's departure from Cambridge, was the rally on May 2 for Governor George Wallace at the Firemen's Arena. That skating rink, the focus of so many desegregation efforts, was the site of his appearance and was a slap in the face to blacks. His presence sparked spontaneous reactions from all over the country. Catholic priests, white students, Southern civil rights leaders who had never been to Cambridge, and others, came to a rally at the Elks Club the same evening. John Lewis spoke, along with minister Lonnie 3X, Jessie Gray (Harlem rent strike leader), and Lawrence Landry of ACT. After the rally, Gloria Richardson led the marchers to Race Street, where along with thirteen others, she was arrested. The National Guard dispersed the crowd with tear gas.

General Gelston, who did not give the order, would later chuckle that the gas affected the white community more because of the shift of the wind. Stokely Carmichael and Gloria Richardson later had the gas analyzed and discovered it was poisonous.[72]

The National Guard officially withdrew from Cambridge on July 7, 1964, at Governor Tawes's direction. The governor's decision was based on a recommendation from the Miles Committee, a mediation committee he had appointed. Additionally, the committee recommended continuation for three months of the controversial food program. Although Richardson was out of town when the report was given, she was cited in it with commendations.

In July 1964, Lyndon Johnson signed into law the momentous Civil Rights Act. Immediately, the Colony Lanes Bowling Alley, Dorset Theater, Dizzyland, and several restaurants were successfully tested (the initial test at Dizzyland resulted in an assault warrant being sworn out on Fehsenfeld).

Gloria Richardson left Cambridge the next month to move to New York with her newly wed spouse, Frank Dandridge, who was a free-lance photographer who had been on assignment in Cambridge. She believed that the Johnson administration's War on Poverty and the Civil Rights Act would make a substantial difference in the lives of blacks.

The CNAC continued, but the vacuum left by Richardson's departure was an awesome tribute to the pensive woman who successfully fielded all manner of criticism from Kennedy, King, the NAACP, columnists, and TV commentators. She held true to her faith in a moral cause, her belief in how to achieve results, and her compassion for the alienated. Her direct action had been a powerful weapon in the civil rights movement. When she left Cambridge, Charles Cornish, ironically, had just been elected president of the five-man city council. Blacks continue to live in the segregated Second Ward; full school integration did not come for nearly seven more years. It took nearly a decade and a half before unemployment figures in Cambridge fell to the range of the national average.

Credit must be given to Gloria Richardson for creating a climate for change in Cambridge. Even today, citizens assert that without the demonstrations, little progress would have been made. Yet, the existing literature on the civil rights movement contains almost no discussions of Gloria Richardson, the CNAC, or Cambridge during the 1962-1964 period. Future historians should underscore the significance of her leadership and give the Cambridge movement she led the attention it deserves.

NOTES

1. Interview with Gloria Richardson, New York, (Ja Jahannes), 1988. Copy in the possession of the author.
2. George Robert Kent, "The Negro in Politics in Dorchester County, Maryland, 1920-1960." Masters Thesis, University of Maryland, 1961, p. 63.
3. *Ibid.*, p. 57.
4. CNAC Summer Staff, "The Negro Ward of Cambridge, Maryland: A Study in Social Change," Cambridge, Maryland, 1963, pp. 34-37.
5. *Ibid.*, p. 32
6. Interview with Gloria Richardson (Gil Noble), February 26, 1981. Copy in the possession of the author.
7. CNAC Summer Staff, "The Negro Ward of Cambridge, Maryland: A Study in Social Change," p. 13.
8. Gloria Richardson interview (Noble).
9. Paula Giddings, *Where and When I Enter* (New York: William Morrow Company, 1984), pp. 290-291.
10. CNAC Summer Staff, "The Negro Ward of Cambridge," p. 13.
11. Kent, "The Negro in Politics in Dorchester County, Maryland, p. 13.
12. *New York Times*, January 21, 1962, p 60.
13. *Wilmington News*, June 13, 1963.
14. Gloria Richardson Interview (Noble).
15. Gloria Richardson Interview (Jahannes)
16. *Newsweek*, August 5, 1963, p. 26.
17. Gloria Richardson Interview (Noble).
18. *Wilmington News*, June 13, 1963.

19. Gloria Richardson Interview (Jahannes).
20. Gloria Richardson Interview (Noble).
21. CNAC Summer Staff, "The Negro Ward of Cambridge, Maryland: A Study in Social Change," p. 3.
22. *Salisbury Times*, August 13, 1962.
23. *Wilmington News*, June 13, 1963.
24. *Ibid.*
25. CNAC Summer Staff, "The Negro Ward of Cambridge, Maryland: A Study in Social Change," p. 47.
26. *Ibid.*, p. 47.
27. *Baltimore Sun*, May 15, 1963.
28. *Daily Banner*, May 15, 1963.
29. *Washington Post*, May 19, 1963, p. 1.
30. *Washington Post*, May 19, 1963, p. 4.
31. *Daily Banner*, May 27, 1963.
32. *New York Times*, June 2, 1963, p. 61.
33. *Ibid.*, June 4, 1963, p. 26.
34. *Ibid.*, June 2, 1963, p. 61.
35. *Ibid.*, June 11, 1963, p. 19.
36. *Ibid.*
37. *Ibid.*
38. *Ibid.*, June 13, 1963, p. 17.
39. Robert Liston, "Who Can We Surrender To?", *Saturday Evening Post*, October 5, 1963, pp. 78-80.
40. *New York Times*, June 16, 1963, p. 1.
41. *Ibid.*
42. *Ibid.*, July 2, 1963, p. 14.
43. *Ibid.*, July 3, 1963, p. 10.
44. *Washington Post*, July 11, 1963.
45. *New York Times*, July 4, 1963, p. 38.
46. *Ibid.*, July 9, 1963, p. 18.
47. *Washington Post*, July 11, 1963.
48. *New York Times*, July 11, 1963, p. 18.
49. *Ibid.*, July 12, 1963, p. 18.
50. *Afro-American*, July 20, 1963.
51. *New York Times*, July 12, 1963, p. 1.
52. *Afro-American*, July 12, 1963.
53. *New York Times*, July 11, 1963, p. 18.
54. *Ibid.*, July 17, 1963, p. 1.
55. *Ibid.*, July 18, 1963, p. 1.
56. *Ibid.*, July 19, 1963, p. 7.
57. *Ibid*, July 22, 1963, p. 10.
58. *Ibid.*
59. *Ibid.*, July 23, 1963, p. 17.
60. *Ibid.*

61. *Ibid.*, July 24, 1963, p. 16.
62. Photocopy of newspaper article received from Gloria Richardson. Source unidentified.
63. *Daily Banner*, September 3, 1963.
64. *Ibid.*, September 25, 1963.
65. Murray Kempton, "Gloria, Gloria," *New Republic*, November 16, 1963, pp. 15-17.
66. CNAC Summer Staff, "The Negro Ward of Cambridge, Maryland: A Study in Social Change," p. 23.
67. *New York Times*, October 10, 1963, p. 25.
68. *Ibid.*, February 27, 1964, p. 20.
69. *Ibid.*, March 7, 1964, p. 52.
70. *Ibid.*, November 30, 1963, p. 8.
71. *Ibid.*, January 31, 1964, p. 11.
72. Gloria Richardson Interview (Jahannes).

The Women of Highlander

DONNA LANGSTON

Introduction

Highlander Folk School (HFS) was founded in 1932 in Monteagle, Tennessee, and served as a regional model for progressive education and politics. During the 1930s and 1940s, HFS was a training ground for labor union organizers. In the 1950s and 1960s, it was closely involved in the civil rights movement. In the 1970s and 1980s, HFS focused on environmental issues and on poverty in Appalachia. The history of HFS provides an important role model for the multifaceted political struggles we now face.

Traditional historical accounts of HFS have not adequately stressed the role that women played in the school's struggles and successes. The school's very existence came about as a result of the donations of Dr. Lillian Johnson of Memphis. The contributions of women such as Zilphia Horton, Septima Clark, and Bernice Robinson were instrumental in the development of HFS's social, cultural, and educational programs. The school was also publicly supported during difficult times by prominent women such as Eleanor Roosevelt.

Civil rights movements have often used a variety of strategies and tactics in their struggles, including legal tactics; nonviolent direct action such as boycotts, arrests, mass marches, and sit-ins; the use of the vote; cultural programs; and education. While women in civil rights movements have played central roles in all of these strategies, their involvement in cultural programs and education has been pivotal. The women of HFS recognized the political significance of culture and education. They devoted much of their talents to shaping programs that fostered the formation of class and race identity and raised consciousness.

HFS is an exciting example of men and women from varying class and race backgrounds working together in common endeavors. Examining both the strengths and weaknesses of their efforts can provide important lessons concerning the possibility of coalition politics.

Workers' Education

HFS came into existence through the generous land and building donations of Dr. Lillian Johnson. Johnson came from a wealthy Memphis banking and merchant family. She was a graduate of Wellesley, had a doctorate in history from Cornell, had been president of Western State College in Oxford, Ohio, was a leading suffragette, and was a member of the Women's Christian Temperance Union.[1] Johnson had studied the cooperative movement in Italy. She returned to the South interested in spreading the idea and started a community center for the mountain people.

She bought land in Grundy County, Tennessee, one of the poorest counties in the nation, built a two-story house, and started a school. Johnson had two women from the University of Tennessee at Knoxville train two women from the mountain community, May Justus and Vera McCampbell, to teach. By 1930, she was interested in retirement and looked for others to carry on her community center work. Johnson chose HFS as her replacement. She gave them a year's probationary lease, which was extended indefinitely.

Highlander Folk School started operations in November 1932. The name of the new school was based on the popular name for an Appalachian (Highlander) and after the folk schools in Denmark that were used as a model for this adult education center. At first HFS opened along the lines of a settlement house in a rural setting, serving as a community center. The staff worked without pay.

The first activities of the school were social evenings. Social and cultural activities provided a rich resource of outreach services to the surrounding community and the women of HFS were particularly involved in this development. In the middle of a poverty-stricken community, HFS was a place where working people could check out books from a well-stocked library and send their children to take free music lessons.[2] Residents of the

146

community were invited to plays and weekly dancing. Zilphia Horton from Arkansas, who married Myles Horton, one of the founders of HFS, arrived at the school in 1935 and played a central role in nurturing community relations.

During its first three years, HFS established a union for WPA workers, a community cannery, a community nursery school, and a quilting cooperative set up by Myles Horton's mother. The nursery school was organized by Claudia Lewis. Later it was run by Johanna Willimetz, a graduate of Wellesley who used her personal contacts to raise money and acquire supplies for the school.[3] By the end of 1935, HFS had become the social center of the community.

Starting its first year, four evening classes were held weekly, with an average attendance of twenty men and women between the ages of eighteen and eighty.[4] The subjects were psychology, cultural geography, revolutionary literature, and current political and economic problems. Class discussion was based on the current situations in the South, as staff soon learned that education was most effective when it was based on people's lived experiences. For example, when asked to explain the theory of surplus value, one student, an unemployed nurse who had paid for her HFS tuition with a basket of onions, beans, and canned fruit, explained, "When I was working at the hosiery mill in Chattanooga, we were told that we would have to take a wage cut or the mill would go out of business. Of course, we took the cut. About ten weeks later, I read in the paper that the daughter of the mill owner was sailing for Europe to spend the winter. I suppose it was the surplus value we had produced that paid her way."[5]

HFS staff were increasingly drawn into the labor struggles that affected the people they served. The school opened during a time of intense class conflicts. The South in the 1930s was extremely violent. Blacks and labor leaders were targeted as offenders against Southern white purity. One of the first attempts to bomb HFS was due to the school's support of workers during the 1933-34 Wilder coal strike. HFS provided a refuge for the struggling Southern labor movement. The early initial goals of HFS were to: (1) serve as a community center for residents in the area based on ideas of unionism and cooperation; (2) develop a workshop program in order to train hundreds of Southern labor leaders; and (3) develop a field and extension program that would enable HFS staff to teach in other communities and in strike situations whenever requested.[6]

The school developed intensive-study residence terms lasting from four to six weeks. Classes were offered in labor history, economics, strike tactics, public speaking, current events, and parliamentary law. One- or two-week "workshops" were held, as were weekend conferences, focusing on a single subject, such as political action or race relations.[7]

On request from a local union, HFS also sent staff to troubled areas in its fieldwork and extension program. This branch of their workers' education program was dangerous and controversial. An example of the school's services occurred in the Wilder coal strike. The HFS staff held unionism classes on the picket lines, wrote letters to secure relief for the strikers, and organized cooperative garden projects to feed the strikers' families.

Zilphia Horton played an important role in HFS labor education programs, particularly through her extensive collection of songs about working-class struggle. She collected labor songs and directed school music and drama work. Pete Seeger and Horton modified "We Shall Overcome" (originally a black spiritual); it was sung by tobacco workers on strike in the 1940s. During the Richmond Hosiery Mill strike at Soddy-Daisy in 1934-35, Horton led singing at the mill gate. Moments after seven strikers were wounded by gunfire from inside the mill, she rallied the strikers to sing "We Shall Not Be Moved."[8]

Staff members were directly involved in community struggles. Hilda Hulbert, HFS librarian, was shot in the ankle during a march in the Chattanooga clothing workers' strike in which machine gun fire was opened.[9] In the Rockwood Hosiery Mill strike in 1936, staff again taught on the picket lines and organized food drives for the strikers.

In 1937, HFS was requested by the CIO to assist in its "Dixie Drive," an attempt to organize the entire South. HFS was asked to manage the educational aspects of the drive. In order to train workers for the CIO, classes were conducted in labor history, economics, public speaking, parliamentary procedure, journalism, and union solidarity. Weekly classes were held in Nashville and Chattanooga on steward training, parliamentary law, and political action; a six-week extension school was held at LaFollette, Tennessee, during the summer of 1937; a writers' workshop was started in 1939; and a special program to train union officials was launched in 1941 in New Orleans. Some staff members went on to become union organizers.

By 1941, HFS was the most noted workers' education center in the South. Thousands of workers were influenced by HFS through resident terms, institutes, workshops, or extension programs. Promising union leaders

Singing was an essential part of Highlander Folk School and Zilphia Horton (wife of Highlander founder Myles Horton) was not only the song leader, but also arranged songs. She and Pete Seeger modified "We Shall Overcome" (originally a black spiritual) to be sung by striking tobacco workers in the 1940s.
[Photo: *Highlander Folk School*]

149

attended residential workshops. In 1942, the school drew 425 students, primarily from labor organizations.[10]

Its success as a labor education institute soon brought attention and repercussions from Southern society. Southern elites charged HFS with being a Communist training camp. Conservative newspapers, mine and mill owners, the American Legion, and state and local WPA officials were some of the most vocal public critics. In addition to verbal attacks, sporadic physical attacks against school property and personnel occurred. By October 1939, a series of articles began to appear in the *Tennessean*, which "exposed" the school as a laboratory for spreading Communist doctrine, with a library full of Communist literature and leaders directly connected to Moscow.[11] In 1940, a band of vigilantes, the Grundy County Crusaders, organized a campaign to drive HFS out of the county. The Crusaders planned a march and talked of bombing the school. The leader was a Tennessee Consolidated Coal Company official.

Reaction from labor and progressive groups throughout the nation was immediate. The Communist accusation had reduced funds to the school, so a fund-raiser was organized in Washington, D.C. It was attended by many prominent citizens, including Eleanor Roosevelt, and respectability was returned to HFS.

Until the late 1940s, HFS served as a labor school for the CIO and some AFL unions. Workers learned to publish a local union newspaper, speak publicly, and print leaflets. By the end of the decade, HFS's role as a labor school had diminished greatly, largely due to its continued relationships with unions that were kicked out of the CIO for refusing to sign the anti-Communist oath required by the Taft-Hartley Act.[12] The red purge that swept the country and sanitized unions affected Highlander's working relations with the CIO. Some union leaders were displeased with what they perceived as left-wing influence on HFS. They pointed to HFS's continued support of the Mine, Mill and Smelter Workers' Union, one of the last militant unions in the South, as evidence of the school's leftist leanings. By 1949, the CIO was no longer holding its usual workers' sessions at Highlander, and it dropped HFS from its list of approved institutions for labor education.[13]

Among its early goals, HFS efforts to improve the economic conditions of the residents in their rural community were generally failures. They were least successful in organizing cooperative farming in an area of insufficient natural resources. Strikes were not successful either in an area that the companies could easily abandon for more profitable ventures.

The most successful aspects of their early programs were the social and cultural services organized primarily by the women. HFS's community library, community picnics, discussion groups, music lessons for children, square dancing and singing, and play productions made it the community center for many local residents. HFS was also successful in its program of workers' education: it was the only year-round resident labor school with a permanent base in the South. It was instrumental in the CIO drive to organize the South beginning in 1937. By 1947, more than 6,900 workers and labor leaders had been trained at HFS, and over 12,300 union members had been reached through field or extension classes.[14]

Efforts at Desegregation

From its beginning in 1932, this Southern school was an integrated institution. The very first announcement produced by HFS stated that it was open to blacks and whites. It wasn't until 1944 that blacks began to attend as students, but beginning with sociologist Charles Johnson from Fisk University during the first year, blacks were invited as speakers. Whenever HFS staff was called on to assist in organizing drives, they would set up only integrated unions, co-ops, and other groups. HFS believed that democracy in the unions should apply to both sexes and all races.[15] The facilities had no provisions for segregation.

During the early 1930s, a few black leaders, such as J. Herman Daves of Knoxville College and Charles Johnson, visited HFS. HFS produced a filmstrip, "Of a New Day Begun," for the Race Relations Department of Fisk.[16] In 1935, the interracial All Southern Conference for Human Rights was chased out of Chattanooga by vigilantes. They managed to elude the group of bigots and continued their proceedings at HFS that same day. HFS was a unique institution in the South where blacks and whites could meet.

The explicit policy of HFS was to operate on an integrated model not only among its students, but also among its staff and policymakers. The first black to join the HFS board was Dr. Lewis Jones, a sociologist at Fisk University, in 1942. Dr. P. A. Stephens, a physician and surgeon, and the most influential black man in Chattanooga, refused several invitations before finally joining the Board of Directors in 1947.[17] That same year, Grace

Hamilton, of the Urban League in Atlanta, joined the board, followed by Dr. B. R. Brazeal, dean of Morehouse College in Atlanta, who joined in 1949.

One of the most controversial issues during the period HFS worked primarily with unions was race. Unions were reluctant to sponsor integrated schools. Not until 1944 was an integrated session held at the school by the United Auto Workers.[18]

HFS conducted numerous workshops for labor groups. Segregation was practiced by many unions and racism was an entrenched problem among the white working class. In 1940, HFS informed all unions it served that the school would no longer hold worker education programs for unions that discriminated against blacks.[19] In 1944, after refusing for four years, the UAW finally accepted an invitation to attend an integrated workshop. Forty black and white members participated. Other unions followed.

In 1949, a meeting for UAW president Walter Reuther's reelection campaign invited only white leaders. When a black union leader arrived uninvited, the HFS staff interrupted the meeting with an ultimatum to integrate or leave before the next meal. The meeting proceeded on an integrated basis.[20] This policy of nondiscrimination was viewed by Southern society as Communist-inspired and immoral.

HFS was active in union organizing years before unions were legal, and in the 1950s they became involved on the same level in the Southern black civil rights movement, well before the movement gained national prominence and support. Before the 1954 Supreme Court *Brown* decision, HFS workshops were addressing problems of desegregated schools and full citizenship.

In 1952, the HFS Board of Directors decided that race relations should become the school's primary focus. At an April 1953 session of the executive council, the governing body agreed that race relations was the most pressing Southern problem. Members of the board emphasized the immediacy of the issue as a result of *Brown*: "The next great problem is not the problem of conquering poverty, but conquering meanness, prejudice, and tradition. Highlander could become the place in which this is studied, a place where one could learn the art of practice and methods of brotherhood. The new emphasis at Highlander should be on the desegregation of the public schools in the South."[21]

HFS prepared a curriculum for community leaders, black and white, who expected to be involved in implementing the decision. Two summer workshops were held in 1953 on "The Supreme Court Decisions and the Public Schools," and subsequent workshops on school desegregation were held in 1954, 1955, 1956, and 1957.[22] This was the first curriculum developed in the South to assist local leaders in desegregating their schools.

The 1953 workshop group developed a guide, "Working Toward Integrated Public Schools in Your Own Community," which was widely printed and distributed. In addition to the guide, a series of recommendations for local community leaders, entitled "Basic Policies for Presentation of Local School Boards," was composed.

Both direct and indirect effects can be traced to HFS activities. For example, weeks after attending a HFS workshop in 1955, Rosa Parks refused to give up her bus seat and her arrest sparked the Montgomery bus boycott. Another example is Esau Jenkins, who after returning from the 1954 workshop to his home on Johns Island, South Carolina, attempted to integrate school leadership on the island by running as the first black candidate for school trustee since Reconstruction.[23] He was defeated in the election, but he succeeded in raising black interest in registering to vote and in demanding improved schools.

With increased attendance of blacks at HFS, the FBI started watching the school, harassing neighbors, and asking questions about the black students. At this time attendance of black students was equated with the presence of communism. The charges of communism continued to plague the activities of the school, often leading to reduced contributions. The closure of the nursery school was attributed to such losses.[24]

Community leaders from across the South came to the 1953 summer sessions. Until the passage of the first civil rights bill in 1963, HFS remained one of the few places available for interracial meetings. Specifically during this time, HFS brought black leadership together, provided a model of an integrated society, and developed a successful citizenship program that was later transferred to the Southern Christian Leadership Conference. An outgrowth of its efforts with community leaders on school desegregation, HFS next worked on literacy and the voting rights project in South Carolina.

Citizenship Schools

In 1953, HFS received a three-year grant from the Schwartzhaupt Foundation, which gave them the freedom to experiment in adult education.[25] South Carolina legislators declared membership in the NAACP a criminal act sufficient to warrant dismissal of a public school teacher, shortly after the 1954 *Brown* decision. In 1956, eleven black teachers, members of the NAACP in Charleston, were fired.[26] One of them was Septima Clark. In 1954, Clark had been elected vice president of the local chapter of the NAACP.[27] Shortly thereafter, she received a letter from the South Carolina school system informing her that she could no longer teach in the system. After she was fired, Clark came to HFS as the director of education. (She subsequently turned down several teaching jobs in New York to stay in the South and continue her work at HFS.)[28] Clark traveled across the South, setting up schools in beauty parlors, country stores, and private homes. Her work at HFS and later with the SCLC required coordinating the citizenship schools throughout the South.

In 1954, Clark attended a workshop on school desegregation at HFS. That summer she returned for another workshop, this time bringing Esau Jenkins and Bernice Robinson. Robinson was Clark's cousin, a Charleston beautician who had completed high school at night.[29] She became the first citizenship school teacher volunteer and later an HFS staff member and member of its Board of Directors.[30]

Esau Jenkins was a poor farmer with seven children who drove a bus between Johns Island and Charleston.[31] He had instructed a handful of students on his route, using the bus as a classroom. His first pupil was Alice Wine, who went on to become a registered voter.

Jenkins viewed the most pressing problem in his community as illiteracy, because adults had to pass a literacy test to be eligible to vote. Jenkins persuaded HFS to set up a school in his community. The Johns Island principal was afraid to let HFS use the local school, and the preacher was afraid to let them use the church. So HFS lent Bernice Robinson $1,500 without interest to buy an old school building and paid for her transportation, materials, equipment, and supplies.[32]

Previous adult literacy programs had been held in children's chairs and adult students had to read material that was of little practical use to them—"See the red ball." The adult literacy program formulated by Septima Clark and Bernice Robinson provided an adult setting of peers with learning based on their life experiences. The students were respected as adults and were provided with dignified reading material. They learned to read and write using practical materials, filling out, for instance, replicas of Sears mail-order

Septima Clark, the director of Highlander's citizenship schools, first came to the school for a School Desegregation Workshop. She is shown here (far left) at a workshop in August of 1955, along with Dr. Parish, University of Louisville, Dr. Fred Patterson, President of Tuskegee Institute, and (at the end of the table) Rosa Parks, whose refusal to give up her seat would begin the Montgomery bus boycott two months later.

[Photo: *Highlander Folk School*]

155

forms. Students were taught how to fill out voter registration material, mail orders, driver's license exams, and how to sign checks.

The citizenship schools were thus begun as one night school for adults with fourteen students. Within a few months, enrollment had increased to thirty-seven students.[33] When the school started in 1954, there were two hundred registered black voters on Johns Island. Fifty new voters were registered in 1955, and by 1958 over four hundred had been added to voter registration rolls.[34]

Bernice Robinson taught her pupils what they wanted to learn. First, they wanted to learn how to write their names, how to read South Carolina election laws to qualify and register to vote, and how to fill in money orders at the post office.[35] HFS made mimeo sheets of voter information and workbooks were composed. For other tasks, such as money orders, replicas of the order forms were made, leaving blanks to be filled in. The kinesthetic method was used, too, so that by tracing the students got the feel of writing their own names. The school was run two nights a week for two hours. Bernice Robinson received compensation only for her expenses.

Textbooks were developed, containing pertinent information on Social Security laws, the rules of safe driving, laws on sanitation and public health, and consumer problems.[36] The earliest booklets in 1959-60 were eighteen mimeo papers stapled together. On the front cover was "My Reading Booklet," with space for the student's name, address, and occupation. They contained copies of actual forms, such as voter registration applications. The chapters included "Political Parties in South Carolina," "Taxes You Must Pay in South Carolina," "Social Security," "Your Health Services," "How to Address Officials," "How to Write My Name," and "Mail Order Blank." Words and letters were taught by linking letters to words they would need to use, for example, a—attorney, amendment; c—congressional, country, circuit, citizen, Constitution; g—government, governor, govern; n—national, nation, nominated; v—voucher, voter, voting; w—witness, world, White House.[37]

After three months of instruction, fourteen students took the voting test and eight of them passed and were registered. This night school for adults became the model for the citizenship schools that spread throughout the South in the 1960s and provided thousands with voter education.

The Schwartzhaupt Foundation continued to support the community leadership and citizenship school programs until 1959. By 1960, most funding came from the Marshall Field Foundation. Between 1954 and 1961, HFS had 37 programs with over 1,295 participants.[38]

Septima Clark recruited teachers and students for the schools. By February 1961, workshops to train citizenship school teachers were being held for twenty to twenty-five persons per month.[39] The only requirements for teachers were that they had to be from the same community as the students, be at least twenty-one, and hold a high school diploma. People of diverse ages and occupations were drawn to teaching at these schools—farmers, union members, housewives, dressmakers, and ministers.

Four sessions held in February, March, April, and June of 1961 trained eighty-eight teachers from forty communities. Women offered their time, homes, and businesses to the schools. The singing of spirituals was an important technique used by citizenship instructors to teach students to read and write. Dorothy Cotton of the SCLC was a great church singer who used her musical skills to train teachers.

Clark highlighted the political role of the citizenship schools: "You see, people having been living on plantations for so many years, had a feeling that they were afraid to let white people know that they wanted to be a part of the governing body. They were afraid to do that. So, we used to put up a regular form on our blackboard with the government at the head and all the people who would come under. Then on down to the masses, and show how you too can become a part of this great governing body, if you will register and vote. In that way, they learned that in a country like the United States they had the right to be a part."[40]

A number of great civil rights leaders, including Fannie Lou Hamer, attended the citizenship schools. Teachers returned home and became actively involved in their communities. The schools were so effective that Andrew Young thought the training program was the base upon which the whole civil rights movement was built.[41] Septima Clark explained that the citizenship school instructors prepared a community so that they "were already prepared to listen to a black man and to know that the government of that state can be handled by blacks as well as whites. They don't know it before. We used to think everything white was right. We found out differently, though."[42]

The citizenship school was one of the most effective organizing tools of the movement. Though education was often viewed as less militant than other strategies and tactics, these schools were a significant mobilizing factor. The Citizenship Education Program that Septima Clark and Bernice

Robinson developed for HFS became the basis for future voter registration work throughout the South. By 1959, due partially to the success of the citizenship schools, HFS was investigated by the Tennessee legislature.

As HFS increased its involvement in the civil rights movement and students were drawn from predominantly black communities, the school lost its strong ties with the local community. But it was antagonism from the state, not from local residents, that eventually closed the school.

Trial

Southern public officials were always eager for opportunities to link the civil rights movement with Communist subversion. They equated integration with communism. Some focused on HFS. The governor of Georgia, Marvin Griffin, wanted to discredit Martin Luther King, Jr., and the state legislature of Tennessee wanted to discredit HFS. At HFS's twenty-fifth anniversary celebrations, King was a keynote speaker. Photographer Ed Friend was sent by Governor Griffin's Georgia Commission on Education to the conference. (The commission was a tax-funded body the governor set up to attack desegregation.)[43] Abner Berry, a columnist for *The Daily Worker*, registered as a free-lance writer and did not reveal his association with the Communist Party at the conference. Perhaps not by coincidence, Friend kept setting up shots into which Berry would jump with leaders such as King. The photos were used to red-bait the school and King. Friend returned, with photographs of whites and blacks dancing and swimming together and a group photo including King and Berry. Billboards shortly appeared across the South with pictures of King and Berry at the conference and the slogan "King Attended a Communist Training Center."[44] Also, 250,000 four-page brochures and postcards featuring Ed Friend's photos were sent throughout the South.

Governor Griffin's plan backfired; a statement written by HFS and signed by Eleanor Roosevelt and other prominent Americans appeared in *The New York Times*. Still, the tactic played on the strong belief that those who favored integration must be Communist. In the next stage of harassment by government officials, the IRS revoked the school's tax-exempt status and the Tennessee legislature adopted a resolution to investigate HFS.

A resolution was introduced in the Tennessee Central Assembly in February 1959 to investigate the subversive activities of HFS. It passed both

This photograph of a civil rights group was taken in front of the Highlander Library. Septima Clark is at the far left.
[Photo: *State Historical Society of Wisconsin*]

houses without opposition and was signed by Governor Buford Ellington.[45] Five members of the legislature appointed by the governor held closed and open hearings. A two-day hearing was held on February 21 and 22. The circumstantial evidence and testimony consisted of accusations such as few people ever saw an American flag flying at the school. The committee presented a condemnatory report to the House and Senate, urging them to direct the district attorney general to bring a suit against HFS and revoke its state charter. The legislature quickly passed such a resolution, which Governor Ellington signed. The legislative committee could find no proof of Communist activity, but it directed the district attorney general, A. F. Sloan, to revoke the school's charter since integrated schools were in technical violation of state laws.

HFS survived its first decade probably only because the prolabor Roosevelt administration was in office. In particular, Eleanor Roosevelt had lent public support when the school was attacked. Since government officials were unsuccessful in their attempts to close the school through legislative procedures, they now pursued the judicial route, beginning with a raid. The crux of the problem was that HFS had always been integrated and was increasing its focus on race relations. The literacy training program was viewed as particularly threatening to Southern white society.

On July 31, at 8:30 P.M., Attorney General Sloan and twenty state troopers and local sheriff deputies in plainclothes raided HFS. Their official purpose was to search for whiskey, as the school was located in a dry county. Myles Horton was in Europe serving as co-chair of an international conference on adult education, but Septima Clark was conducting a weekend workshop on school desegregation. Clark was arrested and charged with illegal possession and sale of whiskey and resisting arrest, the latter charge due to her request to phone a lawyer. Three others were arrested with her on charges of public drunkenness and interfering with an officer. None of them was ever brought to trial.[46]

Initial reports contained many apparently prepackaged fabrications. First was the accusation that Horton had been drinking on the premises, which was obviously untrue since he had been in Europe at the time. Then there was the accusation that black men and white women had been having intercourse in the library, but it hadn't been built yet.

Three months later, in September, a three-day hearing in circuit court upheld Sloan's request for an injunction closing the school because it was a public nuisance. The school was padlocked and used for target practice by the Elks Club and American Legion. The raid in which HFS staff were arrested on trumped-up charges of drunkenness appeared to have accomplished what the legislative committee could not.

The trial opened on November 3 and lasted only four days. The state claimed that HFS's charter should be revoked for three reasons: it had sold beer and other items without a commercial license; Horton had received property and money from the school; and the school had permitted whites and blacks to attend together in violation of a 1901 state law. The state argued that the *Brown* decision applied only to public schools, not private ones such as HFS.

All members of the jury admitted that they opposed integration. A few enemies of HFS sat on the jury, including a cousin of the chief state witness and a cousin of the sheriff who conduced the raid. The state strategy was clear—it paraded witnesses who presented HFS as a place where illegal and immoral behavior between whites and blacks went on. The witnesses testified to having observed wild parties, drunkenness, and open sexual intercourse between whites and blacks at the school.[47] *The Chattanooga Times* observed that HFS witnesses were as impressive as the state's were unsavory.[48] The state had accused the school of engaging in commercial activities—the sale of soft drinks, beer, candy, gum, and razor blades. Since blacks at the school weren't allowed to go into local establishments to purchase items, HFS provided them on a rotating fund basis. Participants could take beer from a cooler and leave twenty-five cents.[49] Selling beer without a license was the technicality that closed the school.

The state also accused Myles Horton of operating the school for personal gain. The truth of the matter was that he had worked for over twenty years at no salary. When the staff did begin receiving salaries in the 1950s, they were below those at comparable institutions. For example, in 1959, Horton earned around $5,000.[50]

It took the jury less than one hour to arrive at a guilty verdict.[51] On February 17, 1960, Judge C. C. Chattin ruled HFS guilty on all three counts. It was ordered that the HFS charter be revoked, and the property liquidated and put in receivership. It was the first time in Tennessee history a corporate charter had been revoked.

Two futile appeals were made. During the appeals process vandalism and a fire destroyed the original house. The school appealed to the State Supreme Court, which in April 1961 upheld the lower court's ruling, except that it threw out the integration violation. There was no constitutional issue left.

The appeal to the U.S. Supreme Court was denied a hearing on October 9, 1961 and HFS reached the end of its course of appeals. At this point HFS extension schools were serving nearly 20,000 students and about 350 teachers were working in the area of literacy and citizenship.[52]

On November 7, HFS was placed in receivership and the school property was confiscated. It had taken the state more than two years to close HFS. On Saturday, December 16, 1961, HFS property was sold at auction. HFS had assets of about $175,000, including 200 acres of land, a dozen buildings, and a library containing several thousand volumes.[53] The state netted $10,000 from the sale of property and an additional $43,700 from the sale of land for a total of $53,700. (Several prosecuting lawyers bought some of the land).[54] The state had taken over the building, land, equipment, school, library, and the director's private home. HFS never received any remuneration.

The investigation, raid, hearing, trial, and conviction took place with amazing speed. The appeals process postponed closure for almost two years, but segregationists had successfully used the courts to deny the right to teach integrated classes. Horton took out a new charter for a new school the day after the first one was revoked. The Highlander Research and Education Center relocated to an urban setting in Knoxville, Tennessee. This, however, was not the end of its harassment by white vigilante groups and the state. During the 1960s, the school was investigated by Senator James Eastland's Internal Security Subcommittee, the FBI, and the IRS.[55] Several years later, when Ellington was again governor of Tennessee, the legislature tried to investigate the new Highlander for alleged subversive activities. This time Horton and the ACLU went to federal court and got an injunction blocking the investigation.[56]

Conclusion

It was the integrated citizenship schools that brought HFS under scrutiny of the authorities in the state of Tennessee in 1959. To ensure the survival of the schools, in late 1961 their operation was turned over to the SCLC. SCLC officials had been looking for an education program, and Clark and Robinson's Citizenship Education Program had nearly outgrown HFS capacities. Arrangements were made to give the program, funds, and staff to the SCLC.

The SCLC financed the citizenship schools with a grant from the Marshall Field Foundation.[57] Septima Clark and Andrew Young joined the Atlanta SCLC staff to administer the schools, with Clark also serving as a consultant to the new HFS establishment.[58] Bernice Robinson eventually left Highlander and joined the SCLC.[59] SCLC-sponsored citizenship schools became a mass-education effort supported by foundation grants and Septima Clark had direct responsibility for these efforts. In 1963, she reported that since the program had been transferred to the SCLC, twenty-six thousand blacks in twelve Southern states had registered to vote.[60] At this time volunteer teachers were running four hundred schools for sixty-five hundred adults.

Clark continued her work with the citizenship schools, which eventually prepared over 140,000 adults for registration tests and taught them to read and write.[61] She was one of the few women on the SCLC board until she retired in 1970.[62] The importance of the citizenship schools to the movement and the role that Septima Clark played cannot be adequately stressed. When Ralph Abernathy asked why Septima Clark was on the board of directors of the SCLC, Martin Luther King, Jr., replied, "Because she sets up the programs that allowed us to expand into eleven Southern states and she deserves to be on our board."[63]

Two months after the sit-ins began at Woolworth's in Greensboro, North Carolina, students from all over the South met at HFS. For three days, April 1-3, 1960, eighty-two students (forty-seven blacks and thirty-five whites) from twenty colleges attended a workshop entitled "The New Generation Fights for Equality."[64] Key leaders in the student movement attended, including James Bevel and John Lewis. Three weeks later, a new regional organization was founded, the Student Nonviolent Coordinating Committee (SNCC).

In 1975, Septima Clark was elected to a seat on the same board of education from which she had been fired nineteen years earlier. She was the third woman and the first black woman ever to sit on the Charleston County School Board. That same year, she also received the highest award of the National Education Association, the H. Council Trenholm Humanitarian Award.[65]

Although Septima Clark had forty-one years of teaching service, it was twenty years before black legislators were able to reinstate her pension.[66] In 1976, the state of South Carolina issued her a check for thirty-six hundred dollars, the sum she was entitled to annually. The governor apologized for her unfair firing. She was never reimbursed for the years between 1956 and 1976. In February 1979, Clark received the Living Legacy Award from President Jimmy Carter.[67]

The Citizenship Education Program Septima Clark developed for HFS became the basis for the black voter registration drive throughout the South. As she observed, "Many of the achievements we made in the civil rights movement started with that Highlander program. You can see the results everywhere—in black elected officials, in voters, and now in the efforts of Indians, and Appalachian whites to get their rights."[68] Most citizenship school projects came to an end in 1966 after passage of the Federal Voting Rights Act.

On August 28, 1961, Highlander reopened. The center carried on its work by holding workshops with students participating in the sit-in movement, actively participating in the training of civil rights workers for the Freedom Summer of 1964, and continuing training up to the time of the Poor People's March on Washington in 1967. The reorganized institution continued to train community people in leadership positions, specifically for the voter registration activities of SNCC.[69] SNCC was one of the last black civil rights groups to continue using Highlander. Nightriders attacked one of their last meetings at the center; one of those narrowly missed by rifle shots was Stokely Carmichael. Among the participants at the annual college workshops were Bernard Lafayette, Marion Berry, James Bevel, John Lewis, Diane Nash, and Julian Bond.[70] At the new Knoxville center Highlander ran workshops on voter registration for twenty SNCC volunteers at SNCC executive secretary James Forman's request.[71] Highlander was then asked by John Lewis and James Forman to set up education programs for SNCC. Debate about the role of whites in the movement increased over the years, with many leaders feeling that whites should work within their own communities.

In the late 1960s, Highlander established an extension facility in the Southwest to work with Chicanos and also set up extension programs in the uptown area of Chicago.[72] In 1971, the school moved from Knoxville to rural New Market, Tennessee. The school's projects focused on a health program, a resource and education center, and a cultural program. Once again, it worked in the field of labor education with programs for the Amalgamated Clothing and Textile Workers Union and the United Furniture Workers Union.[73]

In the 1970s, Highlander again shifted priorities. Beginning in 1967 with the Poor People's March on Washington, HFS staff was increasingly drawn to the dream of King and others of a multiracial poor people's coalition. Highlander moved into poverty work in Appalachia, although it maintained its involvement in civil rights. For example, in 1965, SNCC held five meetings and workshops at the center. In March 1964, a workshop entitled "Appalachia People and their Problems" was held.[74]

In the early 1980s, twelve staff members were working with Appalachian people on issues of poverty, unsafe coal mines and textile mills, and toxic waste. In 1983, Highlander was nominated for a Nobel Peace Prize by Atlanta Mayor Andrew Young and Representative Ronald Dellums of California.[75]

NOTES

1. Frank Adams, *Unearthing Seeds of Fire: The Idea of Highlander* (Winston-Salem, N.C.: John Blair, 1975), p. 26.
2. Glyn Thomas, "The Highlander Folk School: The Depression Years," *Tennessee Historical Quarterly* 23, 4 (1964): 362.
3. Sue Thrasher, "Fifty Years with Highlander," *Southern Changes* 4, 6 (1982): 5, 7.
4. Thomas, "Highlander Folk School," p. 360; Adams, *Unearthing Seeds of Fire*, p. 30.
5. Adams, *Unearthing Seeds of Fire*, p. 35.
6. Thomas, "Highlander Folk School," p. 359.
7. *Ibid.*, p. 364.
8. *Ibid.*, p. 365.
9. Adams, *Unearthing Seeds of Fire*, p. 75.
10. *Ibid.*, p. 84.
11. Thomas, "Highlander Folk School," p. 367.
12. Thrasher, "Fifty Years with Highlander," p. 6.
13. Frank Adams, "Highlander Folk School: Getting Information, Going Back and Teaching It," *Harvard Educational Review* 42, 4 (1972): 509.
14. Thomas, "Highlander Folk School," p. 370.
15. Myles Horton and Mary Frederickson, "The Spark That Ignites," *Southern Exposure* 4, 1/2 (1976): 155.
16. Adams, *Unearthing Seeds of Fire*, p. 162.
17. *Ibid.*, p. 91.
18. Thrasher, "Fifty Years with Highlander," p. 6.

19. Aimee Horton, "An Analysis of Selected Programs for the Training of Civil Rights and Community Leaders in the South," ERDS-ED011058, June 1966, p. 8.
20. Adams, *Unearthing Seeds of Fire*, p. 85.
21. Horton, "Analysis of Selected Programs," p. 10.
22. *Ibid.*, p. 11.
23. *Ibid.*, p. 29.
24. Thomas Bledsoe, *Or We'll All Hang Separately: The Highlander Idea* (Boston: Beacon Press, 1969), p. 77.
25. Adams, "Highlander Folk School," p. 511.
26. Steve Hoffius, "I Expect I'll Get a Plaque," *Southern Exposure* 7, 2 (1979): 74.
27. Septima Clark, *Echo in My Soul* (New York: E.P. Dutton and Co., 1962), p. 111.
28. Hoffius, "I Expect I'll Get a Plaque," p. 76.
29. Septima Clark, *Echo in My Soul* (New York: Dutton, 1962), p. 140.
30. Jerome Donald Franson, "Citizenship Education in the South Carolina Sea Islands, 1954-1966," *DAI* 38, 9 (1978): 43.
31. Clark, *Echo in My Soul*, p. 134.
32. Bledsoe, *Or We'll All Hang Separately*, p. 220.
33. Adams, *Unearthing Seeds of Fire*, p. 114.
34. Bledsoe, *Or We'll All Hang Separately*, p. 221.
35. Clark, *Echo in My Soul*, p. 147.
36. *Ibid.*, p. 193.
37. *Ibid.*, pp. 196, 201, 203.
38. Franson, "Citizenship Education," pp. 82, 89.
39. *Ibid.*, p. 93.
40. Aldon Morris, *The Origins of the Civil Rights Movement: Black Communities Organizing for Change* (New York: Free Press, 1984), p. 238.
41. *Ibid.*
42. *Ibid.*, p. 239.
43. Adams, *Unearthing Seeds of Fire*, p. 124.
44. *Ibid.*, p. 514.
45. John Edgerton, "The Trial of the Highlander Folk School," *Southern Exposure* 6, 1 (1978): 82.
46. *Ibid.*, p. 84.
47. *Ibid.*
48. Bledsoe, *Or We'll Hang Separately*, p. 126.
49. *Knoxville News-Sentinel*, April 24, 1983, p. 7.
50. Edgerton, "Trial of Highlander Folk School," p. 87.
51. Bledsoe, *Or We'll All Hang Separately*, p. 120.
52. Clark, *Echo in My Soul*, p. 211.
53. Edgerton, "Trial of Highlander Folk School," p. 86.
54. Adams, *Unearthing Seeds of Fire*, p. 139; Edgerton, "Trial of Highlander School," p. 88.
55. Franson, "Citizenship Education," p. 2.

56. Edgerton, "Trial of Highlander Folk School," p. 89.
57. Morris, *Origins of Civil Rights Movement*, p. 237.
58. Clark, *Echo in My Soul*, p. 232.
59. Morris, *Origins of Civil Rights Movement*, p. 237.
60. Adams, *Unearthing Seeds of Fire*, p. 119.
61. Alvin Hughes, "A New Agenda for the South: The Role and Influence of the Highlander Folk School, 1953-1961," *Phylon* 46, 3 (1985): 245.
62. Hoffius, "I Expect I'll Get a Plaque," p. 76.
63. *Ibid.*
64. Hughes, "New Agenda for the South," p. 247.
65. Hoffius, "I Expect I'll Get a Plaque," p. 76.
66. Edgerton, "Trial of Highlander Folk School," p. 86.
67. Hoffius, "I Expect I'll Get a Plaque," p. 76.
68. Edgerton, "Trial of Highlander Folk School," p. 86.
69. Adams, "Highlander Folk School," p. 515.
70. Adams, *Unearthing Seeds of Fire*, p. 144.
71. *Ibid.*, p. 167.
72. Thrasher, "Fifty Years with Highlander," p. 8.
73. *Ibid.*
74. Adams, *Unearthing Seeds of Fire*, p. 180.
75. *Knoxville News-Sentinel*, p. 7.

The South Carolina Sea Island Citizenship Schools, 1957-1961

SANDRA B. OLDENDORF

> I'm a Negro, born black in a white man's land. I am a teacher. I have spent my whole life teaching citizenship to children who really aren't citizens. They have fulfilled all the requirements for citizenship; many of their fathers and brothers have died for their country; but this is not enough to qualify them to vote, to receive a decent education . . . I can no longer aid in their education, because I joined in the movement to help them claim their citizenship.
>
> —Septima Poinsette Clark, 1958[1]

The Citizenship School Story

In 1957 under the guidance of Septima Clark, Myles Horton, Esau Jenkins, and Bernice Robinson, Highlander Folk School established the first Citizenship Schools on the Sea Islands of South Carolina. The initial purpose of these schools was to teach black adults to read and write in order to pass the South Carolina literacy tests for voter registration, but the more far-reaching goal was citizenship education for democratic empowerment. Received enthusiastically by students, teachers, and the black community, the schools eventually spread throughout the South during the 1960s, leading Aldon Morris in his book *The Origins of the Civil Rights Movement* to conclude: "[civil rights] activists of various persuasions stated repeatedly that the Citizenship Schools were one of the most effective organizing tools of the movement."[2]

The South Carolina Sea Islands are part of a chain of coastal islands that extend from North Carolina to Florida. Johns Island, the largest and the site of the first citizenship school, is located six miles south of Charleston.

169

Citizenship schools were also started on Wadmalaw and Edisto islands, both south of Johns Island.[3]

Until recently, the majority of the population on the Sea Islands were black descendants of former slaves who worked on huge rice and cotton plantations. Historically they have engaged in truck farming and raising cotton on small farms that they own. Most blacks have owned land since Reconstruction, but their isolation from the mainland for hundreds of years created a "people [who] have been substantially by-passed by the mainstream of American life and development."[4] This isolation has meant poor education, poor health care, and little economic opportunity. Today bridges have eliminated the physical isolation, but part of the culture of an earlier time remains. For example, Gullah, a language composed of Standard English, archaic English, and corruptions of English words and African words can still be heard: "Old-time talk we still de talkem here!"[5]

Today many young blacks leave the islands and subsistence farming to work in cities on the mainland. The old culture is gradually disappearing, due partly to white real estate corporations developing the land for recreation and retirement. Although these developments offer employment for some of the island blacks, they also threaten the sea island culture: "The islanders' ineffectiveness in resisting the often reckless advances of developers must be laid at the door of the very insularity that for so long protected their culture."[6]

One aspect of this insularity was disenfranchisement. Blacks on the Sea Islands and throughout the rest of the South were essentially disenfranchised beginning in the late nineteenth century. Devices such as the grandfather clause, the white primary, the poll tax, and the literacy test were created to keep Southern politics free of black influence. By the 1950s, there were few black registered voters on the Sea Islands because there were few literate adult blacks. On Johns Island about ten percent of the black residents were registered to vote and about the same number were literate.[7]

The 1950s were characterized by problems other than lack of voting power. Sea Islanders suffered from discrimination, lack of education, few jobs, and insufficient health care.[8] Black schools were old, crowded, and drafty in the winter. The teachers had few supplies and attendance was sporadic because of the growing season. Venereal disease was epidemic. There were many unwed young mothers, most of whom knew little about child care. Poor sanitation and health habits led to almost continuous cases of hookworm and skin rashes. Black farmers had to use middlemen to sell their produce. Since many of them were illiterate, they were often cheated. And, of course, everything was segregated—churches, stores, schools, parks, and beaches.

In addition to understanding the place, four personalities are also crucial to understanding the development of the Citizenship Schools: Myles Horton, a white, "radical hillbilly" and director and cofounder of Highlander Folk School; Septima Clark, a black schoolteacher from Charleston; Esau Jenkins, a black bus driver and farmer from Johns Island; and Bernice Robinson, a black beautician and seamstress from Charleston and Clark's cousin.

Myles Horton and Don West co-founded Highlander Folk School in Monteagle, Tennessee, in 1932. Under Horton's leadership, the school became known throughout the South as a school for labor organizers in the 1930s and 1940s and by the 1950s as a school for civil rights. At Highlander adults learned to work cooperatively on problems in their communities; they ate together, sang together, and planned actions together. Highlander measured the success of its programs by the activities of its students when they went back to their communities. Highlander was established as a school for social change, a school that would upset the status quo in the South. It was at a Highlander workshop in 1954 that the seed for the Citizenship Schools was planted.

Septima Clark, a well-educated black schoolteacher and local civil rights leader from Charleston, became Highlander's director of education in 1956. She had been fired from her teaching job in South Carolina for being a member of the NAACP. As a former teacher from Johns Island, she was aware of the education and political needs of the Sea Islands. She invited Esau Jenkins, a black leader from Johns Island, to a 1954 Highlander workshop. Out of this workshop the Citizenship Schools began.[9]

Jenkins, a self-educated bus driver and farmer, had been attempting to increase the number of black voters by teaching them the section of the South Carolina constitution that they needed to know for voter registration. But this was a tedious process, and he could not teach two thousand people. At the 1954 workshop he asked Horton to help him establish schools to teach people to read and write in order to vote. Horton agreed. Jenkins would provide the local leadership and the place; Highlander would provide the funds through the Field Foundation and the Schwartzhaupt Foundation.[10]

The next step was finding a teacher. Horton recommended that a black man or woman with knowledge of the islands but no formal training as a

171

teacher be found. Earlier efforts by the public schools to start adult education classes on Johns Island had failed because black adults were embarrassed to admit their illiteracy to college-educated whites, and learning to read using children's books was humiliating. Bernice Robinson, an NAACP recruiter in Charleston County, was exactly the teacher Horton had in mind.[11]

Teaching the Disenfranchised

Robinson began teaching in January 1957, in the back of a cooperative store organized by Jenkins and other island residents. On the evening of her first class she told her students, "I'm not really going to be your teacher. We're going to work together and teach each other."[12] She asked her students what they wanted to learn and then developed teaching materials to meet those needs. Her students wanted to fill out order blanks for catalogues, read the newspaper, read letters from their children, do simple arithmetic, read the Bible, and register to vote.

Robinson developed a number of successful techniques. She taught students to write their names using the kinesthetic method. She provided reading material relevant to their needs. She developed vocabulary and spelling lists from words they needed to know from the South Carolina constitution and their everyday lives. Words such as *tomato*, *cotton*, *register*, and *imprisonment* were more relevant to their lives than *cat*, *dog*, *Dick*, and *Jane*. She asked them to tell her stories about their work in the fields and their homes. Then she put their stories on paper and told the students, "This is your story. We're going to learn how to read your story."[13] Robinson knew this was a good way to teach, without ever having heard of the "language experience" approach. Math was made relevant by using grocery ads and problems with practical applications: "How much do you expect to receive when you sell your crops?" Later Robinson and Septima Clark combined resources and methods to create *My Citizenship Booklet*. One story problem not likely to be found in standard math texts reads as follows: "Ten students were arrested in the sit-in movement and were fined $75 apiece. How much fine was paid?"[14]

By 1959, Robinson was teaching students songs to help them learn. Music became a regular part of the classes through the work of Guy Carawan, Highlander's music director. Carawan and his wife Candie recorded songs that were part of the islanders' heritage, such as "Michael, Row Your Boat Ashore," which had originated in the islands in the 1850s.[15] Myles Horton once said that in addition to action, people "need something to cultivate the spirit and the soul." Music was that "something" both at Highlander and at the Citizenship Schools.[16]

By February 1958, Robinson had taught two classes on Johns Island and twenty-six students who had attended all five months registered to vote by reading a paragraph from the South Carolina constitution and writing their names. The classes had met twice a week for two hours a night. Adult students, some of whom could not write their names when they began, passed the literacy test after only eighty hours of classes.[17]

The new voters on Johns Island influenced others to get their certificate and before long, Johns Island was "infested with voters." Word spread to adjoining islands, Wadmalaw and Edisto, and to North Charleston. Expansion coincided with additional grant money from the Schwartzhaupt Foundation. Potential leaders on these islands were identified and they attended a workshop at Highlander.[18]

The class on Wadmalaw was taught by Ethel Grimball, Esau Jenkins's daughter, in a small building belonging to the Presbyterian Church. Grimball was a college-educated teacher but had close ties to the people of Johns and Wadmalaw islands. Although she developed her own methods, Grimball, as Robinson, was tuned in to the needs of the students who wanted to read and write, do arithmetic, and to learn to sew or crochet.[19]

A class was started on Edisto Island in 1958 by Alleen Brewer (now Wood). Brewer was a social worker from the Presbyterian Church, which, in turn, furnished a meeting place. Although thirty-eight men and women enrolled (the largest class so far), Brewer met the challenge by grouping students so that they could help one another. She also taught reading, writing, arithmetic, citizenship, sewing and leathercraft, and the history of the United States and the civil rights movement based on expressed student needs.[20] For many of the students, the social part of each class session was extremely important. One man said, "Now we don't have to wait until Sunday to fellowship together."[21]

From December 1958 to February 1959, four Citizenship Schools were held on Edisto Island, Johns Island, Wadmalaw Island, and in North Charleston. With 106 students enrolled in these new classes, ranging in age from 15 to 76, Bernice Robinson became a supervisor, overseeing the development of new classes. By the end of the school term, 66 students were registered to vote.[22]

The students' responses to these early classes were enthusiastic; most wanted classes to continue. Student comments were recorded on tape and some wrote letters to the teachers and to Highlander:

> I enjoyed the school very good and I hope it will be a little longer if its able to continue.
>
> —Ms. Wright, Johns Island[23]

> The adult school means so much to me I cannot express my appreciation and thoughts by words. The only think I am so sorry the school terms was so short. I would like to thank our teacher Mrs. Brewer for helping us out so wonderful in sewing, arithmetic.
>
> —Minnie R. Washington, Edisto Island[24]

In 1959-60, 182 adults enrolled in Citizenship School classes on Johns Island, Promise Land (northern section of Johns Island), Wadmalaw, Edisto, and North Charleston; 65 became registered voters. By March 1960, there were 200 black voters on Edisto, up from 40 in 1958. Johns Island black voters had increased by 300 percent from 1956 to 1960. In 1960-61, classes were held in North Charleston, Edisto, and Wadmalaw, and 105 out of 111 black students registered to vote. In 1950-61, Bernice Robinson and Septima Clark organized 8 classes in Huntsville, Alabama, and Savannah, Georgia. By the end of this session 245 students, ranging in age from 17 to 65, had attended the school and 232 had registered to vote.[25]

In 1961, the Citizenship Schools plus the teacher-training workshops Highlander had developed were transferred to the SCLC, with Highlander remaining as a consultant for the program. Andrew Young, who had joined the Highlander staff earlier that year, and Septima Clark went to the SCLC to organize the schools along with Dorothy Cotton of the SCLC. Bernice Robinson remained at Highlander and acted as a consultant to the SCLC.[26]

The spread of the schools under the SCLC was rapid. By September 1963, there were seven hundred teachers and fifty thousand new voters who could be traced to the Citizenship School movement.[27] These figures represent dramatic growth considering the humble beginning on Johns Island with fourteen students and one inexperienced teacher. But voter registration is only one part of the story. Highlander's goal was that the Citizenship School students would become leaders in their communities, "empowered citizens" who would address problems of health, education, jobs, and discrimination.

Alleen Brewer (at left, standing) began a citizenship school class on Edisto Island in 1958. She was a social worker from the Presbyterian Church, which furnished the meeting place.
[Photo: *Highlander Folk School*]

Empowerment and the Citizenship Schools

In 1981 Myles Horton used the word *empower* to explain Highlander's purpose: "We try to empower people to take more control over their lives."[28] Horton points out that at Highlander the subject matter may range from labor issues to civil rights to multinational corporations, but the purpose remains the same. Horton also stresses that people must be able to see beyond "what is" and try to envision a better world and universal principles that apply to all cultures. Empowerment, according to Horton, is a creative process that enables people to participate in shaping a better world.[29]

But how can teachers and students become convinced that they can shape their social, political, and economic reality? According to Sissela Bok, we must teach that one person can make a difference; an individual can "spark an action" that can lead to a larger movement. Major problems in society must be addressed by individuals who believe that they have the power to effect change by working together for common goals.[30]

The key question to address is: Did the Citizenship Schools empower people? To discuss this question, empowerment in a democratic society will be defined as: (1) believing that people can be effective in addressing injustice and oppression in their lives; (2) asking questions about the differences between democratic ideas and the realities of society; and (3) acting to change society based on universal principles of benefit to all.

There is evidence that the Citizenship Schools helped people identify their problems by looking critically at their own culture and history. Many of the students had acquired "learned helplessness." They believed that it was better for whites to make the big decisions about politics and that blacks had no need to vote. Robinson, however, validated their backgrounds and helped them recognize that their ideas and experiences had worth. By learning together students realized that they had a responsibility in the learning process. Robinson also tried to open their minds to a bigger world, to shed light on the lives of the people who were formerly illiterate. Students were encouraged to learn to use local resources so that they could get help to solve their own problems.

The second step in the empowerment process is critical awareness, developing skepticism. Esau Jenkins told his students that the Lord wanted them to be aware and involved. He said that they could honor the Lord by becoming active citizens and that a good Christian was not passive but took an active role and addressed problems.[31]

Students also became more aware of problems in their culture: lack of political power, apathy, fear of whites, and poor schools. Robinson posted the United Nations Declaration of Human Rights in her classroom. Although the rights in the document were supported by the United States for the rest of the world, they were not a reality for many poor people and minorities in the United States. Democracy, or lack of it, took on new meaning for a number of Citizenship School students. Solomon Brown, a student on Edisto, said, "We learned much of what democracy means that we did not know before. We were inspired to help others toward first-class citizenship."[32]

Bernice Robinson taught students to be more skeptical about what they read in the newspapers and the promises made to them by people who wanted their support. She taught how "to read between the lines" by bringing newspaper articles to the class and discussing what they really meant or what was left out. She was sensitive to the fact that many blacks on the islands had been taken advantage of, and she urged them to take a more critical view of their world by not being so accepting of what whites handed out. She urged them to speak up, telling them that being heard was an important part of becoming effective citizens.[33]

The ultimate evidence of empowerment, however, is action. Although Esau Jenkins was a leader in his own right, through the organization of the Citizenship Schools, he increased his influence. He encouraged students on six islands and two mainland communities to start "second step" political action groups that would address issues, discuss candidates, analyze political power, and develop strategies for practical problems in their communities, such as driving safety.[34] Jenkins' influence spread beyond the islands, through the Palmetto Voters Association and the Citizen's Committee of Charleston County. Through these organizations, Jenkins persuaded candidates to address black needs. He pointed out that the magistrates on Johns Island no longer assumed that blacks were guilty when they entered court because the magistrates needed black votes to get elected.[35] Jenkins was appointed to the school board, thirteen years after he ran unsuccessfully for that same board. He is credited with being instrumental in establishing racial harmony at St. Johns High School, the integrated high school on Johns Island today.[36]

With help from Citizenship School students and other island residents, Jenkins helped establish adult education, a kindergarten, a credit union, a nursing home, The Sea Islands Comprehensive Health Center, and a low-income housing project.[37] Today a number of places bear testimony to his work. The Esau Jenkins Bridge between Wadmalaw and Johns islands in particular symbolizes the strength of Jenkins's leadership as a link between people on the Sea Islands and his work to promote the welfare of all. Jenkins died in an automobile accident in 1972.

Septima Clark and Bernice Robinson increased their activity in the civil rights movement as a result of the Citizenship Schools. Clark became a board member of the SCLC, a close friend of Martin Luther King, Jr., and in her eighties a member of the Charleston school board that fired her in 1956. Clark, who died in December 1987, was remembered by South Carolina governor Caroll Campbell as "not only a leading civil rights activist but a legendary educator and humanitarian."[38] A recent book about her life and work documents her courage and leadership.[39]

After teaching with the first Citizenship Schools, Robinson became a consultant for teacher-training workshops all over the South and worked on voter registration in Mississippi. She is currently a member of Highlander's Board of Directors and in the early 1970s ran for the office of state representative from her district in Charleston and narrowly lost.

Ethel Grimball, the teacher on Wadmalaw Island, and Alleen Brewer Wood, the teacher on Edisto, also grew in their roles as activists. After serving as a Citizenship School teacher, Grimball became a director for Head Start, a director of programs for migrant families, and an executive assistant for the Charleston County Economic Opportunity Commission.[40] Wood led a group to Washington, D.C., to meet with the secretary of education to protest the practice of integrating Edisto Island schools by putting black children in trailers and white children in the buildings. She continues today to be involved with the Edisto Community Center, the Presbyterian Church, and adult education.[41]

The Board of Concerned Members of Wadmalaw Island was formed by the students of the first Citizenship School class. They helped raise the number of registered black voters from zero in the mid-1950s to over one thousand in 1973. A black woman was also elected as a precinct leader and another elected to the school board in 1973. Willie Smith, a Wadmalaw student, helped establish Second Step voter education classes and a community center on Wadmalaw.[42]

Anderson Mack, Sr., credits the Citizenship Schools with helping him become a leader. He came to the Wadmalaw Island school as a student in his early twenties with a second-grade education. Encouraged by the Citizenship School experience, he took more classes through adult education at Haut Gap High School over the next few years. Together with Citizenship School students Willie Smith and Mary Steed, he helped establish a community center on Wadmalaw, which sponsors a senior citizen's program. He worked to get home mail delivery, paved roads, a kindergarten, and more parent involvement in the local school. All three of his children received college educations. Today he is a community leader and works as a supervisor for the County Public Works Department.[43]

Many students experienced greater leadership roles and autonomy in their communities as a result of the schools. One student from Johns Island came to the Citizenship Schools as a cleaning woman for a white family, but she learned to read, write, and figure well enough to become bookkeeper for the Progressive Club and clerk in the cooperative store.[44] One student on Edisto became an officer in the Voter's Association of Edisto Island in 1961.[45] Another finished high school, went to a Baptist training center, and today is the minister of a large Baptist church. Other students finished high school, became church leaders, and helped to establish a community center.[46] Fifty percent of the class on Wadmalaw finished high school. A few went to college,[47] but for most students the primary function of the schools was to help them develop personally and/or socially. The skills they gained in reading, writing, speaking, sewing, and crocheting enabled them to become less dependent on others and to make greater contributions to their communities and families. The evidence from letters, tapes, and interviews is clear: many of the students, teachers, and others in the Sea Island communities were empowered because of the presence of the Citizenship Schools.[48]

Conclusion

First-class citizenship is a process of continued growth and change. Herman Blake, after he studied the effects of the schools in 1969, noted: "It is no longer possible to speak of the citizenship program in terms of the Sea Islands only . . . for the program has reached out to embrace the entire county of Charleston, and its impact is felt statewide since Charleston is the largest county in South Carolina."[49] The Citizenship Schools got people moving, first on the Sea Islands, then throughout the South. According to

Bernice Robinson: "The Citizenship School program became the basis for the civil rights movement because it was through these classes that people learned about their rights and *why* they should vote."[50] The schools, in Myles Horton's opinion, were probably Highlander's most successful program, a spark that helped ignite the civil rights movement throughout the South.[51]

The Citizenship Schools furnish an example of education that is based on the belief that people have the power within themselves to effect change in their own lives. Although the relationship of education and power is the theme of the work of educators such as Michael Apple and Henry Giroux,[52] there are few examples of schools or programs that have actually put this belief into action. Paulo Freire's literacy schools in Brazil[53] and Highlander Folk School's programs are two of the most notable. The Citizenship Schools, therefore, were unique—and successful. The Citizenship Schools, a key program in the civil rights movement, challenge us to ask today what Septima Clark asked in 1958: Do our schools confront the conflict inherent in our world and aspire to promote dignity, justice, and first-class citizenship for all?

NOTES

1. W.A. Parris, "Highlander Folk School: An Adult Education Program with a Purpose," *Negro History Bulletin*, 21 (1958), p. 185.
2. Aldon Morris, *The Origins of the Civil Rights Movement* (New York: The Free Press, 1984), p. 239.
3. M.A. Twining and K.E. Baird, "Introduction to Sea Island Folk Life," *Journal of Black Studies* 10 (1980); C. Tjerandsen, *Education for Citizenship: A Foundation's Experience* (Santa Cruz, Calif.: Schwartzhaupt Foundation, 1980).
4. H. Blake, The Visions of Myles Horton, 1961, State Historical Society of Wisconsin, Madison, box 82, folder 8.
5. C.L. Blockson, "Sea Change in the Sea Islands," *National Geographic* 172 (1987).
6. P. Jones-Jackson and C. Joyner, *When Roots Die: Endangered Traditions on the Sea Islands* (Athens: University of Georgia Press, 1987).
7. U.S. Department of Commerce, Bureau of the Census, *Characteristics of the Population, South Carolina* (Washington, D.C.: GPO, 1960), vol. 1, part 42.
8. G. Kearney, Highlander Folk School Uses Practical Sociology in Facing Racial Integration, 1955, State Historical Society of Wisconsin, box 83, folder 5; Z. Horton, notes on trip to Johns Island and Charleston, 1954, State Historical Society of Wisconsin, box 67, folder 3; G. Carawan and C. Carawan, *Ain't You Got a Right to the Tree of Life?* (New York: Simon and Schuster, 1966); S.P.

Clark, letter to Highlander: interview with farm agent, July 30, 1959, State Historical Society of Wisconsin, box 67, folder 3; Miscellaneous Notes on Dafuskie, January 30, 1959, box 67, folder 4.

9. Tjerandsen, *Education for Citizenship*; Septima Clark, interview by S.B. Oldendorf (January 13, 1986, Charleston, S.C.).

10. Tjerandsen, *Education for Citizenship*.

11.. M. Horton, personal interview, October 26, 1985.

12. B. Robinson, personal interview, January 15, 1986.

13. *Ibid*.

14. B. Robinson and S. Clark, *My Citizenship Booklet*, 1961-62, p. 13, Highlander Research and Education Center Archives, New Market, TN.

15. G. Carawan, report of Sea Islands work, 1960-61, State Historical Society of Wisconsin, box 8, folder 9; Edisto Island Citizenship School class, January 7, 1960, State Historical Society of Wisconsin, tape 515A, reel 101, side 1, part 1.

16. B. Moyers, interview with Myles Horton, June 5 and 11, 1961, Boston, WGBH, "Adventures of a Radical Hillbilly," *Bill Moyers's Journal*.

17. Tjerandsen, *Education for Citizenship*.

18. J.D. Franson, "Citizenship Education in the South Carolina Sea Islands," unpublished Ph.D. diss., Vanderbilt University, 1977; Tjerandsen, *Education for Citizenship*.

19. E.J. Grimball, personal interview, January 30, 1987.

20. Teachers discuss methods, 1961, State Historical Society of Wisconsin, tape 515A, reel 205, side 1, part 2; A. Brewer, final report, Edisto Adult School, 1959-60, State Historical Society of Wisconsin, box 67, folder 4; S. Clark, *Echo in My Soul* (New York: Dutton, 1962).

21. Clark, *Echo in My Soul*, p. 159.

22. Tjerandsen, *Education for Citizenship*, p. 167.

23. Final class, 1st Citizenship School, Johns Island, State Historical Society of Wisconsin, tape 807A, reel 7, part 1.

24. Letters from Citizenship School students to Highlander Folk School, 1959, State Historical Society of Wisconsin, box 67, folders 9, 5.

25. Tjerandsen, *Education for Citizenship*; J.M. Glen, "On the Cutting Edge: A History of the Highlander Folk School, 1932-1962," unpublished Ph.D. diss., Vanderbilt University, 1985; Highlander Folk School, *Fiscal Year Report*, 1960, State Historical Society of Wisconsin, box 1, folder 7; Charleston and Sea Island Activities, 1960-61, box 1, folder 7; news release, May 4, 1961, box 38, folder 2.

26. Glen, "On the Cutting Edge."

27. S.P. Clark, "Success of SCLC Citizenship School Seen in 50,000 New Registered Voters," *SCLC Newsletter* 1, 11 (1963).

28. Moyers, interview with Miles Horton.

29. M. Horton, "Decision-Making Processes," in N. Shimahara, ed., *Educational Reconstruction: Promise and Challenge* (Columbus, OH: Charles E. Merrill, 1973).

30. R.M. Kidder, "Sissela Bok," *Christian Science Monitor*, October 22, 1986, pp. 16-17.
31. Edisto Island Citizenship School class, tape 515A.
32. Letters from Citizenship School students.
33. Robinson discusses newspapers, 1965, State Historical Society of Wisconsin, tape 515A, reel 57, side 1, part 2.
34. Highlander Folk School, news release; Second Step Voter Education Schools, 1963-65, State Historical Society of Wisconsin, box 68, folder 1, 6; Franson, *Citizenship Education*.
35. Esau Jenkins and Bernice Robinson talk to Sea Island civic voter clubs, June 7, 1962, State Historical Society of Wisconsin, tape 515A, reel 223, sides 1, 2.
36. B. Saunders, personal interview, January 31, 1987.
37. N. Woodruff, *Esau Jenkins: A Retrospective View of the Man* (Charleston, SC: Avery Institute of Afro-American History, 1984).
38. "Septima Clark's Living Legacy," Charleston *News and Courier*, December 17, 1987, p. 10-A.
39. C.S. Brown, *Ready from Within: Septima Clark and the Civil Rights Movement* (Navarro, Calif.: Wild Tree Press, 1986).
40. Grimball, interview.
41. A.B. Wood, personal interview, March 12, 1988.
42. A. Mack, personal interview, January 31, 1987.
43. *Ibid*.
44. Clark, *Echo in My Soul*.
45. L. Bligen, letter to Septima Clark, July 6, 1961, State Historical Society of Wisconsin, box 67, folder 4.
46. Wood, interview.
47. Tjerandsen, *Education for Citizenship*; Mack, interview; Grimball, interview.
48. For a more detailed discussion of the history, methodology, and effect of the schools, see S. Oldendorf, "Highlander Folk School and the South Carolina Sea Island Citizenship Schools: Implications for the Social Studies," unpublished Ph.D. diss., University of Kentucky, 1987; Tjerandsen, *Education for Citizenship*; Glen, *On the Cutting Edge*; Franson, *Citizenship Education*; H. Neufeldt and L. McGee, *Black Adult Education in the United States* (Westport, Conn.: Greenwood, 1989).
49. Tjerandsen, *Education for Citizenship*, p. 171.
50. Robinson, interview.
51. Horton, interview.
52. M. Apple, "The Hidden Curriculum and the Nature of Conflict," in W. Pinar, ed., *Curriculum Theorizing: The Reconceptualists* (Berkeley: McCutchan, 1975); H.A. Giroux, *Theory and Resistance in Education, a Pedagogy for the Opposition* (South Hadley, Mass.: Bergin and Garvey, 1983).
53. P. Friere, *Pedagogy of the Oppressed* (New York: Herder and Herder, 1972).

The Role of Black Women in the Civil Rights Movement

ANNE STANDLEY

The role of black women in the civil rights movement has received scant attention from historians. Most studies of the movement have examined such organizations as the Southern Christian Leadership Conference, the Student Nonviolent Coordinating Committee, the Congress of Racial Equality, and the National Association for the Advancement of Colored People, and accordingly have focused on the black ministers who served as officers in those organizations, all of whom were men. Harvard Sitkoff's list of the leaders of the movement, for example, consisted exclusively of men—Martin Luther King, Jr., of SCLC, James Forman and John Lewis of SNCC, James Farmer of Core, Roy Wilkins of the NAACP, and Whitney Young of the National Urban League. The accounts of other historians, such as Aldon Morris, Clayborne Carson, and August Meier, also showed male preachers spearheading the various protests—boycotts of bus companies and white-owned businesses, voter registration drives, and marches—that constituted the movement. Likewise, the vast majority of students leading the sit-ins and freedom rides named by Sitkoff were men. He cited only two of the many women who held positions of leadership in the movement—Fannie Lou Hamer, who was elected delegate to the Democratic National Convention by the Mississippi Freedom Democratic Party in 1964, and Ella Baker, executive secretary of SCLC—and understated their influence.

The omission of women from many of the histories of the movement is also apparent in the widespread use of the metaphor of reaching manhood to describe the self-confidence that blacks gained from the movement. Sitkoff, for example, observed: "Sit-ins transformed the young blacks' image of themselves . . . Each student had his own way of expressing 'I became a man.' "[1] Although this image accurately described the emergence of a new, male-defined black identity, historians' use of this analogy reveals their failure to consider the impact of the movement on black women's consciousness, and to recognize the contributions of women in making this racial pride possible.

The argument that men were the principal leaders of the civil rights movement is not wholly inaccurate. According to women who achieved prominence within the movement, such as Septima Clark, who trained teachers of citizenship schools for SCLC, or Ella Baker, and historians Jacqueline Jones and Paula Giddings, the ministers' sexism and authoritarian views of leadership prevented women from assuming command of any of the movement organizations. Indeed, in light of the advantages men possessed in establishing themselves as leaders of the movement—the preachers' virtual monopoly on political power within the black community and the exclusion of women from the ministry in many black churches—it is remarkable that any women achieved positions of authority.

Yet, in fact, women exerted an enormous influence, both formally, as members of the upper echelon of SNCC, SCLC, and the Mississippi Freedom Democratic Party, and informally, as spontaneous leaders and dedicated participants. Many of the protests that historians describe as led by ministers were initiated by women. For example, Martin Luther King, Jr., is usually cited as the leader of the Montgomery Bus Boycott, since it was King who was appointed director of the organization that coordinated the boycott, the Montgomery Improvement Association. Yet the boycott was started by a woman, Jo Ann Robinson, and by the women's group that she headed, the Women's Political Council. Black women directed voter registration drives, taught in freedom schools, and provided food and housing for movement volunteers. As members of the MFDP, women won positions as delegates to the national Democratic convention in 1964 and as representatives to Congress. They demonstrated a heroism no less than that of men. They suffered the same physical abuse, loss of employment, destruction of property, and risk to their lives.

Black women also deserve credit for the refusal within the movement to accept halfway measures towards eradicating Jim Crow practices. Fannie Lou Hamer's rejection of the compromise offered the MFDP delegation at the Democratic National Convention in 1964 typified the courage of black women, who formed the majority of the preachers' congregations and whose pressure forced the ministers in SLCL, CORE, and the other movement associations to persist in the face of white opposition to their demands. Paula Giddings reported that when the minsters of Montgomery met after the first day of the bus boycott to discuss whether to continue the boycott, they agreed on the condition that their names not be publicized as the boycott leaders. E. D. Nixon, former head of the Montgomery NAACP, shamed them into giving their public endorsement by reminding them of the women to whom they were accountable: "How you gonna have a mass meeting, gonna boycott a city bus line without the white folks knowing about it? You guys have went around here and lived off these poor washerwomen all your lives and ain't never done nothing for 'em. Now you got a chance to do something for 'em, you talking about you don't want the White folks to know about it."[2]

As well, black women were responsible for the movement's success in generating popular support for the movement among rural blacks. Ella Baker convinced SCLC to jettison plans to take control of SNCC, allowing the student-run group to remain independent of the other movement organizations and to adopt, with Baker's encouragement, an egalitarian approach to decisionmaking. Because SNCC workers formulated the organization's objectives by soliciting the views of members of black communities in which the volunteers worked, they were able to build considerable grass-roots support for the movement.

Despite the exclusion of black women from top positions in movement organizations and the little recognition they received from either blacks or whites for their contributions, the published accounts of black women activists suggest that the movement gave women as well as men a sense of empowerment. Bernice Reagon, who was suspended from Albany State College for participating in civil rights demonstrations, and who sang with the Freedom Singers of Albany, credited the battle for equal rights with giving her the confidence necessary to combat all forms of oppression. For Reagon, the significance of the movement lay not in the abolition of specific forms of discrimination, nor in the impact of particular protests on the strategic position of the movement's official leaders, but rather in its liberating effect on her sense of self.

There was a sense of power, in a place where you didn't feel you had any power. There was a sense of confronting things that terrified you, like jail, police, walking in the street—you know, a whole lot of Black folks couldn't

185

even walk in the street in those places in the south. So you were saying in some basic way "I will never again stay inside these boundaries." There were things asked for like Black police and firepeople and sitting where you wanted on the bus . . . But in terms of what happened to me, and what happened to other people I know about, it was a change in my concept of myself and how I stood . . . When I read about the Albany movement, as people have written about it, I don't recognize it. They add up stuff that was not central to what happened. Discussion about Pritchett [the police chief]; discussion about specific achievements; discussion about whether it was a failure or success for King. For me, that was not central. I had grown up in a society where there were very clear lines. The older I got, the more I found what those lines were. The Civil Rights Movement gave me the power to challenge *any* line that limits me . . .[3]

I learned that I did have a life to give for what I believed. Lots of people don't know that; they feel they don't have anything. When you understand that you do have a life, you do have a body, and you can put that on the line, it gives you a sense of power. So I was empowered by the Civil rights Movement.[4]

Similarly, Anne Moody, who grew up in Centreville, Mississippi, and who began working for SNCC in the summer of 1963 after her junior year at Tougaloo College, reported that the movement became an inseparable part of her identity that prompted her to fight segregation wherever she went. She described her attempts to take a vacation from the movement:

Before the train pulled in, I found myself sitting in the white waiting room . . . Sitting there in the station, I got the same feeling I had in all the other sit-ins I had participated in. I remember getting up once, and going to the Negro section to ask the Negroes there if they knew the white section was desegregated. Then I knew that I would never really be leaving the Movement.[5]

The other women activists who wrote about their experiences in the battle for equal rights confirmed Moody's and Reagon's observation that the movement raised their self-esteem. Yet these women differed in their analyses of the cause of the racial oppression that they combatted. Two of the older women leaders—Daisy Bates, who was president of the NAACP State Conference of Branches, and who led the integration of Central High School in Little Rock, Arkansas, and Jo Ann Robinson—and a younger leader, Diane Nash, who organized sit-ins and freedom rides for SNCC, viewed racism as politically motivated. They believed that if blacks could obtain the vote, white politicians would be forced to act against racial discrimination at the polls, segregated schools, and the varied forms of extralegal violence carried out against blacks. Blacks could use their political influence to improve their economic status, which in turn would enhance their image among whites.

Because they saw themselves as having to convince whites to support the movement, and because they identified so completely with the struggle for civil rights, Bates, Robinson, and Nash refrained from making critical judgments about the movement or their roles within it. Nor did they, according to their memoirs, question or challenge the other black leaders who were mostly men, leading one to infer that as Morris, Sitkoff, and other historians maintained, they played subordinate roles to the ministers in the black community. Consequently their behavior showed contradictions—on the one hand a boldness in initiating protests and applying pressure on whites in power, while at the same time a submissiveness in their acceptance of the authority of the black male clergy.

Jo Ann Robinson was born in 1916 in Colloden, Georgia, twenty-five miles from Macon. She was the youngest of twelve children. Her family subsequently moved to Macon, where she graduated first in her class from an all black high school. Robinson received a bachelor's degree from Georgia State College in Fort Valley, taught for five years at a public school in Macon, and earned a master's degree in English literature from Atlanta University. In 1949, after teaching for a year at Mary Allen College in Crockett, Texas, she moved to Montgomery to join the faculty at Alabama State University. Robinson chaired the Women's Political Council in Montgomery, an organization of professional women that sought to raise the status of blacks by working with juvenile and adult delinquents and organizing voter registration. She also served on the Executive Board of the Montgomery Improvement Association and edited the MIA newsletter.

Robinson declared that in publishing her memoir, she hoped to improve whites' image of blacks by demonstrating blacks' courage, dedication, and self-discipline in their fight for their rights. Robinson saw the movement as blacks' attempt to overcome the circumstances that degraded them—to secure the same living conditions and opportunities as whites—so as to live decently and thereby prove their equality with whites.

I have chosen to record the facts of the Montgomery Bus Boycott for several reasons . . . so that the world will know that black people of America are not, as stereotypes have depicted them for generations, a "Happy-go-lucky," self-satisfied, complacent, lazy, good-for-nothing race that has nothing good or worthwhile to offer society. People the world over should know that any group, if given equal opportunity in education, employment, civil rights, and the like can be desirable citizens anywhere, with as much . . . to offer as any group. Debasement or degeneracy of character is not confined to one race, but is found in all races. From this record future generations may know that black Americans are just people like other people, wanting the same things, doing the same things, enduring the same things, and fighting against the same things that destroy the soul as well as the mind and body. When this is understood, a pure democratic government may survive in the American land of freedom, with justice and opportunity for all . . . [I am also writing this book] . . . to show that black Americans can endure hardship and suffering for the cause of justice. If given the same chance to get an education and to obtain jobs on all levels for which they are trained, oppressed people can control emotion and discipline feeling, even when tension is high and justice is derelict.[6]

Robinson's view of the movement as the first step towards blacks' redemption in the eyes of whites, and the role she assumed as the movement's publicist, left little room for a candid evaluation of the male leadership or for challenging its authority. She briefly criticized the ministers in Montgomery for their timidity, stating that only when they read a circular advertising the bus boycott and realized that "all the city's black congregations were quite intelligent on the matter and were planning to support the one-day boycott with or without the ministers' leadership" did they endorse it. She offset this reproach, however, with praise for the preachers' work, and attributed the boycott's success to the clergymen.

Had it not been for the ministers and the support they received from their wonderful congregations, the outcome of the boycott might have been different. The ministers gave themselves, their time . . . and their leadership . . . which set examples for the laymen to follow. They gave us confidence, faith in ourselves, faith in them and their leadership, that helped the congregations to support the movement every foot of the way.[7]

In her memoir, *The Long Shadow of Little Rock*, Daisy Bates displayed similar contradictions between her readiness to confront her white oppressors, which she demonstrated both as a child and as an adult, and her acceptance of what she regarded as a flawed black leadership. Bates grew up in southern Arkansas, in a town controlled by a sawmill company. She first experienced discrimination at the age of eight, when a white grocer refused to serve her until he had waited on all of the white customers. Bates also learned, at about the same age, that the couple who raised her were not her real parents, and that her mother had been raped and murdered by three white men. Her anger led her to reject all whites in her community, including a white friend, and to search for her mother's killers. When she discovered that one of them was a drunk who slept on a bench outside the commissary, she walked every day to stare at the man and to torment him with her resemblance to her mother. One day she shook him awake and glared at him.

> I don't know how long we stayed there, staring at each other. Finally he struggled to his feet. In a low, pleading voice, he said "In the name of God, leave me alone."[8]

Bates not only challenged whites while growing up; she also defied the authority of her parents and members of the black community. Although her mother believed in leniency, Bates frequently succeeded in provoking her wrath. "I was often clobbered, tanned, switched and made to stand in the corner. The floor in the corner was slightly worn from the shuffling of my feet."[9]

In another anecdote, Bates described making fun of a group of devout and prominent women. These "Church Sisters" had come to pray for Bates while she lay sick in bed. Bates secretly let loose her guinea pigs, which proceeded to run across the legs of one of the women.

> That night the Church Sisters, who met each week at the church or at the home of some sick person to pray, gathered at our home. They knelt around my bed and prayed for my soul. I noticed the fat knees of one praying lady. It gave me an idea I couldn't resist. I eased the box [of guinea pigs] to the floor and released [them]. One of them ran across the fat lady's leg. Unable to lift her weight upon the chair beside her, she lumbered around the room, screaming hysterically. The other ladies, managing to keep a few paces ahead of her, joined in the wild demonstration.

Bates admitted her own amusement at the woman's distress. "Helpless with laughter, I could not reply . . . I got my behind properly spanked."[10]

Bates's narrative showed that as an adult, she continued to challenge those in power. She met with the governor of Arkansas and the U.S. Attorney to urge them, unsuccessfully, to respond to the whites' violence. In contrast, however, she appears to have deferred to the male leadership in the black community. She made only a passing reference to her irritation at the black ministers' silence in the face of the whites' terrorism carried out against the black students, suggesting that she suppressed her frustration.[11] In her conclusion, she assailed Congress and the Eisenhower administration for their lackluster support of desegregation, but like Robinson, refrained from placing any blame for the movement's slow progress on its leadership.

One can see similar inconsistencies in the actions of Diane Nash, a SNCC volunteer. Nash grew up in Chicago and came to Nashville to attend Fisk University. Nash's shock at the segregation of restaurants, water fountains, and other public facilities in the south prompted her to join SNCC.[12] In 1965, Nash wrote an article for *Ebony* that implied that she accepted the prevailing view that the civil rights movement, and specifically SCLC, should be led primarily by men. Nash's article, "The Men Behind Martin Luther King" profiled the male staff members of SCLC. She depicted the women on the staff, who numbered three out of a total of twelve, as important but peripheral figures. She reported, "Although most of SCLC's programs constitute 'men's work,' a few of the 'men' behind King are women. In addition to SCLC wives who do a lot of reading for their husbands and keep in touch with the public reaction to SCLC projects, a few women provide major leadership in the various education programs."[13] In describing the different points of view expressed in staff meetings, Nash mentioned only those of the male staff members, suggesting that the men's opinions carried the most weight, and that the women were not included in the inner core of the staff. At no point did Nash question the women's secondary status within SCLC.

Nash's prominence in protest efforts, however, seemed to contradict the unspoken assumption of her article that men should lead the movement. Nash chaired the central committee of the sit-in movement in Nashville. She also assembled a second group of freedom riders to continue the journey when harassment forced the first group to disperse in Birmingham before they reached their destination of New Orleans. Juan Williams' quotation from Nash shows her determination.

> If the freedom riders had been stopped as a result of violence, I strongly felt that the future of the movement was going to be cut short. The impression would have been that whenever a movement starts, all [you have to do] is attack it with massive violence and the blacks [will] stop.[14]

While Bates, Robinson, and Nash attributed racism to blacks' lack of representation in the political process, the majority of black women leaders who left accounts of their experiences regarded racial oppression as symptomatic of a structurally flawed society. Disheartened by the movement's fragmentation in the late sixties and by what they regarded as its limited success, they concluded that racial oppression formed part of a larger system of inequities that characterized American society and that could not be eradicated without addressing the other injustices to which it was connected. One activist who became disillusioned was Jean Smith, a student at Howard University who registered voters for SNCC in 1963 and who organized the MFDP meetings that elected an integrated delegation to the Democratic National Convention in 1964. Smith maintained that the right to vote, while unifying the black community and giving blacks the confidence to assert themselves and challenge racist laws or customs, had proved ineffectual in diminishing white hegemony and improving the living conditions of blacks.

> The best way to understand is to look at what the Negro people who cast their lot with the Movement believed. They believed, I think, that their participation in the drive for voting rights would ultimately result in the relief of their poverty and hopelessness. They thought that with the right to vote they could end the exploitation of their labor by the plantation owners. They thought they could get better schools for their children; they could get sewers dug and sidewalks paved. They thought they could get adequate public-health facilities for their communities. And of course they got none of these . . . They believed there was a link between representation in government and making that government work for you. What they—and I—discovered was that for some people, this link does not exist. For most black people, voting has not much more benefit than the exercise of walking to the polls. Why is this the case? Because the link between voting and partaking of the benefits of society exists at the pleasure of society. The society must be willing to respond to the legitimate needs of the people; only then can the channels for the expression of these needs, such channels as voting, be meaningfully employed.[15]

Anne Moody expressed similar bitterness.

> I came to see through my writings that no matter how hard we in the Movement worked, nothing seemed to change; that we made a few visible little gains, yet at the root, things always remained the same; and that the Movement was not in control of its destiny—nor did we have any means of gaining control of it. We were like an angry dog on a leash who had turned on its master. It could bark and howl and snap . . . but the master was always in control. I realized that the universal fight for human rights, dignity, justice, equality, and freedom . . . [is] the fight of every ethnic and racial minority . . . every one of the millions who daily suffer one or another of the indignities of the powerless and voiceless masses. And this trend of thinking is what finally brought about an end to my involvement in the Civil Rights Movement . . . [16]

Joyce Ladner, a SNCC volunteer, decided at an early age that the deprivation and degradation she suffered formed part of a larger system of oppression. Ladner grew up in Hattiesburg, Mississippi. Her father worked as a diesel engine mechanic. Her mother stayed at home, because her father "insisted that she not work for whites and be subjected to the abuse his mother had experienced."[17]

Ladner helped organize the first NAACP Youth Council in Hattiesburg in 1959, when she was a junior in high school. In the summer of 1963, she registered voters for SNCC in Albany, Georgia.

> Growing up in the segregated South meant that I had severe restrictions placed on almost every facet of my life. I did not have the freedom to express myself and to explore many of those things in which I was interested. I felt like a caged animal . . . It is very difficult to describe how oppressed I felt during those years: to be stifled, to be poor and subjugated, to be humiliated by ignorant whites whom we regarded as the scum of the earth and to realize that people in powerful positions didn't care what happened to you. I was acutely sensitive to those less fortunate than ourselves. I always defended the underdog. When I was in the sixth grade I had a classmate named Hattie Mae Naylor. Hattie Mae was one of about 18 children from a very poor family . . . I remember going off into the corner crying when the other children made fun of Hattie Mae because of her tattered clothing and her worn, dusty shoes . . . In some sort of way I understood that Hattie Mae and her parents were victims of the same system that created both the abject poverty in which they lived and [our] vicious [white] bus driver [who Ladner recalled "frequently swore at the black passengers."][18]

This disenchantment with the civil rights movement led some activists to temporarily embrace separatism. Smith, for example, in 1968 argued for a self-sufficient black community as the solution to blacks' political impotence.

> . . . the call for black power . . . I consider the other side of the coin of black consciousness. One cannot exist without the other . . . We have to build a broad-based black consciousness so that we can begin to depend on one another for economic, political, and social support. We have to build our own businesses to put money into the development of the Negro community . . . We have to make our politicians responsible to us so that either they improve our communities or they go . . . Our immediate objective must be the strengthening of the black community instead of the apparently unattainable goal of diffusion of all black people into the mainstream of American life. We have to become strong so that we can depend on one another to meet our needs and so that we'll be able to deal with white people as we choose to, not as we are obliged to.[19]

Two years earlier, in 1966, Ladner had also abandoned integration as a goal, convinced by the unrelenting brutality of whites that black power offered the most effective means of improving the status of blacks.

> When Vernon Dahmier [Ladner's mentor] was killed, my faith in integration was shaken. I found myself trying to justify my belief that "Black and white together" was still the solution to the race problem . . . What Blacks needed to do, I thought, was to unite as a group and develop their own institutions and communities. What they needed was Black power! Only then, I felt, would whites give in to our demands. I gave up on trying to appeal to the conscience of whites. Racial power politics seemed to be a more viable way to effect fundamental changes. Institutional racism became the target instead of individual racial prejudice . . . I suppose the most painful time of all came when I rejected long-time white friends solely because they were white . . . I felt that my ideological commitment to integration had never brought the freedom and dignity [I had been told to] fight for when I was a young child.[20]

In addition to embracing separatism, Ladner turned to marxism for a diagnosis and a solution to racial oppression, along with Frances Beal, a former SNCC activist. Ladner asserted that in aspiring to middle-class goals of upward mobility and wealth, blacks condoned a structure of economic inequality. For Ladner, it was not blacks' lowly position in the hierarchy, but their acceptance of a capitalist economy which required a hierarchy, in which the fortunes of a few came from the exploitation of many, that oppressed them. [21] Similarly, Frances Beal claimed that the feminists who sought only to improve their own position, demanding, for example, equal pay for equal work, failed to attack capitalism as the root of inequality and thus perpetuated an unjust system.[22]

Perhaps because they published their views twenty years after the movement, when American society had become significantly more integrated, Bernice Reagon and Septima Clark did not share the disillusionment of Moody, Smith, Ladner, or Beal, although they shared those activists' opinion that racism was inseparable from other forms of oppression. They expressed hope in the possibility of progress, and emphasized the power of ideas to bring about social change. They argued that the movement succeeded because it increased consciousness of a variety of social problems, which in turn would prompt the necessary broad based reform.[23]

For many Civil Rights Movement organizers and supporters, leaving a specific project or struggle didn't mean the end of political activity. These people came away from their Civil Rights Movement experience with a greater facility for seeing a wide range of questions. For many, there was no end nor rest. The Civil Rights Movement was only a beginning. Its dispersion continues to be manifested in ever widening circles of evaluation of civil and human rights afforded by this society . . . The Movement continues . . . People are being threatened in almost every way. If it runs its course, no institutions or values will be left unexamined or untested.[24]

Robinson, Bates and Nash sought to present a united front to white authorities. Consequently, they suppressed their differences with the male leadership. In contrast, the other activists aired their disagreements with the men managing the movement organizations, although most did so only in hindsight.

Only two of the women, Ella Baker and Septima Clark, confronted the male leaders of the movement while working with them to challenge their policies. Baker, like Robinson and Bates, belonged to the older generation of women civil rights leaders. She was 57 when SCLC appointed her as executive secretary in 1960. Baker was born in 1903 in Norfolk, Virginia. Her family moved to Littleton, North Carolina when Baker was seven. Baker's father waited on tables for the Norfolk-Washington ferry; her mother tended to the sick in the community.[25] After graduating from Shaw University in Raleigh, Baker began a long career of activism. She worked for a WPA consumer education project in New York City during the depression. The NAACP hired her in 1938 to recruit members and raise money in the south, and five years later named her national director of branches. Baker helped found SNCC in 1960. In 1964 she gave the keynote address at the MFDP convention in Jackson and established the MFDP Washington office.

Baker's readiness to confront the male officers in SCLC may have come in part from her commitment to participatory decisionmaking. She disapproved of King's autocratic style of leadership, insisting that a true leader gave others the opportunity to acquire skills in managing and speaking for an organization or effort. Baker said of SNCC, "I had no ambition to be in the leadership. I was only interested in seeing that a leadership had a chance to develop . . . My theory is strong people don't need strong leaders."[26]

Baker's account of the debate within SCLC on a strategy to bring SNCC under SCLC's control showed her opposing SCLC's hierarchical style of management—her efforts to democratize the leadership of the movement by lobbying for an autonomous SNCC, and her refusal to defer to King.

> The Southern Christian Leadership Conference felt that they could influence how things went. They were interested in having the students become an arm of SCLC. They were most confident that this would be their baby, because I was their functionary and I had called the meeting. At a discussion called by the Reverend Dr. King, the SCLC leadership made decisions [about] who would speak to whom to influence the students to become part of SCLC. Well, I disagreed. There was no student at Dr. King's meeting. I was the nearest thing to a student, being the advocate, you see. I also knew from the beginning that having a woman be an executive of SCLC was not something that would go over with the male-dominated leadership. And then, of course, my personality wasn't right, in the sense I was not afraid to disagree with the higher authorities. I wasn't one to say, yes, because it came from the Reverend King. So when it was proposed that the leadership could influence the direction by speaking to, let's say, the man from Virginia, he could speak to the leadership of the Virginia student group, and the assumption was that having spoken to so-and-so, so-and-so would do what they wanted done, I was outraged. I walked out.[27]

Septima Clark, the other activist who challenged the male staff of SCLC, was also a member of the older generation of women civil rights leaders. Clark was born in 1898 in Charleston, North Carolina. She taught in the Charleston public schools until she lost her job in 1956 when the legislature passed a law prohibiting state employees from belonging to the NAACP. The Highlander Folk School, which brought blacks and whites together to discuss social issues at a farm in Tennessee, hired Clark to lead workshops training members of rural communities to teach their neighbors to read and to register to vote. In 1961, when the Tennessee legislature moved to close Highlander, SCLC and the United Church of Christ provided the funds to enable Clark to continue organizing citizenship schools, which in 1964 numbered 195.

Clark talked freely about what she saw as the sexism of the SCLC staff.

> I was on the executive staff of the SCLC, but the men on it didn't listen to me too well. They like to send me into many places, because I could always make a path in to get people to listen to what I have to say. But those men didn't have any faith in women, none whatsoever. They just thought that women were sex symbols and had no contributions to make. That's why Reverend Abernathy would say continuously, "Why is Mrs. Clark on this staff?" Dr. King would say, "Well she has expanded our program. She has

taken it into eleven deep south states." Rev. Abernathy'd [sic] come right back the next time and ask again."

I had a great feeling that Dr. King didn't think much of women either . . . when I was in Europe with him, when he received the Nobel Peace Prize in 1964, the American Field Service Committee people wanted me to speak. In a sort of casual way he would say "Anything I can't answer, ask Mrs. Clark." But he didn't mean it, because I never did get the chance to do any speaking to the AFS committee in London or to any of the other groups.[28]

Like Baker, Clark communicated to King her differences with his style of leadership, urging him in a letter to run SCLC more democratically by delegating authority. She also attacked other ministers for their dependence on King, in which they assumed that only King could lead the movement, and for their belief that to suggest expanding the leadership of the movement cast doubt on King's own capabilities.

When I heard the men asking Dr. King to lead the marches in various places, I'd say to them, "You're there. You going to ask the leader to come everywhere? Can't you do the leading in these places?"

I sent a letter to Dr. King asking him not to lead all the marches himself, but instead to develop leaders who could lead their own marches. Dr. King read that letter before the staff . . . they just laughed. I had talked to the secretaries before about it, and when the letter was read they wouldn't say a word, not one of them. I had a feeling that they thought Dr. King would have to do the leading. If you think that another man should lead, then you are looking down on Dr. King. That was the way it was.[29]

Clark insisted that her capacity to criticize King and the other SCLC staff members came from the influence of the National Organization for Women (NOW) which she joined in 1968. She observed that while she worked for SCLC in the early and mid-sixties, she was blind to its leadership's sexism.

. . . in those days I didn't criticize Dr. King, other than asking him not to lead all the marches. I adored him. I supported him in every way I could because I greatly respected his courage, his service to others, and his non-violence. The way I think about him now comes from my own experience in the women's movement.[30]

Yet Clark also stated that she joined NOW because she resented the subordination of women to men in the south, which suggests that she was not as unaware of sexism in the movement as she later claimed to be. "I found all over the South . . . whatever the man said would be right, and the wives would have to accept it."[31] Clark first attended a NOW conference in

1968 at the request of Virginia Durr, a white southern liberal. She spoke to its members about

> . . . the women of the South who failed to speak up when they knew what they wanted, about white women who would see their husbands doing wrong but dared not tell them, about black women who wouldn't speak at all because the husband had the right to say whatever.[32]

Kathleen Cleaver also discussed her perceptions of sexism in the movement. She reported in 1971 that she joined the women's movement because she observed while working for SNCC, beginning in 1966, that women did most of the work but that few women held positions of authority. Those women who obtained administrative posts, Cleaver noticed, carried the double burden of their jobs and their duties as wives and mothers, and also had to contend with the male staff members' refusal to accept them as their equals. Cleaver attributed the death of Ruby Doris Smith, Executive Secretary of SNCC, to sheer exhaustion from the many demands and from having to fight racism and sexism simultaneously. "What killed Ruby Doris was the constant outpouring of work, work, work, with being married, having a child, the constant conflicts, the constant struggles that she was subjected to because she was a woman."[33]

A letter written in 1977 by Cynthia Washington, who directed a freedom project for SNCC in Mississippi in 1963, suggested that the position of black women in the movement was more ambiguous than the deference of Robinson, Bates, or Nash to the male leadership, or the anger of Baker, Clark, or Cleaver at women's subordinate status indicated. Washington contended that she did not recognize sexism in the movement because, although women were rarely appointed to senior positions, they were frequently given jobs with responsibility, such as the job Washington herself held of project director. Although she recalled observing that white women were typically assigned the most menial tasks, Washington reasoned at the time that it was because they lacked the competence required for more challenging jobs.

> During the fall of 1964, I had a conversation with Casey Hayden about the role of women in SNCC. She complained that all the women got to do was type, that their role was limited to office work no matter where they were. What she said didn't make any particular sense to me because, at the time, I had my own project in Bolivar County, Mississippi. A number of other black women also directed their own projects. What Casey and other white women

seemed to want was an opportunity to prove they could do something other than office work. I assumed that if they could do something else, they'd probably be doing that.[34]

Washington said that while some black men viewed the women as inferior—she quoted Stokely Carmichael's jeer that the only position for women in SNCC was prone—she believed that the authority she enjoyed as project director demonstrated that few shared his view. "Our relative autonomy as projects directors seemed to deny or override his statement. We were proof that what he said wasn't true—or so we thought."[35]

In addition, according to Washington, women who participated in the movement may not have been aware of sexism because they assumed that black men did not question their abilities, for historically, the poverty of blacks had forced the women to work as well as the men in order to support their families, while also caring for their children. These multiple responsibilities, said Washington, were not seen as evidence of an inferior status. On the contrary, women were honored for their labor.

> I did not see what I was doing as exceptional. The community women I worked with on projects were respected and admired for their strength and endurance. They worked hard in the cotton fields or white folks' houses, raised and supported their children, yet still found the time and energy to be involved in struggle for their people. They were typical rather than unusual.[36]

Yet Washington also implied that she later concluded that sexism did exist, despite her lack of awareness of it at the time. "In fact, I'm certain that our single-minded focus on the issues of racial discrimination and the black struggle for equality blinded us to other issues."[37]

The ambiguity in the status of women in the movement brought out by Washington's letter paralleled the activists' ambivalence towards the male leaders, in which even those women who criticized the male activists for their condescending attitudes towards women did not hold the men responsible for their sexism. Some, such as Clark, saw the men's treatment of women as reflecting their hostility towards a racially oppressive society that put down black men even more than black women. Clark thought that black men's sexism was a reaction against their overprotective mothers, who tried to shield their sons from the violence of whites to which black men were particularly susceptible. Clark's insights shed light on one source of the stereotype, expressed by Andrew Young, that " . . . a system of oppression tends to produce strong women and weak men."[38]

I see this as one of the weaknesses of the civil rights movement, the way the men looked at women. I think I know how the men got that way. I think about my mother, who had a feeling that black boys in the south could be conspired upon. She wanted to keep her boys right under her nose; she never wanted them away from her. She would always say, "A girl will bring you one trouble, but a boy can bring so many others. He can be arrested for stealing. He can be arrested for looking at a white." She'd name all these things that I think caused black mothers to feel as if black boys have to be very docile. Because they resented that, the black boys grew up feeling that women should not have a say in anything.[39]

Other movement workers, such as Beal and Cleaver, blamed capitalism as well as racism for black men's discrimination against women. Sexism, like racism, they argued, was a device by which whites reinforced the exploitation of the masses. Just as racism perpetuated lower-class whites' poverty by preventing them from joining forces with blacks to overthrow their oppressors, so too, by internalizing the sexism of whites, black men contributed to the marginal economic status of blacks. Their complicity in the segregation of jobs by sex, which limited black women's access to all but the lowest paid jobs, and which treated women as a source of surplus labor and as strikebreakers, impoverished blacks as a group.

Cleaver agreed with Clark that black men developed sexist attitudes because they were oppressed, although Cleaver saw their oppression as economic. The black men, according to Cleaver, resented the "strong" role black women had had to assume as breadwinners as well as mothers. They vented their frustration by asserting their power over women—treating them as inferior, abusing them—or by abandoning their families to escape their guilt at their inability to find employment.

The oppression of the woman by the black man is something that is perpetuated and encouraged by the system of colonialism run by the white man. We must always remember that the basic enemy of the black woman is not her own man because her own man, the black man, is not the creator or perpetrator of the system that is dedicated to depressing women. However, as black men move to assert themselves . . . to regain a sense of dignity . . . of manhood . . . of humanity, and to become strong enough and powerful enough and manly enough to fight against the oppressor, they many times take out their resentment of their position against their own black women. And many times flee from the guilt that they know is theirs in their refusal and inability to protect the black woman . . . the violence that black men direct toward their own women, the brutality, the hostility, the bitterness, the antagonism, and all this resentment, is something that black women are subjected to as a result of the colonization of the man.[40]

All of the women leaders agreed that discrimination against women was of secondary importance to the subjection of all blacks and the inequitable distribution of power in society. Cleaver, for example, insisted that to focus on sexism diverted blacks from attacking the root of all injustice, "colonization," or economic exploitation of white women and minority men and women.[41] Likewise, Reagon believed that "the basic structure of the country . . . as it's set up, cannot sustain itself without oppressing someone,"[42] and Fannie Lou Hamer asserted that the liberation of one required the liberation of all. [43]

Moreover, these activists held differing views of the relationship between the status of black women and that of blacks as a whole. Cleaver thought that women's equality was a necessary precondition to achieving the equality of all blacks—a means of ensuring the full utilization of blacks' resources.

> As long as the men deny the women their full role and their full respect in that struggle (to destroy the system of colonialism) . . . they are cutting themselves short and they're selling the struggle short because the women have as much to give as the men . . . Therefore the black woman must be given her full respect in life and not hampered in her abilities, in her desires, and her activities towards forwarding the liberation of her people.[44]

Ladner, on the other hand, feared that the assertiveness of women made black men look relatively weak, as Andrew Young suggested, and hindered the men from proving their equality to whites.

> What is clear, however, is that an alteration of roles between Black males and females must occur. The traditional "strong" Black woman has probably outlived her usefulness because this role has been challenged by the Black man, who has demonstrated that the white society acknowledge his manhood and deal with him directly instead of using his woman—considered the weaker sex—as a buffer . . . I am not suggesting that the distinctive positive character of Black womanhood forged by centuries of oppression be abolished . . . I am proposing, however, that the stereotyped "Sapphire" ("Sapphire" is the name applied to the typical strong Black woman) cannot continue to operate in the traditional manner but must make the necessary adjustments that will allow for the full development of male and female.[45]

The inconsistencies in the behavior of these women leaders, in which they challenged white authorities but deferred to black ministers, or criticized the male activists, but only in hindsight, or directly challenged the male officers of movement organizations, yet nevertheless accepted their leadership, cannot entirely be explained by their various theories on the source of racism. Indeed, only in the case of three of the activists, Robinson, Bates, and Nash, do their ideologies seem consistent with their actions. A more plausible explanation for their contradictory behavior is that these women, for the reasons given by Washington, did not consider themselves oppressed by black men, either in or out of the movement, and in some respects believed that black men were worse off than black women. Consequently they did not seek to change their roles in the movement. In addition, the women had conflicting feelings about whom to hold responsible for sexism, if they thought that it did exist, and were uncertain as to how the assertion of their rights as women would affect the status of blacks as a group. These women leaders' reflections suggest that the role of black women in the civil rights movement, largely ignored by historians, was complicated by their ambivalence about what it ought to be and defies a definitive answer.

NOTES

1. Harvard Sitkoff, *The Struggle for Black Equality*, (New York: Hill and Wang, 1981), p. 90.
2. Paula Giddings, *When and Where I Enter* (New York: Bantam Books, 1984), p. 266.
3. Dick Cluster, ed., *They Should Have Served That Cup of Coffee*, (Boston: Sought End Press, 1979), pp. 22-23.
4. *Ibid.*, p. 29.
5. Anne Moody, *Coming of Age in Mississippi* (New York: Dial Press, 1968), p. 310.
6. David Garrow, ed., *The Montgomery Bus Boycott and the Women Who Started It: The Memoir of Jo Ann Gibson Robinson* (Knoxville: University of Tennessee Press, 1987), pp. 10-11.
7. *Ibid.*, pp. 53-54.
8. Daisy Bates, *The Long Shadow of Little Rock* (New York: David McKay, 1962), p. 22
9. *Ibid.*, p. 25.
10. *Ibid.*, p. 13.
11. *Ibid.*, pp. 85-86.
12. Juan Williams, *Eyes on the Prize*, (New York: Viking Penguin, 1987), p. 130.
13. Diane Nash, "The Men Behind Martin Luther King," *Ebony*, 1965, p. 170, as cited in Mary Mace Spradling, ed. *In Black and White*, Vol. 2, (Detroit: Gale Research Company, 1980), p. 211.
14. Williams, *Eyes on the Prize*, p. 149.

15. Jean Smith, "I Learned to Feel Black," in Floyd Barbour, ed., *The Black Power Revolt*, (Boston: Porter Sargent, 1968), p. 211.

17. Quoted in Jane E. Bowden, ed., *Contemporary Authors*, (Detroit: Gale Research Company, 1977), vol. 65-68, p. 418.

18. Joyce Ladner, "Return to the Source," *Essence*, June 1977, p.126.

18. *Ibid.*, p. 127.

19. Smith, "I Learned to Feel Black," pp. 214-217.

20. Ladner, "Return to the Source," p.129.

21. Joyce Ladner, *Tomorrow's Tomorrow*, (New York: Doubleday, 1971), pp. 273-275.

22. Frances Beal, "Slave of a Slave No More: Black Women in Struggle," *The Black Scholar*, March, 1975, p. 9.

23. Septima Clark, *Ready From Within* (Navarro, California: Wild Tree Press, 1986), p. 126.

24. Cluster, *They Should Have Served*, p. 36.

25. Ellen Cantarow, *Moving the Mountain* (Old Westbury: The Feminist Press, 1980), pp. 59-60.

26. *Ibid.*, pp. 86, 53.

27. *Ibid.*, p. 84.

28. Clark, *Ready from Within*, p. 77.

29. *Ibid.*, p. 77.

30. *Ibid.*, p. 78.

31. *Ibid.*, p. 79.

32. *Ibid.*, p. 80.

33. Sister Julia Herve, "Black Scholar Interviews Kathleen Cleaver," *The Black Scholar*, December 1971, p. 55.

34. Cynthia Washington, "We Started From Different Ends of the Spectrum," *Southern Exposure*, Vol. 4, No. 4, 1977, p. 14.

35. *Ibid.*, p. 15.

36. *Ibid.*, p. 14.

37. *Ibid.*, p. 15.

38. Giddings, *When and Where I Enter*, p. 313.

39. Clark, *Ready from Within*, p. 79.

40. Herve, "Black Scholar Interviews Kathleen Cleaver," p. 59.

41. *Ibid.*

42. Cluster, *They Should Have Served*, p. 25.

43. Fannie Lou Hamer, interview with Anne Romaine and Howard Romaine, 1966, Fannie Lou Hamer papers, Wisconsin State Historical Society, p. 14.

44. Herve, "Black Scholar Interviews Kathleen Cleaver," p. 59.

45. Ladner, *Tomorrow's Tomorrow*, p. 285.

Women as Culture Carriers in the Civil Rights Movement: Fannie Lou Hamer

BERNICE JOHNSON REAGON

Understanding Fannie Lou Hamer and her role as a cultural carrier becomes clearer when we recognize that she opened many mass meetings by pulling the congregation into a community of singing.

> Remember me
> Remember me
> Oh Lord, remember me.
>
> Father, I stretch
> My hands to thee
> No other help I know.
>
> You remembered my mother, remember me
> You remembered mother, remember me
> Oh Lord, remember me.

There is something I feel when sound runs through my body. I cannot sing without experiencing a change in my mood, a change in the way I feel. In the African American culture, that is a major function of singing. People come to singing because of how they feel in it and on the other side of the song. The aim is to be sure that whatever shape you were in before you started to produce this sound is transformed when the singing is over. There are cultures where one can engage in singing without having one's inner self aroused, but this is not the case with the African American congregational song tradition.

Fannie Lou Hamer was an activist and a cultural leader who assumed major responsibility for the creation and maintenance of the environment within which those who struggle for freedom lived and worked. She positioned herself so that she was constantly in great danger; she operated in the open, aboveground, confronting an entire system that was organized to keep her and all Black people subjugated. When Mrs. Hamer found her voice as a fighter, she became a transmitter of the culture of that struggle. Her work as an organizer was grounded in her own testimony. She called and urged others to join in battling racism, poverty, and injustice. A natural and fearless community leader, master orator, and song leader, she used her stories and songs to nurture the air we breathed as fighters.

The first time I saw Fannie Lou Hamer she came up to me and thanked me for everything we had done for her. I couldn't figure out why this giant was thanking me. I struggled a long time to figure out whom she was talking about. She was talking about the young people who made up the staff of the Student Nonviolent Coordinating Committee (SNCC).

I was in the Atlanta SNCC office, and she was a SNCC field secretary by then, primarily organizing in Mississippi, but increasingly traveling throughout the South and the nation telling stories about what it took for a citizen of the United States of America of African descent to vote in the state of Mississippi. In expressing her thanks to SNCC, Mrs. Hamer was defining and validating the work of the movement from a new perspective. She was saying that the movement was the best thing that had ever happened to her. She sounded as if we in SNCC had rescued her. When I thought about it, I understood what she meant. The movement gave all of us choices about how we would live, and it gave us the chance to act as people with power.

Fannie Lou Hamer was expressing thanks—as I have done many times since—for the opportunity to become, for her time and her community and her people, more like herself. We all have souls, an inner voice that wants to find its essence through the expression of our living. Often we feel that the world would not tolerate us if we followed our hearts. The movement provided a nurturing ground that encouraged us to open up and move beyond our fears and become who we were in our hearts. One who answered that call was Fannie Lou Hamer.

Fannie Lou Hamer was born in Montgomery County, Mississippi, in 1917. She was the youngest of twenty children born to Jim and Lou Ella Townsend, who worked as sharecroppers. From the age of two, she lived in Sunflower County and she began to pick cotton at six. Of her childhood years, she said: "Life was worse than hard. It was horrible! We never did have enough to eat and I don't remember how old I was when I got my first pair of shoes, but I was a big girl. Mama tried to keep our feet warm by wrapping them in rags and tying them with string."[1]

One year after a good season, her father cleared enough to rent land and buy stock and a car. A white neighbor envious of this progress struck a devastating blow by poisoning the stock with Paris green, an insecticide. This plunged the family back into poverty, from which they never recovered. The family's situation was complicated by an accident that left her mother blind. As the plight of the family worsened, Fannie Lou Hamer was forced to leave school at twelve years of age, just able to read and write. So in 1962, when the movement came to Ruleville, Mississippi, she was working weighing cotton and serving as timekeeper for B. D. Marlowe, a job she held for eighteen years until she made her first attempt to register to vote.

We know about Fannie Lou Hamer because of her tireless efforts to change the conditions of African Americans in Mississippi in particular and the country in general. We know about her because of the price that she paid to participate in the struggle for change. We know about her because of the power of her voice. Everywhere she went she spoke, sang, and shared her life and her vision of a better world. It was a powerful message; her delivery was Southern, Black and riveting.

The first time I heard her speak was in Town Hall in New York City. It was the first time I had ever been to Town Hall. I owe a lot to the movement that the first time I entered this hallowed hall of the land was to hear Fannie Lou Hamer tell the stories of our fight for justice. Walking into Town Hall, New York City, for the first time to hear Mrs. Hamer, E. W. Steptoe, and Hartman Turnbow, all from Mississippi, was the way to learn about that place and others like it. Because of the movement, such places became ours, to use for our forums and our messages. They were never beyond our lives and our reach. The first time I ever heard about Carnegie Hall, I was invited to sing there as a Freedom Singer.

205

Listening to the story of Fannie Lou Hamer took me to a place I had witnessed so many times in Black church services. Someone rises and through her or his offerings begins to charge up the air. Sometimes after a service has begun somebody will just come out of a corner and with the support of the congregants will do something to bring the space under his or her power. This refocusing and transforming spaces goes beyond content and data; it deals directly with the power to establish the tone and tenor of the environment. Within the African American oral tradition our stories and our legacies travel through time in a bed of rich cultural sound. I am not talking about simply starting something in a room and changing the space the people in the room have to deal with. It goes much farther because the oral tradition requires the transmission of its lode across generations. When you are a part of such an environment the experiences that are passed in that space become forever a part of who you are. In order to serve and extend the process and keep alive these treasures for others living in your time and beyond, you walk out of that space with responsibility for the stories you now carry within your soul. For example, I know

> Walk with me, my Lord, walk with me
> Walk with me, my Lord, walk with me
> While I'm on this tedious journey
> I want Jesus to walk with me.

I cannot tell you when I learned that song. I did not get it out of a book and I did not learn it in a classroom. It was traveling to me through time, an integral element of the cultural world into which I was born. I know the song and the singing because when I was surrounded by it, its power moved me and became a comfort to me, and I now continue its life in sharing it.

> Make a way for me, now Lord, make a way for me
> Make a way for me, now Lord, make a way for me
> While I'm on this tedious journey
> I want Jesus to walk with me.

It is important to talk about cultural transmission, how ideas, analysis, social stances, and worldviews move through communities and across time. A lot of us do not understand what it really would take to make our work available to the next generation—not only for those who follow us to read about what we believed and valued and tried to do with our living, but also to receive our stories as models and the base from which our children may move in the world they struggle to shape. The idea that the world you live in is one you should work to shape moves across time only if it is a part of the cultural environment you create and put in motion.

This work within African American culture—the work of passing on the stories of life in song, in ceremonies, in games, in the sounds around us—has been carried to a large extent by the women. You know who you are before you remember that you don't know who you are. And you know that from the women. They whisper it to you in the cracks between feeding and the air you breathe. Fannie Lou Hamer understood that what she experienced was not for her alone but for those who would be moved by the sound of her voice and the power of her living.

That night at Town Hall, Mrs. Hamer told the story of her arrest and the severe beating she and Annelle Ponder received because of their efforts to register voters in Mississippi. It was a story I was to hear many times, but that night it was engraved in my heart. I was transformed by the intensity of her identification with struggle. There was no separation; she had stepped onto a path and found joy amid unspeakable danger. As a young woman beginning to find my own voice, it was crucial that I sat in an environment created by the life and struggle of Fannie Lou Hamer.

She began, "My name is Fannie Lou Hamer. I live in Ruleville, Mississippi. . . ." She told how she and five other people had been returning from a voter registration training session in Charleston, South Carolina. Their bus was stopped in Winona, Mississippi, and they were arrested. From her cell, Mrs. Hamer could hear Annelle Ponder, a student from Atlanta who worked with the Southern Christian Leadership Conference (SCLC), screaming as they beat her. When Annelle Ponder, her face swollen, walked past Mrs. Hamer's cell, she whispered, "Pray for me."

Then Mrs. Hamer heard her own name called and they came and got her and made her lie down on a bench. She was beaten by two Black men, prisoners called trustees, who were charged to beat her by two white guards who held guns on them to make sure they gave her a good whipping. As they lashed her about her legs, her dress started to move up her thighs and as she reached to try and pull it down, one of the guards pulled her dress over her head. They beat her with leather straps until her thighs were as hard as a board, until pain came and went. When they told her to get up she didn't think she could move. When she finally was able to get up, she knew that although they had whipped her body, they had not whipped her soul. She knew that freedom was when you understood that not even an attempt to kill you would determine what you did or said.

Fannie Lou Hamer's participation in the movement seemed to come from a long-held desire to do something about the way her people had been forced to live. This pride was instilled in her by her mother: "Sometimes when things were so bad and I'd start thinking maybe it would be better if we were white, she'd [Hamer's mother] insisted that we should be proud to be Black, telling us, 'nobody will respect you unless you stand up for yourself.' "[2]

Growing up believing in God and being taught not to hate, Mrs. Hamer discovered that there were many things "dead wrong" with the lives of Blacks and whites in Mississippi. "I used to think . . . let me have a chance, and whatever this is . . . I'm gonna do somethin' about it."[3]

Her chance came one night when she went to a mass meeting at a church in Ruleville, where she heard James Forman and James Bevel speak about voter registration. Reverend Bevel told those gathered about how many Black people there were in the county and how, if they were voters, they could remove from power the racist politicians who controlled their state. They also learned that in Washington, many of the senior members of the House and Senate were from the South because they were able to hold on to their seats for the most terms. Their longevity was directly related to Blacks not participating in the political system; they did not have to be accountable to the majority of people in their districts since most of them were not allowed to vote.

Mrs. Hamer was one of those who volunteered to try to register, and she was made the leader of the group. This resulted in her losing her job and her family being kicked off the plantation. She often told this story in mass meetings to encourage others to join the movement.

It was 1962, thirty-first of August that eighteen of us traveled twenty-six miles to this place to the county courthouse to try to register to become first-class citizens. When we got here to Indianola to the courthouse, that was a day I saw more policemen with guns than I'd ever seen in my life at one time. They were standing around, and I never will forget that day. One of the policemen called the police department in Cleveland, Mississippi, and told him to bring some type of big book back over there. Anyway, we stayed in the registrar's office—I was one of the first persons to complete, as far as I knew how to complete, my registration form and I went and got back on the bus. During the time we were on the bus, the policeman kept watching the bus and I noticed a highway patrolman watching the bus.

After everybody had completed their forms and after we started back to Ruleville, Mississippi, we were stopped by the policeman and highway patrolmen and was ordered to come back to Indianola, Mississippi. When we got back to Indianola, the bus driver was charged with driving the bus the wrong color. This is the gospel truth. This bus had been used for years for cotton chopping, cotton picking, and to carry people to Florida to work in the wintertime to make enough to live on to get back here in the spring and summer. But that day the bus had the wrong color. We got to Ruleville about five o'clock.

Reverend Jeff Sunny drove me out to the rural area where I had been working as a timekeeper and a sharecropper for eighteen years. When I got there I was already fired. My children met and told me, "Mama, this man is hot! Said you will have to go back and withdraw [your registration application] or you will have to leave." . . . It wasn't too long before my husband came and he said the same thing. I walked in the house, set down on the side of my little daughter's bed, and then this white man walked over and said, "Pap, did you tell Fannie Lou what I said?" I said, "He did." "Well, Fannie Lou, you will have to go down and withdraw or you will have to leave." And I addressed and told him, as we have always had to say "Mr., I didn't register for you; I was trying to register for myself." He said, "We're not ready for that in Mississippi." He wasn't ready, but I been ready a long time. I had to leave that same night.[4]

While organizing in Mississippi, Mrs. Hamer never hesitated to speak of the cost and danger of entering a life of activism against racism: "On the tenth of September in 1962, sixteen bullets were fired into the home of Mr. and Mrs. Robert Tucker for me. That same night two girls were shot at Mr. Herman Sissan's in Ruleville. They also shot Mr. Joe McDonald's house that same night."[5] She then moved from her personal testimony to sharply focused analysis: "Now the question I raise, is this America? The land of the free and the home of the brave? Where people are being murdered, lynched, and killed because we want to register and vote!"[6]

As a good organizer, she never failed to return to the immediate goals of the project. "You know I feel good. I never know what's gonna happen to me tonight. But you see, you know the ballot is good. If it wasn't good, how come he trying to keep you from it and he still doing it? Don't be foolish, folks. They go in there by the droves and they had guns to keep us out of there the other day, and dogs. And if that's good enough for them, I want some of it too."[7]

Mrs. Hamer was much more than a talker, organizer, and singer; her efforts brought results. She failed the literacy test the first time she tried to register to vote. She told the registrar she would return every thirty days until she passed the test. And she did. She wore them out with her living and became one of the first African Americans to register to vote in the Sunflower County voting campaign.

It was perhaps these two stories—Mrs. Hamer and Annelle Ponder being beaten in jail and her first efforts to register to vote—that pushed me to write this song when I heard that she had passed.

> Fannie Lou Hamer, Fannie Lou Hamer
> Fannie Lou Hamer, Fannie Lou Hamer
>
> This Little Light of mine
> Her song would fill the air
> She rocked the state of Mississippi
> Now a few more Black people stand there.
>
> For twenty years she weighed cotton
> Down on a white man's farm
> She received threats on her life, fired from her job
> Scorned and kicked off the farm.
>
> We're sick and tired of being sick and tired
> That's what the lady would yell
> Her body was beaten and she walked crippled
> Trying to vote, she was thrown in jail.
>
> Land of the tree and home of the slave
> She criticized the law of this land
> For hundreds of years Blacks had lived in fear
> Now we marched took our lives in our hands.
>
> She came by here and she didn't stay long
> Helped to turn a few things around
> Cancer took her body, the struggle's got her soul
> Now we've laid her body in the ground.

When I look at the words of Fannie Lou Hamer, I am always struck by how she defined who she was. She was a religious woman, and whenever she got up to speak she took a text or she quoted from the Scripture. In this case, she defines the work she felt she was called to do. The first thing she did was to lead out on "This Little Light of Mine." Then right out of the song she said:

> From the fourth chapter of St. Luke, beginning at the eighteenth verse: "The Spirit of the Lord is upon me because he hath anointed me to preach the gospel to the poor; he hath sent me to heal the broken-hearted, to preach deliverance to the captives, and recovering of sight to the blind, to set at liberty them who are bruised, to preach the acceptable day of the Lord."
> Now the time have come, that was Christ's purpose on earth, and we only been getting by paving our way to hell, but the time is out. When Simon Cyrene was helping Christ to bear his cross up the hill, he said; "Must Jesus bear this cross alone and all the world go free? No, there's a cross for everyone and there's a cross for me. This consecrated cross I'll bear, till death shall set me free. And then go home a crown to wear, for there's a crown for me."[8]

When she finished quoting that hymn (and I understood that Simon Cyrene had not said those particular words), she added, "It is not easy out there. We just got to make up our minds and face it, folk, and if I can face the issue, you can too." In this sermon, she is saying that she is charged to do the work from the highest source she has operating in her life. The preaching of the gospel, and the anointing, and the giving of sight to the blind are activities that Jesus did. She claims that territory where seemingly impossible changes are brought forth, for herself. And before she finishes, she calls the congregation to action by saying, "If I can do it, you can too."[9]

Fannie Lou Hamer placed Jesus where his experiences, as passed through the traditions of the Black church, could be used in the freedom struggle. She used all of this material and she brought its full force to bear on the work she had to do.

There was the time in the mass meeting in Greenwood when Mrs. Hamer talked about how long she had been concerned about the system she was now risking her life every day to challenge.

> And brothers, you can believe this or not—I been sick of this system as long as I can remember. Heard some people speak of the Depression in the thirties; in the twenties it was always "pression" with me! Depression! I been as hungry. . . . You know it's been a long time, people, I have worked, I have worked as hard as anybody. I have been picking cotton and would be so hungry and one of the poison things about it, wondering what I was gone cook that night, but you see, all of them things were wrong? And I asked

God, and I have said, "Now Lord," and it ain't no need a lying and saying you ain't, "open a way for us. Please make a way for us, Jesus, where I can stand up and speak for my race and speak for my hungry children," and he opened a way and all of them mostly backing out.

It's a funny thing since I started working for Christ—it's kinda like in the Twenty-third Psalm, He said, "Thou preparest a table before me in the presence of my enemies; thou anointeth my head with oil; and my cup runnest over," and I have walked through the shadows of death, because it was on the tenth of September in 1962 when they shot sixteen times in a house—and it wasn't over a foot over the bed where my head was—but that night, I wasn't there. Don't you see what God can do? Quit running around trying to dodge death, because this book says, "He that seeketh to save his life is gonna lose it anyhow."[10]

Mrs. Hamer walked the ground that was the Twenty-third Psalm as a fighter. These Bible stories became concrete in her attempt to register to vote. She always drew on this source in her speeches. For instance, she used the Israelite story of Moses to describe Bob Moses, the head of the Mississippi Freedom Project: "You see, He made it so plain for us: He sent a man to Mississippi with the same name that Moses had to go to Egypt and tell them to go down in Mississippi and tell Ross Barnett to let my people go."[11]

She directly addressed the fear of the Black people in that church. After telling everyone that they might get killed if they joined the movement, she used this story to show them how that was exactly what they were supposed to do. She was telling Black people that this was the time. How do we know it? Bob Moses was the sign of Moses. And though Bob Moses was not always comfortable with this analogy, Fannie Lou Hamer the organizer used it like a guarantee that the time had arrived. She believed that the movement was an unmistakable door that the people had opened in their own lives and now must be fortified to walk through. Whenever she talked, you felt that she was processing material that had come to her and was analyzing it and blending it with the challenges of the day.

She became a national voice, moving throughout the nation, speaking to the issues of the day. In one speech she was asked to talk about women. In the opening part of the speech, she speaks to white women.

You know I work for the liberation of all people, because when I liberate myself, I'm liberating other people. But you know, sometimes I really feel sorrier for the white woman than I feel for ourselves because she been caught up in this thing, caught up feeling special, and folks, I'm going to put it on the line, because my job is not to make people feel comfortable. You've been caught up in this thing because, you know, you worked my grandmother, and after that you worked my mother, and then finally you got a hold of me.[12]

The irony of the issue, still before us today, was the widening of the historic gulfs between white women and their nonwhite servants. As "liberated" women increasingly chose professional careers outside the home as well as motherhood and homemaking, they turned to poorer women to provide the services to make their lives possible. Often these women were not paid enough by their sisters to provide adequate care for the children they had to leave at home so their employees' children would be well cared for.

In speaking to issues like this, Mrs. Hamer was and is timeless and relentless in her honesty. She insisted that the relationships between maids and nursemaids and their employers be a part of any discussion about sisterhood. She acknowledged her experiences, including the mixed families she grew up in, and how many blue-eyed Black people she knew, and how many cousins she had who said they were white in Mississippi who never "sistered" or "cousined" her.

For Mrs. Hamer, Black women were in partnership with Black men in the interest of the family and the future of their people. She was uneasy with the radical edge of feminism that seemed to say that if you are going to fight for your freedom as women and you are going to fight against sexism, it may become necessary and appropriate to separate yourself from your fathers, your brothers, your male lovers, and your sons. Mrs. Hamer took a strong position on what she felt was divisive and destructive to Black American organizing: "I'm not hung up on this about liberating myself from the Black man, I'm not going to try that thing. I got a Black husband, six feet three, two hundred and forty pounds, with a 14 shoe, that I don't want to be liberated from."[13]

Mrs. Hamer's view on the partnership between Black men and women was not a romantic one. As a leader in the movement and in her community, she did not hesitate to criticize men who wanted to lead but were unable to confront their fears. She believed that leadership came from actual work and commitment and was not preordained by sex. She clearly stated her position on this when urging people to face the danger: "You see the thing what so pitiful about it, the men been wanting to be the boss all these years, and the ones not up under the house is under the bed."[14]

Coming out of the poorest state in the nation, from one of the poorest classes, Mrs. Hamer was harsh and frank about the way some college-educated Black women had difficulty embracing her as their sister:

A few years ago throughout the country the middle class Black women—I used to say not really Black women, but the middle class colored women, didn't respect the kind of work that I was doing. But you see now baby, whether you have a ph.d., dd, or no d, we're in this bag together. And whether you are from Morehouse or Nohouse, we're still in this bag together. Not to fight to liberate ourselves from the men—this is another trick to get us fighting among ourselves—but to work together with Black men. And then we will have a better chance to just act as human beings, and be treated as human beings in our sick society.[15]

Fannie Lou Hamer had a realistic sense of how she was perceived by her community. She understood and spoke about the power of class in paralyzing people to organize against their own oppression.

You see in this struggle, some people say, well she don't talk too good. The type of education that we get here, years to come, you won't talk too good. The type of education that we get in the state of Mississippi will make our minds so narrow, it won't coordinate with our big bodies. We know we have a long fight, because our leaders like the preachers and the teachers, they are failing to stand up today. But we know some of the reasons for that. This brainwashed education that the teachers have got.[16]

We have a job as Black women, to support whatever is right, and to bring in justice where we've had so much injustice. Some people say, well I work for $24 per week. That's not true in my case, I work sometimes for $15 per week. I remember my mother working for 25 and 30 cents a day. But we are organizing ourselves now, because we don't have any other choice.
Sunflower County is one of the few counties in the state of Mississippi where we didn't lose one Black teacher. Because I went in and told the judge, I said, "judge, we're not going to stand by and see you take a man with a master's degree and bring him down to janitor help. So if we don't have the principal . . . there ain't going to be no˙ school, private or public."[17]

Looking at the economic reality of slavery and racism, Fannie Lou Hamer blended a familiarity with God with her personal history and testimony to make her point.

A house divided against itself cannot stand. America is divided against itself and without they considering us as human beings one day America will crumble! Because God is not pleased! God is not pleased with all the murdering and all the brutality and all the killing for no reason at all. God is not pleased that the Negro children in the state of Mississippi [are] suffering from malnutrition. God is not pleased because we have to go raggedy and work from ten to eleven hours for three lousy dollars! And then how can they

214

say that in ten years' time we will force every Negro out of the state of Mississippi. But I want these people to take a good look at themselves, and after they have sent the Chinese back to China, the Jews back to Jerusalem, and give the Indians their land back; they take the *Mayflower* back from where they came, the Negro will still be in Mississippi! We don't have anything to be ashamed of in Mississippi and actually we don't carry guns, because we don't have anything to hide.[18]

Fannie Lou Hamer, standing among a chorus of Black women leaders like Ella Baker and Septima Clark, taught something else about being a leader in the movement. These women made their political and social stances primary in their lives. They had jobs of a sort, somebody sometimes paid them wages, but the work never changed. By being in the atmosphere they created and listening to the talk, I learned that it is possible to live in this society and be a radical and always be ready to fight. Sometimes you would get killed, but a lot of times you wouldn't. There was in the midst of pain and effort and the real dangers also a sweetness about struggle that no human being should go through life and not experience.

There is another story Fannie Lou Hamer tells, this one about the 1964 Democratic National Convention in Atlantic City. She described being in a room with Hubert Humphrey, who explained that in his heart he really supported their struggle. The Mississippi Freedom Democratic Party was challenging the seats of the all-white Mississippi delegation on the grounds that Blacks were not allowed to exercise their rights as citizens to participate in electoral politics in that state. However, Humphrey's chance to be on the ticket with Lyndon Johnson would be jeopardized if the issue reached the floor. Mrs. Hamer said:

I was delighted even to have a chance to talk with this man. But here say a little roundeyed man with his eyes full of tears, when our attorney at the time, Joseph Rauh, said if we didn't stop pushing them and fighting to come to the floor, that Mr. Humphrey wouldn't be nominated that night for vice-president of the United States, I was amazed, and I said, "Well Mr. Humphrey, do you mean to tell me that your position is more important to you than 400,000 Black lives?" And I didn't try to force nobody else to say it, but I told him I wouldn't stoop to no two votes at large.[19]

It takes a fresh vision to raise that question and then stand on your position and say that's your ground. Mrs. Hamer refused the compromise offered by the convention—to seat the regular all-white delegation and give the MFDP two seats at-large. "Now they thought they had us sewed up, bag sewed up, but I told it everywhere. You can kill a man, but you can't kill ideas. 'Cause that idea's going to be transferred from one generation 'til after a while, if it's not too late for all of us, we'll be free."[20]

It was this Fannie Lou Hamer who, when I actually met her, said, "I want to thank you all for what you are trying to do for us." I will always stand in her shadow charged by the power of her work.

> I wandered far away from God
> Now I'm coming home
> The path of sin too long I've trod
> Now I'm coming home.

This is a favorite hymn in the Black church. If you are not a Christian, go beyond the specific text and think about being lost from yourself. You cannot understand what the civil rights movement means or what you did if you don't have a space like this where out of the heat of the activity you can sit and ponder it. Fannie Lou Hamer's reality of representing 600,000 people in the state of Mississippi was her home base. No matter where she was, she knew that if she moved with integrity from that reality she would be on solid ground. Committing oneself to long-time struggle requires the search for oneself and the embracing of your vision of the world and yourself in it at your fullest development as "home." Then from that place you can move and return as you struggle to make a way for the life you have to live.

> Coming home,
> Coming home,
> Never more to roam.
> Open wide, thine arms of love
> Now I'm coming home.

NOTES

1. Phyl Garland, "Builders of the South: Negro Heroines of Dixie Play Major Role in Challenging Racist Traditions," *Ebony*, August 1966, p. 28.
2. *Ibid.*
3. George Sewell, "Fannie Lou Hamer," *Black Collegian*, May/June 1978, p. 18.
4. Fannie Lou Hamer, mass meeting, Hattiesburg, Mississippi, 1963, Moses Moon Collection, Program in African American Culture, Archives, National Museum of American History, Smithsonian Institution, Washington, D.C.
5. *Ibid.*
6. *Ibid.*
7. *Ibid.*
8. Fannie Lou Hamer, mass meeting, Greenwood, Mississippi, 1963, Moses Moon Collection.
9. *Ibid.*
10. *Ibid.*
11. *Ibid.*
12. Fannie Lou Hamer, speech, NAACP Legal Defense Fund Institute, New York City, May 7, 1971, in Gerda Lerner, ed., *Black Women in White America* (New York: Vintage, 1972).
13. *Ibid.*
14. Hamer, Greenwood meeting.
15. Hamer, NAACP speech.
16. Hamer, Hattiesburg meeting.
17. Hamer, NAACP speech.
18. Hamer, Hattiesburg meeting.
19. Fannie Lou Hamer, interview, *Southern Exposure*, 9, 1 (Spring 1981).
20. *Ibid.*

Behind the Scenes: Doris Derby, Denise Nicholas and the Free Southern Theater

CLARISSA MYRICK-HARRIS

The experiences of Doris Derby and Denise Nicholas in the Civil Rights Movement demonstrate two symbiotic ideas: African-American women's quest for self-definition and empowerment is often advanced by their political activism; and, African-American women involved in the ongoing struggle for social change contribute most to the black community when they step out of roles defined for them by black males and use both their personal experience as black women and the collective history of all African-Americans to define and empower themselves.

A discussion of the lives of these two women during their involvement in the civil rights movement illustrates the dynamic ways in which women achieved personal empowerment through political activism and the centrality of personal empowerment to the success of the struggle for social change.

I.

Doris Derby's involvement in the movement began in 1962 and became both a continuation and affirmation of her personal and family history of activism. As she was growing up, her parents encouraged involvement in social causes and taught her to value her African-American heritage. Derby first applied these lessons as a student activist at Hunter College.[1] Her individual growth and her contributions to the African-American struggle for self-definition as an organizer, administrator, educator, and artist are illustrated through her involvement with the Student Nonviolent Coordinating Committee (SNCC) in New York and Mississippi, and her work with the Free Southern Theater (FST).

In the summer of 1962 when Doris Derby decided to stop in Albany, Georgia "to see about a friend" who had been jailed because of her involvement in the Albany Movement, the young schoolteacher was drawn directly into the civil rights movement. During the next three months, she worked in Atlanta and Albany with such activists as Martin Luther King, Jr., Septima Clark, and James Forman.[2] Over the next two years, Derby not only defined her own roles but was a key figure in defining three civil rights projects. When she returned to New York after her summer in Georgia, she became a founding member of the New York office of SNCC; then, in the summer of 1963, she travelled to Mississippi as an organizer of an experimental adult literacy program at Tougaloo College; and, that winter she co-founded the Free Southern Theater.

Derby did not come to these activities as a blank slate. Her personal history provided the basis for her to believe that African-American women had the ability and the right to determine the nature of their contributions to the movement. In effect, she was prepared to do what she believed was necessary to advance aspects of the movement in which she was involved.

While a number of women who worked in the offices of civil rights organizations were relegated to secretarial work or coordination of existing programs, Derby went beyond such roles as an original member of the SNCC New York office by conceiving, planning and implementing fund-raising events. She successfully spearheaded a major fund-raising drive of artists for civil rights, and for another fund raiser, she brought in Bob Moses, the leader of SNCC in Mississippi, as the speaker.

When she accepted Bob Moses' invitation to move south to help develop an experimental adult literacy program at Tougaloo College in Mississippi, she continued her flexible activism, transcending the roles that black males thought should determine the tenor and tone of her contributions. On the one hand, Derby's decision to help set up this program can be viewed as an understandable decision made by an educator. Such a role seems consistent with the traditional role of schoolteacher that many would associate with black women. On the other hand, the decision to practice her profession in an environment where the worth and humanity of her pupils—African-Americans—were not acknowledged and where the penalties for being an educated African-American ranged from ostracism to murder meant that Derby was moving beyond the traditional role of educator to that of liberator.

Derby's work in defining and planning the adult literacy program combined her skills as an educator and organizer. Indeed a major reason Moses personally asked Derby to go to Mississippi was because of her effectiveness in the fledgling New York office. For the literacy program, she developed instructional materials and methods to prepare black men and women to take the literacy test required to gain voting rights.[3]

Derby's roles in the SNCC adult literacy program were consistent with her image of herself as an educator and organizer. However, she also possessed creative talents and believed that she could use her background in art and theater to further the aims of the movement.[4] As a co-founder of the Free Southern Theater in the winter of 1963, Derby helped to create an arena in which she believed she could function as an educator, organizer and artist. Her skills as an organizer and educator were most useful in the conceptual stage of the FST as she and the two black male co-founders of the theater—John O'Neal and Gilbert Moses—attempted to define the theater as a vehicle for educating African-Americans of the South about their history and about the civil rights movement. Derby's talents as an artist were to be utilized as scenic designer for the theater.[5]

Eventually, Derby's vision of the leadership she could provide in the theater and chauvinistic notions O'Neal and Moses held about what her day-to-day roles should be clashed. They agreed that the best use of Derby's artistic talents was as the scenic designer for the theater. Yet, O'Neal has admitted, he and Moses also expected her "to do the filing, the typing, the bookkeeping—because she's a woman."[6] Derby was so secure and clear about her chosen role in the FST that O'Neal's and Moses's attitudes about women's roles were irrelevant to her. "I never felt I was discriminated against

One aspect of Doris Derby's movement work was national fundraising and public relations for Mississippi projects. She is shown here on the Rosey Grier Show in Los Angeles.

This photograph of Doris Derby was taken while she was doing grassroots organizing in Mississippi during "the long hot summers."
[Photo: *Bob Fletcher*]

because I was a woman," she has said in recent years. "I was going to do what I wanted to do no matter what they thought."[7]

The impetus for Derby's departure from the FST was not so much the sexism of O'Neal and Moses as it was the two men's decision to move the FST from Tougaloo College in Mississippi to New Orleans, on the periphery of the movement.[8] That decision dramatically demonstrated major differences in the perspectives of Derby and her two co-founders. Derby believed in the power of creative endeavors to raise the consciousness of black people, but because of the importance of historical referents in her own life, she was also unwavering in her belief that the productions and programs of the FST could be effective only if they were informed by the history and the environment of the black people of the rural South. Derby's decision not to move with the theater attested to her consistency and dedication to the roles she had chosen for herself: "I didn't think we should move the theater to New Orleans, to Tulane, a white university. We had this base in Mississippi. And as an educator, I felt it was more important that I stay and develop materials for the literacy program."[9]

In contrast to Derby's unwavering pragmatism, O'Neal and Moses were unabashed idealists who were unsure about the best way to build a strong political theater. Sometimes they believed that moving to New Orleans away from tension-filled movement activity would provide a better context in which to build a theater; at other times—even after the move—they believed that their separation from the movement would make the FST a missionary theater.[10]

In 1965, as O'Neal and Moses grappled with the consequences of moving the FST to New Orleans, Derby continued to define her own roles in Mississippi. Even after the civil rights movement ebbed and the center of activism moved North, Derby remained in Mississippi, working as an educator, organizer/administrator and artist until 1972. She taught and trained others to teach children in the first Headstart Program in the state, she directed a cooperative program and trained others to form cooperatives, and she blossomed as an artist and photographer documenting the lives of African-Americans of the rural South.[11]

II.

Denise Nicholas came into the movement without Derby's history of personal involvement in activism. Nicholas's father, like men in Derby's family, was a "race man," but Nicholas was not encouraged by her family to become an activist.[12] The nineteen-year-old college student's decision to leave her insulated world in Ann Arbor, Michigan, and join the Free Southern Theater in Mississippi was primarily a function of her decision to marry Gilbert Moses, one of the theater's three founders. Her early roles as an actress, script reader and office worker in the FST were, for the most part, those assigned her by her husband and other male leaders of the theater.

Nicholas's developing empowerment was most clearly reflected in the socio-political orientations she adopted during her two-year affiliation with the theater. She went from being an idealistic integrationist actress "molded" by her husband to being a pragmatic advocate of black consciousness who planned and implemented community programs.

Denise Nicholas began a process of self-discovery and empowerment as she toured the rural South in an integrated FST production of Martin Duberman's play *In White America* during the Mississippi Freedom Summer of 1964, one of the most volatile periods of the movement. Until that time, Nicholas, a political science major at the University of Michigan, had only the vaguest idea about what life was like for African-Americans in the South. Although she felt it was important to make a contribution to the movement, her decision to participate in Freedom Summer against the will of her parents had been based primarily on the desire to seek adventure and continue her relationship with Gilbert Moses, the young man she met and fell in love with at a party in New York during a school break in 1963. Moses urged her to join the FST as an actress in spite of her inexperience and naivety.[13]

During their marriage, Moses continued to influence the theatrical and real-life roles Nicholas played. However, over the next three years, Nicholas continued her process of self-discovery and empowerment that eventually enabled her to define her own life. She came progressively closer to achieving self-empowerment as she became one of the leaders of the faction working to make the FST a black theater and developed a black resource center in a depressed area of the black community in New Orleans. In 1967 she made the decision to leave the theater and direct involvement with the movement to pursue an acting career on her own.

Two of the catalysts that sparked Nicholas's growth during Freedom Summer in 1964 were the experience of meeting people of rural Mississippi and Louisiana who had lived their entire lives surviving the most brutal forms of racial oppression and her personal exposure to racists' terrorist tactics. Nicholas was impressed and inspired by the courage and strength of the African-Americans of the rural South she encountered while performing in the FST's adaptation of Martin Duberman's *In White America*. This compilation of scenes of significant events in African-American history was meant to help educate the audiences about their heritage. However, Nicholas and others involved in the production learned even more valuable lessons from their audiences about the indomitable spirit and strength that have historically helped African-Americans triumph over the day-to-day pressures of oppression. "I remember the quietness that these people had," Nicholas recalled. "It was overwhelming, but you knew you wanted to absorb it; you wanted this strength, spirit and the soul that these people had to be a part of yours. And they gave it to you."[14]

Surviving the explosion of a bomb near a performance in McComb and being picked up and driven around by a redneck policeman in Jackson for handing out flyers announcing a FST performance also sped Nicholas's maturation. The bombing, while startling, did not interrupt the performance: "You just keep going." And though terrified by the arrest, she went back to her work with the theater immediately after being released. Nicholas has said of her experiences on the frontlines of the movement: "It's like being in the trenches and you're testing yourself. In a way you are in the process of developing and growing into what you want to be as a human being and those kinds of situations of danger help you to find yourself."[15]

Nicholas's day-to-day roles behind the scenes in the theater and interactions with the male leaders of the FST demonstrate that she did not "find herself" immediately after the Mississippi Freedom Summer. In late 1964, as the institution attempted to build a base in New Orleans, Nicholas willingly assumed the roles she was assigned by Moses and O'Neal. When the theater was not on tour, she performed the mundane tasks of script reading and office work. Moreover, while she sometimes openly disagreed with the male leaders of the FST, she accepted the fact that she was excluded from the decision making process of the theater—even though she was one of its core members. "Then I was not as strong as I am now," she admits. "Then I was able to be led because I was so young and so ignorant about so many things."[16]

Although the intensity of her civil rights movement activities ignited Nicholas's period of growth, her process of self-discovery and empowerment was advanced most during the period of decline of the civil rights activity and emergence of the black consciousness movement. Nicholas's education about her racial heritage spurred this period of growth. She was among the hundreds of young African-American activists who began to ·question the integrationist thrust of the movement in the wake of the disappointments of Freedom Summer, the rejection of the integrated Mississippi Freedom Democratic Party at the National Democratic Convention in 1964, and the assassination of Malcolm X in the winter of 1965. Immediate catalysts for what Nicholas called her "first rebirth" were a period of introspection, the reading of books about black history and works by such figures as Malcolm X and Franz Fanon, along with observing growing black consciousness among African-Americans in New York City.[17]

Her emerging black consciousness was a major reason for Nicholas's decisions to become a leader of the black nationalist faction in the FST in the spring of 1966 and to become a community worker in New Orleans later that year. Yet, those decisions were also influenced by her husband and a narrow idea of what was politically correct for the advancement of the black consciousness movement. Therefore, her contributions in these roles were never as successful or fulfilling as she had hoped.

A period of research in New York City in the winter of 1965-1966 accelerated Nicholas's process of self-discovery and empowerment. For the first time she was involved in an intense, self-directed quest for knowledge about African-American history and political ideology. She and her husband, along with others in the theater who were developing a black nationalist perspective, had only superficially discussed the political and cultural precedents and current manifestations of black consciousness.[18]

Her independent, focused search for knowledge and understanding about black nationalism, black culture, and the ongoing quest for freedom among black people was empowering in that it caused her to look inward and resolve some of the conflicts she felt as a "light-brown skinned" woman. It also allowed her to look outward and appreciate such signs of black consciousness among African-Americans in New York as African dress and natural hairstyles. As a result of this consciousness raising, she began "to feel completely black for the first time." Three years later Nicholas said of this period in her process of self-discovery: "I call that winter, that anniversary of Malcolm's death, my first rebirth. Some of us call it 'instant' blackness; but when I think about it, that's hanging a pejorative tag on something that is very real, and very valuable. I don't think when it comes, it's a sign that you should throw your brain and your rationality in the river; it's just consciousness, touch, awareness."[19]

Nicholas's role in the FST shifted as a result of this period of empowerment and self-discovery; it also precipitated the end of her marriage to Gilbert Moses. At first the husband and wife worked together as the leaders of the effort to make the integrated FST a black theater. Some of the problems they encountered as they attempted to become black nationalists within the context of the FST were caused by their ambivalence about ousting the white members of FST who were close friends. The initiative also was stymied by the fact that Moses was not comfortable in the role of black nationalist and was still unclear about the kind of theater he wanted to lead.[20] Despite the challenge, Nicholas was committed to developing a black theater and instituting changes in the theater that reflected her emerging black consciousness.

By the spring of 1966, Nicholas's role in the FST was similar to that of Doris Derby's two years earlier in the conceptual phase of the theater. At crucial points in the development of the theater, both women were ready to take whatever practical steps were necessary to make the FST relevant to the lives of African-Americans in the South. For Derby an important part of that goal was keeping the theater in Mississippi, in touch with the pulse of the civil rights movement and in tune with black people of the rural South. For Nicholas it meant keeping the theater in step with the black consciousness movement and in tune with the black people of Desire, a public housing project in New Orleans.

This first attempt to make the FST a black institution failed, and the marriage of Nicholas and Moses was a casualty of the struggle. The marriage had begun to disintegrate as Nicholas began to have a clearer sense of herself and the role she wanted to play to advance the black consciousness movement. "I think Gilbert saw me as pliable someone he could mold," Nicholas said almost twenty years later. "I think a lot of directors see actresses that way. And that was fine until I got strong enough to resist it; and as soon as I started resisting it and having my own self in the theater then that was over."[21]

Before the end of 1966, Moses left the theater to find himself and clarify his artistic and political orientation. Nicholas remained, determined to create

Denise Nicholas and Joseph Perry in *Does Man Help Man*, Bethel Lutheran Church, New Orleans, August, 1966.
[Photo: *Robert Analauage*]

within the FST a library and information center to enlighten and empower young African-Americans in the black community of New Orleans.

Planning and operating what was called the Afro-American/African Information Center in the FST in the summer of 1966 marked a significant point in Nicholas's process of self-discovery and empowerment. She consciously chose a role based on her personal history as a black female veteran of the civil rights movement and based on the lessons she had recently learned about the collective history and culture of African-Americans. Beyond that, the project helped to clarify Nicholas's ideas about her long-range role and the contributions she thought she could make to the African-American quest for empowerment.

Nicholas's project was, at first, fulfilling and energizing for it provided her with the opportunity to reinforce her own development as she attempted to instill in black children of the community the attitude of confidence, defiance and pride she had acquired as a disciple of the black consciousness movement. "I wanted to see little children walk with their heads high, reading Negro history, understanding fully this bind Whitey put us in," she explained a few years later.[22]

By the end of the year, however, Nicholas's intense, practical work with the information center had drained and disillusioned her. She felt stymied because the role of community worker she had assigned to herself inhibited her personal growth. She had reached a stage in her development when her new independent "self" required both a different form of expression and a new arena.

> For me after that nationalistic mood that we went through a lot of the adventure went out of what we were doing and all of a sudden it became good old-fashioned community work in the unglamorous [sic] sense. I had run out of feeling for it. I had absorbed an extraordinary amount, not just as an artist, but as a human being, from the experiences in the South. I got tired, I got burned out, and I lost the love of the environment I was in. I stopped caring about it.[23]

Working with the information center made Nicholas realize the importance of acting in her life. She left the FST and New Orleans early in 1967 for a role in a play in New York. Her break with the FST was not so much a retreat from activism as it was an embracing of herself, her desires, her aspirations. Over the succeeding years, Nicholas has attempted to reconcile her desire to be both an actress and a contributor to the empowerment of African-Americans by choosing roles that reflect her black consciousness.

Conclusion

The experiences of Doris Derby and Denise Nicholas in the civil rights movement represent two of the many roads African-American women have traversed in their efforts to empower themselves and advance black people's ongoing struggle for social change. While Derby's involvement in the movement as an educator, organizer, administrator and artist was a continuation of roles she had defined for herself early in life, Nicholas's involvement in movement activities launched her on a process of self-discovery and empowerment that eventually allowed her to choose an acting career as the most appropriate role for her.

The roles each woman played behind the scenes and on the frontlines of the movement while involved with the FST validate the idea that African-American women contribute most to their own development and the development of African America when they step out of roles defined for them by black men and step into roles informed by both their personal experiences and an appreciation of their racial heritage. For Derby her experience in the Free Southern Theater affirmed her decisions to contribute to the movement by creating and implementing educational and community programs in Mississippi. Her decade of work in Mississippi, in turn, provided a strong foundation for her current work as a director of the Minority Information Center for the University of Wisconsin system. For Nicholas the Theater provided an intense training ground that has enriched her life and informed her career in theater, television, and film.

NOTES

1. Telephone interview with Doris Derby, January 12, 1987.
2. *Ibid.*
3. *Ibid.*
4. *Ibid.*
5. *Ibid.* See also Thomas C. Dent, Richard Schechner, and Gilbert Moses, *The Free Southern Theater by the Free Southern Theater* (New York: Bobbs-Merrill, 1969), pp. 3-7.

6. Interview with John O'Neal, December 12, 1986.
7. Derby interview.
8. *Ibid.* Although Richard Schechner, a drama professor at Tulane University and later a producing director of the FST, attempted to get permission to establish the FST at the university, that plan was dashed by Monroe Lippman, then head of the Drama department. Lippman told Schechner that he did not see the benefit of such a theater and that he opposed the conscious mixing of art and politics. [Letter to Richard Schechner from Monroe Lippman, July 2, 1964, Amistad Research Center, FST Papers, roll 4, Box 11, folder 6.]

   For a discussion of the impetus and effects of the FST's move to New Orleans see also Clarissa Myrick-Harris, *Mirror of the Movement: The History of the Free Southern Theater as a Microcosm of the Civil Rights and Black Power Movements, 1963-1978* (Unpublished Dissertation, Emory University, 1988), pp. 32-35.
9. Derby interview.
10. Gilbert Moses discusses this dilemma in *Free Southern Theater*, p. 33. John O'Neal speaks of the conflicts in an interview with the author on December 12, 1986.
11. Derby interview.
12. Interview with Denise Nicholas, January 18, 1987.
13. *Ibid.*
14. *Ibid.*
15. *Ibid.*
16. *Ibid.*
17. Denise Nicholas, "A Chapter in the Etymology of the Word Negro," in *The Free Southern Theater*, pp. 181-85.
18. *Ibid.*
19. *Ibid.*
20. These challenges and contradictions are discussed in *The Free Southern Theater*, pp. 93-102 and in the author's dissertation *Mirror of the Movement: The History of the Free Southern Theater*, pp. 85-89.
21. Nicholas interview.
22. *The Free Southern Theater*, pp. 184-85.
23. Nicholas interview.

A Reluctant but Persistent Warrior: Eleanor Roosevelt and the Early Civil Rights Movement

ALLIDA M. BLACK

Eleanor Roosevelt was not always a champion of civil rights. For most of her life, she counseled moderation to those activists who attacked the system instead of the mentality behind it. Yet, once aroused to the racial abuses blacks suffered at the hands of American democracy, Roosevelt reluctantly but persistently confronted this undemocratic behavior and called it by its rightful name. As she continued to grow as an individual, her insight into this "American dilemma" increased. No other noted white American spoke out so consistently, so eloquently, and so brazenly on this issue or encountered such vicious public ridicule for this stand. Consequently, by the time of her death in 1962, Martin Luther King, Jr., could write, "The courage she displayed in taking sides of matters considered controversial, gave strength to those who risked only pedestrian loyalty and commitment to the great issues of our times."[1]

This does not imply, however, that Roosevelt always agreed with civil rights activists or endorsed their tactics. Rather, from the 1930s through the early 1960s, black activists knew that they could trust her commitment to racial equality, her financial support to civil rights organizations, and her outspoken and honest responses to their questions and tactics. Whether serving on the National NAACP Board of Directors, financially contributing to CORE, addressing the Southern Conference on Human Welfare, supporting the black students of Little Rock's Central High School, or campaigning tirelessly for an antilynching bill, Eleanor Roosevelt consistently acted out her commitment and challenged others to do the same. As she aged, her attitudes changed, but she did not grow conservative. She may not have done what everyone wanted her to do—for example, she did not push for a civil rights plank in the Democratic Platform as hard as civil rights activists wished—but after the 1956 campaign, she realized that Adlai Stevenson's stance on the issue was equivocal and she questioned whether another candidate should take his place. When John Kennedy called on her in 1960, she spent the most of the interview grilling him on his position on civil rights issues. In May 1962, just a few months before her death, she chaired the Commission of Inquiry into the Administration of Justice in the Freedom Struggle and attacked those who attacked civil rights workers in the South.

Nor was she silenced by death. In *Tomorrow Is Now*, published posthumously, Eleanor Roosevelt wrote, "it is today that we must create the future of the world." After praising the courage of those involved in the Southern freedom struggle, she compared American racists to European fascists:

> And here, too, emerged another and unmistakable similarity to the Nazism we had believed destroyed. . . . Most of the dictators of the West—Franco, Mussolini, Hitler—claimed that they were "saving" their lands from the threat of Communism. Today, as I have learned over and over to my cost, one needs only to be outspoken about the unfair treatment of the Negro to be labeled "Communist." I had regarded such expression to be the only honorable and civilized course of a citizen of the United States.[2]

The course Roosevelt took to reach this position was fraught with personal struggles, limitations, and political constraints. Yet once she reached a decision, she acted despite the consequences. Sometimes, a public injustice prompted a response. Other times, it was an appeal from unknown individuals who spurred action behind the scenes. I will focus on two of her early decisions—her resignation from the DAR in support of Marian Anderson and her intervention on behalf of Pauli Murray and Odell

Waller—and how they reflect Eleanor Roosevelt's public and private commitment to civil rights.

In 1939, Washington, D.C., like most major urban areas, was a segregated city. Yet it was an erratic form of segregation in which the district government haphazardly enforced the local separatist ordinances. Although the Organic Law of 1906 mandated a dual school system for black and white students, the D.C. School Board relaxed those standards in social situations. White universities and biracial community associations regularly used the recreation facilities and auditoriums of black public schools. Black labor organizations often conducted their meetings in assembly halls of white religious and labor organizations. District citizens frequently overlooked Jim Crow customs when they attended the theater, the symphony, or a public lecture. Consequently, throughout the 1920s and 1930s, black and white patrons integrated the audiences of numerous concerts staged at both federal auditoriums and private concert halls.[3]

This elasticized form of segregation operated fairly smoothly until January 8, 1939, when Howard University School of Music applied to the Daughters of the American Revolution for use of their auditorium, Constitution Hall, by the world-renowned contralto Marian Anderson. Unbeknownst to all initially involved in this application, this request, the subsequent struggle to lease appropriate concert space, and the concert itself merged to become the major event in the civil rights legacy of the New Deal, a pivotal battle in the campaign to end Jim Crow social practices in the nation's capital, and a crucial test of Eleanor Roosevelt's political judgment.

In 1936, after a triumphant European tour, a stunning performance at the Salzberg Music Festival, and a concert for the Roosevelts that Eleanor Roosevelt praised in her daily *My Day* column, Anderson's manager, Sol Hurok, advised his client to focus less on her European following and concentrate instead on her American tour. Following his advice, the contralto devoted 1938 and 1939 to appearances in the finest auditoriums before integrated audiences across the country, receiving rave reviews from the Atlanta, New York, Boston, St. Louis, San Francisco, New Orleans, and Memphis press. Equally praised for her talent and her poise, Anderson crossed the color line and began establishing a devoted biracial following throughout the United States.[4]

As part of her 1936 tour, Anderson had accepted Howard University's request for a benefit performance for their School of Music. For over a decade the University Concert Series had sponsored performances by renowned artists of both races as cultural gesture to the District and as a minor fundraising tool for the University. Marian Anderson's three performances prior to 1939 were the highlights of the series and drew successively larger integrated crowds, which forced the university to seek new concert space. By 1938, the eleven-hundred-seat auditorium of Armstrong High School could not accommodate all the requests for tickets to Anderson's concert and the university rented the larger Rialto Theatre. Although Armstrong High School and the Rialto Theatre were black facilities, the audience for all Anderson's concerts was predominantly white. Therefore, in 1939 when the Rialto was in receivership and Anderson's popularity was steadily increasing, the concert series had to find another, larger location for its most popular annual event.[5]

Constitution Hall was the preeminent auditorium in Washington. Built in 1929 by the DAR to house its national headquarters and host its national conventions, the hall's four thousand seats made it the largest auditorium in the district. The National DAR Board "authorized almost immediately" public use of the hall for "a minimum cost as a tangible contribution to life in the Nation's Capital." As home to the National Symphony Orchestra, the Washington Opera, and the National Geographic Society, Constitution Hall served as the focal point in the district for classical music and international culture. And it was the only hall in the nation's capital comparable to those in which Marian Anderson appeared in other cities around the nation and throughout the world.[6]

Constitution Hall was the only logical stage for the concert. On January 9, Charles Cohen, chairman of the Howard University Concert Series, and V.D. Johnson, university treasurer, applied to the DAR for use of its concert facility on April 9. Fred Hand, manager of Constitution Hall, responded that the hall had a standing policy of not renting concert space to black artists. However, later that day, Hand told the press that Marian Anderson could not perform in Constitution Hall because the date requested had been booked a year earlier by the National Symphony Orchestra and DAR regulations prohibit rental of the hall for two engagements on the same day.

Actions were immediately taken to appeal to the DAR for reconsideration. V.D. Johnson contacted Charles Houston, special counsel to the NAACP as well as a Howard University board member. Houston advised Johnson to inform the press about the dilemma and to request letters of support from Anderson's peers. After requesting such endorsements, the university contacted the Washington press, describing the DAR's restrictive policy.

Eleanor Roosevelt's staunch support helped Highlander Folk School survive accusations of communism in the 1940s and 1950s, while it evolved from a labor school to a center of civil rights education. She is shown here speaking at Highlander, with Myles Horton (the founder of the school) and May Justus. [Photo: *State Historical Society of Wisconsin*]

Within a day after the requests were mailed, such leading performers as Geraldine Farrar, Kirsten Flagstad, Lawrence Tibbet, Walter Damrosh, and Leopold Stokowski telegraphed their disapproval to the DAR. The Washington press, however, was slower to respond. *The Washington Post* ran an editorial expressing dismay at the DAR's action but stopping short of calling for its reversal. *The Washington Star* ignored the issue until February 1. Only *The Washington Afro-American* and *The Washington Times-Herald* challenged the DAR's decision and called on Congress to build a federal auditorium in the District that would be free of racial discrimination.[7]

Action intensified on all fronts the following week. Assured by Anderson's manager Sol Hurok that Constitution Hall was available April 8 and April 10, Johnston and Cohen reapplied to Hand. The DAR again refused permission, this time stating no reason. Howard concert officials appealed the decision. On January 16, in New York City, the Spingarn Committee of the NAACP met and unanimously voted to present its most prestigious award to Anderson for "her special contributions in the field of music . . . and her magnificent dignity as a human being." In Washington, Charles Houston suggested that a community meeting be called to discuss the Anderson ban and to propose alternative strategies, and Walter White, secretary of the NAACP, called on Eleanor Roosevelt to ask her to present the Spingarn Medal to Anderson at the National NAACP conference in July. Roosevelt gladly accepted.[8]

Three days later, Howard University applied to the Community Center Department for permission to use Central High School Auditorium for the April 9 event. The petition was referred for review to the Committee on the Use of Public Buildings of the District Board of Education. As Central High School was a white school, the committee recommended that Superintendent of Schools Frank Ballou decline the request and recommend the use of Armstrong Auditorium instead. Press coverage increased and Howard, through Johnston and Houston, asked prominent Washingtonians to lobby the DAR on its behalf. Interior Secretary Harold Ickes, Agriculture Secretary Henry Wallace, several members of Congress, and Washington Cathedral Canon Anson Phelps Stokes responded to the university's request.[9]

Thus, by February, public pressure mounted. Nevertheless, despite requests from Anderson's agents to book the hall for any date available the first two weeks of April, Constitution Hall continued to ban Anderson from its stage. On February 13, the president general of the DAR, Mrs. H. M. Roberts, Jr., mailed a communique on the matter to her state regents, informing them that "the rules [of the DAR] are in accordance with the policy of theatres, auditoriums, hotels and public schools of the District of Columbia." Two days later, Fred Hand informed Charles Cohen, "the hall is not available for a concert by Miss Anderson."[10] There could be no appeal. Anderson would have to find space elsewhere in the District.

Community response was swift and effective. On February 17, Johnston called a citywide meeting to discuss the board's refusal and to plan the counterattack. By the next day, local organizations were adopting resolutions protesting both the DAR and the School Board's actions. Jascha Heifetz denounced the DAR from the Constitution Hall stage, saying he was ashamed to be on "a stage barred to a great singer because of her race." That same evening, five blocks away, Charles Edward Russell, a liberal white attorney, chaired an interracial gathering that agreed to circulate petitions urging the use of Central High School Auditorium. This audience, formally incorporating itself as the Marian Anderson Citizens Committee (MACC), adopted a resolution instructing its interim officers to request permission to present the petitions to the School Board at its March 1 meeting. By February 22, the MACC was front-page news in the District and the national press roundly criticized the board's decision.[11]

Four days later, as the MACC reconvened to assemble the thirty-five hundred signatures it collected on its petition, Eleanor Roosevelt debated which action to take on Anderson's behalf. Howard University had been lobbying the first lady since the beginning of February to issue a public statement rebuking the DAR, but Roosevelt refused, arguing that such a statement would do no good, as the organization "considered [her] to be too radical." Besides, she told two friends, "she would like to make a statement . . . [but] this situation is so bad that plenty of people will come out against it." This refusal, however, did not mean that Roosevelt sat idly along the sidelines. She carefully mapped a strategy, planning a forceful rebuttal to the snubbing Anderson received in the nation's capital.[12]

Roosevelt was not hiding behind the curtain of public opinion. Her position on race was already well known. Immediately after the DAR's initial refusal to Anderson, Eleanor Roosevelt agreed to present the Spingarn Medal to the diva, met with NAACP secretary Walter White and conference chair Dr. Elizabeth Yates Webb to discuss the broadcast of the awards ceremony, planned to invite Anderson to perform for the British king and queen at the White House in June, and telegraphed her support to Howard University.[13]

The strategical problem for Roosevelt was how to support Anderson without upstaging the local community or further angering the powerful Southern Democrats. Initially, she decided to refrain from direct action and to participate only peripherally in the campaign. On February 20, less than a week after Anderson's appeals to the DAR and the School Board were rejected, Roosevelt mentioned Anderson in her column for the first time. Yet, on February 25, she denied a request from V. D. Johnston to criticize the DAR in her weekly press conferences. However, the following day, she did respond to the MACC request for telegrams in support of the proposed concert. Clearly, Roosevelt did not sidestep the problem. She publicly committed herself to the black performer while she tried to find the most effective way to implement that commitment.

By the end of the week, Roosevelt concluded that for maximum impact her actions must be seen as a response to a national, rather than local, issue. Consequently, the National Society of the Daughters of the American Revolution and not the District of Columbia School Board should be the focus of the rebuttal. Having taken steps to insure Anderson's eventual performance in the District and having carefully limited her association with the local groups appealing a local political decision, Eleanor Roosevelt remained free to act as an individual member of an organization responding to a decision made by that body's leadership. This masterful political strategy resounded with long-range political and public policy implications. Consequently, when Eleanor Roosevelt determined to act as an individual outside the locale directly affected by the policy, she expanded its focus from one of local leasing policies to one of national social import.

More significant than the overt actions Roosevelt took behind the scenes to facilitate Anderson's appearance in the district was the pivotal role she played in highlighting the discriminatory conduct of such a prestigious organization as the DAR. The power of understatement displayed in her *My Day* column of February 28, 1939, revealed Roosevelt's hand on the pulse of the nation. She began her column with the standard account of her social duties of the day before, rather than immediately discussing the controversy. Yet even after introducing her real topic, she refrained from naming the issue or the organization that had caused her distress.

This tactic clearly portrayed the situation in impersonal, nonthreatening terms with which the majority of her readers would identify. She introduced the dilemma simply: "I have been debating in my mind for some time a question which I have had to debate with myself once or twice before in my life. Usually, I have decided differently from the way in which I am deciding now." She then outlined the problem and her response to it:

> The question is, if you belong to an organization and disapprove of an action which is typical of a policy, shall you resign or is it better to work for a changed point of view within the organization? In the past when I was able to work actively in any organization to which I had belonged, I have usually stayed in until I had at least made a fight and been defeated.
>
> Even then I have as a rule accepted my defeat and decided either that I was wrong or that I was perhaps a little too far ahead of the thinking of the majority of that time. I have often found that the thing in which I was interested was done some years later. But, in this case I belong to an organization in which I do no active work. They have taken an action which has been widely talked of in the press. To remain as a member implies approval of that action, therefore I am resigning.[14]

The next day, the column splashed across the front pages of American newspapers from San Francisco to New York City. Although others had resigned from the DAR over this issue, and although major public figures had publicly lamented the DAR policy, Eleanor Roosevelt placed Marian Anderson, the DAR, and racial discrimination on a national stage where it could not be ignored. By putting her political clout and personal popularity squarely behind Anderson and in front of the DAR, she moved the conflict into another arena.

On Monday, March 25, that support was formalized. The White House staff entered the battle. Assistant Secretary of the Interior Oscar Chapman presented Walter White's request to use the Lincoln Memorial to Interior Secretary Ickes. Ickes, a past president of the Chicago NAACP, phoned Franklin Roosevelt and requested an immediate appointment. Roosevelt, who was preparing to leave town that afternoon, delayed his plans and agreed to see the Interior official. When informed of Ickes's request, the president responded, "I don't care if she sings from the top of Washington Monument as long as she sings." Ickes called an afternoon press conference and announced that the Lincoln Memorial would be the site of the April 9 concert.[15]

Once again the Anderson affair made the front pages of newspapers around the country. The struggle to find appropriate space for a world-famous artist outweighed the personal bias of certain members of the press corps toward black civil rights in general and the NAACP in particular. Only the perennial Roosevelt baiter Westbrook Pegler was less than enthusiastic about the sudden turn in events.[16]

The NAACP launched a campaign to assemble as diverse a group of prominent cosponsors for the event as possible. Although Eleanor Roosevelt was the immediate first choice for chairing the event, she was not in Washington and recognized that she would upstage Anderson if she were to sponsor the event. So her close friend, Congresswoman Caroline O'Day, stepped in to assist the coordination of endorsements. Telegrams asking assistance "in sponsoring an open-air free concert by Marian Anderson under the auspices of Howard University from the Steps of the Lincoln Memorial . . . at 5 P.M., Sunday, April 9" were sent to over five hundred people. By the next day, responses were flooding O'Day's office.[17]

By Easter Sunday, over three hundred prominent individuals had agreed to sponsor the event. The concert had become a national cause celebre. The DAR had been rebuked throughout the three-month campaign to stage the event, but the racial policy implications had been virtually ignored. If the event was to effect the change that the NAACP and some MACC members desired, the concert must be viewed in cultural, political, and racial terms. Few who realized the long-range implications of the event had the stature and wide-range popularity to achieve this success. Eleanor Roosevelt had both. Consequently, she was charged with carrying the mantle into the public fray. By inviting Anderson to sing for the king and queen of Britain and agreeing to present Anderson the Spingarn Medal in the midst of the controversy, Roosevelt clearly indicated to the public she intended to stay the course.

Eleanor Roosevelt kept her word and presented the Spingarn Medal to Marian Anderson at the NAACP convention in Richmond. There she delivered a nationally broadcast address urging her audience to protect democracy actively, to insure "the ability of every individual to be a really valuable citizen," and to strive to secure "whatever rights of citizenship are ours under the Constitution." By unabashedly associating herself as a primary power source behind the concert, by allowing herself to be photographed sitting next to black political and social leaders on stage of the NAACP national convention on Independence weekend in a stronghold of Southern conservatism, Roosevelt made the event overtly political two months after Anderson's final encore.[18]

The Marian Anderson venture taught Eleanor Roosevelt a valuable lesson. In 1939, she was just beginning to use *My Day* as her own political forum.

The Marian Anderson controversy and the response it generated from her readers showed Roosevelt the direct impact she had when she spoke out on a political event. She received more mail supporting her resignation from the DAR than she did on any other issue she associated herself with in 1939. Consequently, this experience reinforced Mrs. Roosevelt's venture into the politics of confrontation.

Not all of Mrs. Roosevelt's actions were so public. Or so effective.

In November 1938, Franklin Roosevelt went to the University of North Carolina to receive an honorary doctor of law degree. FDR used the occasion to address those present on the need for social change. "There is change whether we will it or not," the president argued, and all citizens must recognize that the "affirmative action which we have taken in America" is the "maintenance of a successful democracy at home." The president ended his address by praising the college for "typifying as it does American liberal thought and American tradition."

When Pauli Murray read FDR's address in *The New York Times* the following day, she was outraged. Having just applied to graduate school and been rejected by the institution the president praised for its liberalism, Murray wrote the president a stinging rebuttal.

> Yesterday, you placed your liberal approval on the University of North Carolina as an institution of liberal thought. You spoke of the necessity of change in a body of law to meet the problems of an accelerated era of civilization. You called on Americans to support a liberal philosophy based on democracy. What does this mean for Negro Americans? Does it mean that we, at last, may participate freely . . . with our fellow citizens in working out the problems of this democracy? . . . Or does it mean that everything you said has no meaning for us as Negroes, that again we are to be set aside and passed over for more important problems? . . . Do you feel, as we do, that the ultimate test of democracy in the United States will be the way in which it solves its Negro problem?[19]

Despite her misgivings about Eleanor Roosevelt's reluctance to condemn racial segregation, Pauli Murray mailed the first lady a copy of her letter to the president. To her surprise, she received a reply signed by Eleanor Roosevelt herself.

> I have read the copy of the letter you sent me and I understand perfectly, but great change comes slowly. I think they are coming, however, and sometimes it is better to fight hard with conciliatory methods. The South is

changing, but don't push too hard. There is great change in youth, for instance, and that is a hopeful sign.[20]

Both women shared the same goal but differed over the methods used to achieve a democratic society. A few weeks before writing this letter, Eleanor Roosevelt electrified black and white Americans by refusing to comply with the Birmingham segregation ordinances when she attended the Southern Conference for Human Welfare. Pauli Murray was well aware of this when she sent her letter to Roosevelt. Consequently, Roosevelt's admonition, "don't push too hard," was even more difficult for her to accept.

Nevertheless, Murray was impressed that the first lady took the time to acknowledge her frustration. When Murray heard Roosevelt's radio address on behalf of domestic workers, she again wrote the White House urging recognition of the basic human rights of black Americans. Again, Eleanor Roosevelt responded. Only this time, instead of replying directly to Pauli Murray she published part of the woman's letter in her national column.[21] This correspondence started an almost thirty-year friendship between the young black activist and scholar and Eleanor Roosevelt—a friendship that was as blunt and outspoken and committed as the two women were to the causes they espoused.

Although Roosevelt responded to a plea from Murray's sister when Murray was arrested in Virginia for challenging Jim Crow seating ordinances and called the judge involved on Murray's behalf, the two women did not meet until January 1940, when Roosevelt invited Murray to her New York apartment to discuss Murray's plans for National Sharecroppers Week. Impressed with Murray's presentation and well aware of the issues involved, Roosevelt agreed to be the keynote speaker for the conference and donated one hundred dollars to the campaign.[22]

But Roosevelt's efforts on behalf of sharecroppers were just beginning. Not all her actions were as public as this speech and contribution. Nor were they as effective as intervention on behalf of Marian Anderson. But they were nonetheless heartfelt.

In August 1940, Odell Waller, a black sharecropper from Virginia, was convicted by an all-white jury (a jury from which blacks had been excluded via the poll tax requirement) of the first-degree murder of Oscar Davis, his white landlord. Waller was sentenced to death. Pauli Murray was sent to investigate the case for the Worker's Defense League. Eleanor Roosevelt asked Murray to keep her informed.

Despite a nationwide campaign on Waller's behalf and appeals to the state courts, the death sentence stood. The Supreme Court refused to hear the case because the defense had failed to offer specific proof that those who did not pay the poll tax were excluded from jury service. The only way for Waller's sentence to be changed was for Governor Darden to commute it to life imprisonment. The governor agreed to postpone execution until all avenues for appeal were exhausted. When the Supreme Court refused to hear the case, a date for Waller's execution was set.[23]

To Roosevelt the parallels between the jury system Waller encountered and lynching were unmistakable. She wrote A. M. Kroeger, "Times without number Negro men have been lynched or gone to their death without due process of law. No one questions Waller's guilt, but they question the system which led to it." Responding to appeals from Murray, the NAACP, and A. Philip Randolph, Eleanor Roosevelt launched a one-person crusade within the White House to have the sentence commuted. First, she called Governor Darden and pleaded the case. When that proved unsuccessful, she persistently dogged the president to write the governor requesting commutation. Finally, FDR acquiesced and wrote Darden.[24]

On the day of Waller's execution, Eleanor Roosevelt still would not let up. She phoned Harry Hopkins, the president's closest advisor, four or five times. FDR believed that since the governor had given reprieves while Waller appealed, he had acted constitutionally and "doubted very much if the merits of the case warranted the Governor reaching any other decision." This did not deter the first lady, as this memorandum from Harry Hopkins shows:

> Mrs. Roosevelt, however, would not take no for an answer and the President finally got on the phone himself and told Mrs. Roosevelt that under no circumstances would he intervene with the Governor and urged very strongly that she say nothing about it. . . .
> I think, too, in this particular case Mrs. Roosevelt felt that I was not pressing her case with the President adequately, because in the course of the evening he was not available on the phone and I had to act as a go-between. At any rate I felt that she would not be satisfied until the President told her himself, which he reluctantly but finally did.[25]

Two hours before Waller was to be executed, a dejected Eleanor Roosevelt phoned A. Philip Randolph at NAACP headquarters. As Waller's supporters listened to her over five extensions, Roosevelt in a trembling voice informed Randolph: "I have done everything I can possibly do. I have interrupted the President twice. . . . He said this is a matter of law and not of the heart. It is in Governor Darden's jurisdiction and the President has no legal power to intervene. I am so sorry, Mr. Randolph, I can't do any more."[26] At 8:30 A.M., July 2, despite all the efforts on his behalf, Odell Waller was executed.

Eleanor Roosevelt was an extremely powerful person. Yet there were limits to her power. In the cases discussed, her husband was the ultimate power. Not because he was the husband and she the wife, but because Franklin Roosevelt was the president of the United States. The challenge Eleanor Roosevelt confronted on a daily basis from 1932 to 1945 was how to use her influence and her clout to the maximum, how to use her power in her own right. In the same memo in which Hopkins described Roosevelt's efforts on behalf of Odell Waller, he characterized her actions as "typical of the things that have gone on in Washington between the President and Mrs. Roosevelt since 1932."[27]

Once free of the constraints of the White House, Eleanor Roosevelt continued to protest injustice and demand that democracy be practiced without any limits or qualifications.

Her genius lay in her ability to know when to take a symbolic stance in favor of or in protest against an act (as she did in the Marian Anderson affair) and when to apply constant pressure behind the scenes to reach a particular end. Whether confronting the DAR, arguing strategy with Pauli Murray, or pressing the case of those denied justice, Eleanor Roosevelt had the courage of her convictions. She was not afraid to take a stand or face the consequences that stand might arouse. If she was too idealistic in her belief in education as the cure to evils of racism or too reluctant completely to endorse nonviolent resistance as a means to end injustice, she nevertheless realistically confronted the evils of a racist society and devoted her energies to defeating them.

Shortly before her death, Eleanor Roosevelt wrote: "One thing we must all do. We must cherish and honor the word *free* or it will cease to apply to us. And that would be an inconceivable situation."[28] It is to her everlasting credit that throughout her life, Eleanor Roosevelt practiced what she preached.

NOTES

The author wishes to thank the Eleanor and Franklin Roosevelt Institute for funding this research as well as Leo Ribuffo, Helen Veit, Charlene Bickford, Kenneth Bowling and Wendy Wolff for their encouragement and insightful critcism.

1. *Amsterdam News*, November 24, 1962, p. 1.
2. Eleanor Roosevelt, *Tomorrow Is Now* (New York: Harper & Row, 1963), epigraph and p. 52.
3. Harry S. Wender, "An Analysis of Recreation and Segregation in the District of Columbia," (Washington, D.C.: District of Columbia Board of Education, May 1949), pp. 3-11; Gunnar Myrdal, *An American Dilemma* (New York: Harper & Row, 1944), pp. 630-31.
4. For reviews of Anderson's appearances in these cities, see: "It Happened in Memphis," *The Washington News*, April 4, 1939; "Marian Anderson Here for Concert," *The Atlanta Constitution*, April 5, 1939, p. 23; Mozelle Horton Young, "Marian Anderson Thrills 6000 with Rich Voice in Concert Here," *The Atlanta Constitution*, April 6, 1939, p. 13; E. Clyde Whitlock, "Marian Anderson Near Top In Signing Appeal: Negro Contralto Who Appears Here Sunday has Few Rivals in Audience Demand," *The Fort Worth Morning Star-Telegram*, March 12, 1939; "Marian Anderson to be honored in City Tonight," *The New York Daily Worker*, April 18, 1939. See also the following uncited, untitled New York City newspaper articles from the Martin Luther King Library, Washington Collection, Washington, D.C.: " 'I fell downstairs on the Ile de France and broke a bone in my foot and when I gave a recital at the Town Hall I had to give it standing on one foot,' said Marian Anderson"; "Marian Anderson, who has recently been achieving astonishing success abroad appeared tonight for the first time since her return to this country December 23;" and "The steel band of prejudice which has held back allusions to the beauty of Negro women by the New York white press has been broken." See also the press references for Eleanor Roosevelt's resignation from the DAR. For more information on Anderson's White House appearance, see Joseph P. Lash, *Eleanor and Franklin* (New York: W.W. Norton, 1971), p. 684.
5. Various articles mention the dates of different events. For a brief chronology of the struggle for concert space, see Carleton Smith, "Roulades and Cadenzas: Summing up l'affaire Anderson," *Esquire*, July 1939, pp. 79, 167-68. For other individual incidents, see "Ickes Comes to Aid of Colored Singer in Controversy," *The Washington Evening Star*, March 7, 1939; "The Anderson Episode," *The New York Times*, editorial, February 21, 1939; press releases of the Marian Anderson Citizens Committee, March 9, 1939, and their letters to the Board of Education of the District of Columbia of the same date.
6. For discussion of the purpose and history of Constitution Hall, see Martha Strayer, *The DAR: An Informal History* (New York: Greenwood Press, 1958), chaps. 1, 7; National Society of the Daughters of the American Revolution, *In*

Washington: The National Society of the Daughters of the American Revolution Diamond Anniversary (Washington, D.C.: NSDAR, 1965).

7. See articles cited in note 5. See also Marian Anderson Citizens Committee, "Chronology: Marian Anderson Concert Case," group 1, box 2, folder 35, Moorland-Spingarn Research Center, Howard University; John Lovell, "May we have return wire expression from you for mass meeting tomorrow protesting . . .," telegram, n.d. List of names wire sent to attached to telegram draft, Marian Anderson Controversy Collection, collection 1, box 2, folder 35. For press coverage, see "Joins Protest Against Ban on Marian Anderson" and "Opera Stars Protest Marian Anderson Ban," *The Washington Star*, January 31, 1939; "The Anderson Episode," *The Washington Post*, February 21, 1939; "Ban Maintained at Constitution Hall by DAR," *The Washington Afro-American*," January 21, 1939, p. 1.

8. See Anderson Citizens Committee, "Chronology"; John Lovell to Eleanor Roosevelt, February 25, 1939, Eleanor Roosevelt Papers, Series 100, Personal Correspondence, 1939, box 1512; "Press Release—24th Spingarn Medal to Marian Anderson," NAACP Papers, Section I, Administrative Files, box C-214; Walter White to Marian Anderson, January 21, 1939, NAACP Papers, Administrative Files, box C-24; Walter White to Eleanor Roosevelt, January 16, 1939, Eleanor Roosevelt Papers, Miscellaneous Correspondence, 1939, box 1532.

9. See Anderson Citizens Committee, "Chronology"; For information on the School Board petition, see Charles Cohen et al. to District of Columbia Board of Education, February 15, 1939, Marian Anderson Controversy Collection, Collection 1, box 1, folder 21; "Statement on Application for the Use of Central High School Auditorium for a Recital by Marian Anderson," February 16, 1939, box 2, folder 38; Frank W. Ballou, "Statement on the Application for the Use of Central High School . . .," February 28, 1939. See Wallace, Ickes, and Stokes, telegrams in Marian Anderson Controversy Collection, box 2, folder 36.

10. See Smith, "Roulades and Cadenzas," and other articles cited in note 5.

11. For a list of sponsors of the Marian Anderson Citizens Committee, see their press release dated March 9, 1939, Marian Anderson Controversy Collection, box 2, folder 38. "Heifetz, Ashamed D.C. Hall is Denied Marian Anderson," *The Washington Post*, February 20, 1939, p. 1; "Ban on Anderson Attacked by 6000," *Washington Daily News*, February 27, 1939, p. 1.

12. V.D. Johnston to Eleanor Roosevelt, February 4, 1939, and Eleanor Roosevelt to V.D. Johnston, February 9, 1939, Eleanor Roosevelt Papers, Series 100, box 1507; John Lovell, Jr., to Eleanor Roosevelt, February 25, 1939, box 1512; Eleanor Roosevelt to Wilbur La Roe, Jr., February 25, 1939, box 1509.

13. See Eleanor Roosevelt to John Lovell, Jr., February 26, 1939, Eleanor Roosevelt Papers, White House Telegrams, box 2995.

14. "My Day," February 26, 1939, Eleanor Roosevelt Papers, My Day, box 3073.

15. Harold L. Ickes, *The Diary of Harold Ickes*, entry for March 30, 1939, Library of Congress. Charles Houston to Gerald Goode, April 1, 1939, and Walter

White to Charles Houston and V.D. Johnston, March 31, 1939, Marian Anderson Controversy Collection, box 1, folder 1.

16. For examples of press response, see "Anderson Supporters Unsatisfied by Plan for Open-Air Concert," *The Washington Star*, April 1, 1939; "DAR's Ban Upset; She'll Sing Easter," *The New York Daily News*, March 31, 1939; "Anderson to Rise on Easter," *The Norfolk Journal and Guide*, April 8, 1939, pp. 1, 10; "Concert in Capitol for Marian Anderson," *The New York Times*, March 31, 1939; "Marian Anderson Songs to be Heard a Mile," *The Washington Daily News*, April 4, 1939; "Marian Anderson to Sing at Lincoln Memorial," *Chicago News*, March 30, 1939.

17. For the text of O'Day's telegram, see Caroline O'Day to Eleanor Roosevelt, April 1, 1939, Eleanor Roosevelt Papers, White House Telegrams, 2/39-12/39, box 2995. For list of respondents, see Marian Anderson Controversy Collection, box 1, folder 24.

18. "Mrs. Roosevelt Awards Medal," *The Crisis*, September 1939, p. 265.

19. FDR speech quoted in Pauli Murray, *Song in a Weary Throat* (New York: Harper & Row, 1988), pp. 110-11. Pauli Murray to Franklin Roosevelt, December 19, 1939, attached to Pauli Murray to Eleanor Roosevelt, December 19, 1939, Eleanor Roosevelt Papers, Series 100, Personal Correspondence, box 1517. Pauli Murray, interview by Dr. Thomas Soapes, February 3, 1978, transcript, Eleanor Roosevelt Oral History Project, Franklin D. Roosevelt Library.

20. Eleanor Roosevelt to Pauli Murray, December 19, 1939, Eleanor Roosevelt Papers, series 100, box 1517.

21. Murray, *Song in a Weary Throat*, p. 134.

22. *Ibid.*, p. 135.

23. For a detailed account of Waller's trial, conviction, and appeal, see Murray, *Song in a Weary Throat*, chaps. 13, 14. See also Lash, *Eleanor and Franklin*, pp. 865-66. For accounts of Roosevelt and the NAACP's efforts of Waller's behalf, see Eleanor Roosevelt-Walter White Correspondence for 1940, Eleanor Roosevelt Papers, Walter White folder, Series 100, box 1668.

24. Lash, *Eleanor and Franklin*, pp. 865-66; Murray, *Song in a Weary Throat*, p. 173; Eleanor Roosevelt to A.M. Kroeger, August 20, 1942, Eleanor Roosevelt papers, Personal Correspondence, box 1649. See also Eleanor Roosevelt Papers, Series 190.1. Criticism re: Negro Question, 1942.

25. Quoted in Lash, *Eleanor and Franklin*, pp. 865-66.

26. Quoted in Murray, *Song in a Weary Throat*, p. 173.

27. Lash, *Eleanor and Franklin*, pp. 865-66.

28. Roosevelt, *Tomorrow Is Now*, p. 138.

Methodist Women Integrate Schools and Housing, 1952-1959

ALICE G. KNOTTS

In 1952, one of the largest organizations of women in the United States, the Woman's Division of Christian Service of the Board of Missions of the Methodist Church, began to work toward the goal of integrating public schools. Five years later, the Woman's Division began efforts to integrate housing, in the belief that integrated housing provided the key to integrated public schools and strengthened the foundation of democratic principles in the United States. Over one and one-quarter million strong, these organized women provided grass roots leadership that significantly changed racial attitudes, influenced public policies, and resulted in positive steps toward equality. From the 1920s through the 1940s, they comprised approximately half of the southern women involved in efforts to change race relations, and their influence continued in the 1950s even though they belonged to The Methodist Church, which officially segregated most of its black churches and pastors into one large racially determined Central Jurisdiction.

Methodist women changed attitudes both within their own organization and in their communities: first, they affirmed theological foundations for racial equality; second, they understood and illuminated social problems inherent in segregation; and third, they exercised personal moral influence in local communities. From 1940 to 1968, Thelma Stevens, a white Mississippian who headed the Department of Christian Social Relations, interpreted racial equality and its meaning for Christian life to Methodist women. The life of Jesus provided the standard by which she measured social

251

justice. Just as Jesus had included foreigners and women, sick and sinners, among his followers, Stevens expected Christian women to include people of all races on an equal basis in the daily affairs of life.

In 1952, the Woman's Division adopted its first Charter of Racial Policies, a two-page summary of the rationale for and beliefs about inclusive racial policies and a set of guidelines and objectives by which decisions and actions of the Woman's Division could be assessed.[1] Although the document did not specifically state that the Woman's Division would work for the integration of public schools, it stressed its commitment to open its own schools and hospitals to all people without discrimination and to "build in every area it may touch, a fellowship and social order without racial barriers."[2]

The charter provided the rationale for early efforts in school integration. Occasionally schools run by the Woman's Division quietly accepted a few students of color.[3] Methodist women founded, joined, or lobbied existing Human Relations Councils in numerous locations, including Greensboro and Nashville. Before the Supreme Court issued its decision on school desegregation, the Department of Christian Social Relations challenged Methodist women: "Regardless of what the decision may be, our job is clear. Time marches on! The ground swell of human equality under God is becoming unmistakably the ground swell of human equality under law! . . . We must plant the right seeds."[4] With this premise, Methodist women promised to influence public attitudes.

In 1952 and 1953, Methodist women launched early efforts for school integration based on four recommendations of the Woman's Division. Women should: (1) work through their churches and communities to inform the public about the facts related to segregation; (2) work with community agencies to gather and publicize facts about the facilities, teachers, and resources of public schools with reference to minority racial groups; (3) bring together parents and teachers of various races in order to discuss problems; and (4) work consistently to secure necessary state and federal funds for making available adequate opportunities through public schools to all children without discrimination in any form.[5] Methodist women launched neighborhood conversation groups to talk about public schools and segregation and thus influence local practices.

"Every Methodist woman in the nation has a responsibility directly or indirectly for the public schools of this land," heralded *The Methodist Woman*. Responsibility extended to all aspects of education for all the children of a community. Equal opportunities needed to be interpreted in comprehensive terms, including teachers' salaries, length of the school term, teacher-student ratios, and the number and age of school buses. Arkansas spent $114 per white student and $75 per black student in 1951-52; and other states had similarly disproportionate ratios.[6]

The 1954 quadrennial Assembly of Methodist Women met in Milwaukee, Wisconsin, where the Charter on Racial Policies was presented for ratification by approximately one hundred conference units of the Woman's Society of Christian Service. While the assembly met, the Supreme Court issued its long-awaited decision on school desegregation. Immediately Thelma Stevens and Susie Jones, a Woman's Division member and wife of the president of Bennett College, met and drafted a resolution of support for the Brown v. the Board of Education decision. The resolution, adopted by the assembly, was the first public statement to affirm the court's action.[7] A group of Southern delegates to the assembly gathered to rescind their conferences' support of the charter, but Stevens argued that although not every woman's society would be able to implement every part of the charter, the charter was needed to keep long-range goals before Methodist women. In the end, no conference rescinded the charter.[8] Methodist women left the assembly committed to work for the integration of public schools.

The Woman's Division came under sharp criticism for its stand on school desegregation. Some of its members supported a proposal to "commend those leaders in the several states and the national government who counsel that the time and manner of instituting integrated schools be left to the federal courts in the local communities."[9] The measure was defeated.

The Supreme Court decision freed the Woman's Division from social and legal constraints to move toward integrating the institutions it operated. The Woman's Division announced:

> We welcome this opportunity to expand our program of racial integration in these institutions and expect our schools to stand by, ready to enroll students and to appoint faculty regardless of race or color. We also affirm our intention to accept our full responsibility to work through all available church and community channels to speed the process of transition from segregation to a new pattern of justice and freedom and equality of opportunity.[10]

Public declarations of intent provided backing for specific local changes. One institution owned by the Woman's Division, Scarritt College for Christian Workers, in Nashville, opened its doors to black students when the state law changed to allow white schools to admit blacks in 1952. Other schools and colleges began to appoint nonwhites to their faculties. Edith Carter, the superintendent of Boylan-Haven School, a Methodist school in Jacksonville, Florida, said, "The leaders among the members of the Woman's Society of Christian Service are ready for nonsegregation, I believe."[11] By 1957, Muriel Day was able to report developments in interracial staff appointments at several institutions operated by the Woman's Division. Allen High School, in Asheville, North Carolina, Browning Home and Mather Academy in Camden, South Carolina, Boylan-Haven School, and Harwood Girls' School in Albuquerque had all developed staff arrangements that she described as interracial working relationships.[12]

The Methodist women urged their church to change its discriminatory racial practices. In 1956, the Woman's Division petitioned the General Conference of The Methodist Church to take similar steps by requesting "that the institutions of the church, local churches, colleges, universities, theological schools, hospitals, and homes carefully restudy their policies and practices as they relate to race, making certain that these policies and practices are Christian."[13]

Public school integration proceeded slowly, plagued by tokenism. The NAACP reported that as of May 1955, "Nearly 250,000 Negro and white children were attending classes peaceably together in 500 elementary and secondary schools which until last year had been for the exclusive use of boys and girls of one race or the other."[14] According to the Department of Christian Social Relations the process needed to be speeded up and Methodist women were not to relax their efforts to see that integration was accomplished. Rather than providing a master plan for school integration, the Department of Christian Social Relations trained local leaders to run workshops to address specific local situations.[15] The Woman's Division expressed concern that in the process of integrating schools, competent black teachers might lose their jobs, and in fact that was already happening. The department urged Methodist women to "get to know them and discuss ways of preventing loss to the community of valuable skills."[16]

In many communities church people played an inconspicuous but important role, carrying out the detail jobs, committee meetings and community dialogues essential to school integration. Methodist women participated in community plans that successfully integrated public schools in Oak Ridge, Tennessee, "without undue disturbance."[17] When Clinton, Tennessee, experienced racial violence, the members of the WSCS of Clinton Memorial Methodist Church wrote to the black members of a neighboring

Methodist Church, expressing their regret over the racial incidents and requesting that both groups covenant to pray for the restoration of peace in the community. While the public schools were desegregating, the Clinton Memorial Woman's Society ratified the Charter of Racial Policies, publicly committing themselves to work for the removal of racial barriers in their community.

In Nashville, the interracial Human Rights Council had been formed about four years earlier to study school integration. When tensions reached their peak over school integration, the United Church Women, of which Methodist women were a part, declared their support for the school board's plan for desegregation.

Mrs. J. S. VanWinkle of Danville, Kentucky, attributed the success of local community meetings of interracial groups to the guidance of the Lincoln Leadership School's interracial workshops, held every summer since 1951 at Lincoln University in Pennsylvania. The Woman's Division had contributed money to these workshops and had provided leaders and students. Integrated prayer groups in Danville had grown and become small discussion groups relating to community problems. Interracial Bible study groups met in various churches during 1957. The first black students entered Danville High School in 1956 and three of them graduated with the class of 1957. "The prayer groups, discussion periods, and the fellowship hours brought about understanding between the Negroes and the Whites. This helped to accomplish integration of the Danville High School without fears or misunderstandings."[18]

Similar stories can be recounted for numerous Southern towns that never made the news because desegregation came about without racial violence. Shelbyville, Kentucky, integrated its first-grade classes without incident. The Methodist woman who reported this success felt that the presence of Christian teachers and a Christian principal made the difference, and that they may have been influenced by the Civic Church Woman's Group that had been meeting in Shelbyville for many years. A foundation of Christian understanding and attitudes had been laid by this interracial, ecumenical group who had taken it upon themselves to prepare Shelbyville's citizens for school integration. In hundreds of towns across the South, foundations for community interracial relations had been laid by Methodist women in the three previous decades.[19]

In 1956 in Kentucky, before schools integrated in their community, the white members of the Methodist Youth Fellowship from Flemingsburg

Methodist Church invited their black counterparts from Strawberry Methodist Church to attend a regular Sunday evening meeting. The same white students helped welcome their black friends into the formerly all-white high school in ways that helped ease their adjustment. Methodist women counseled the youth in these choices.[20]

Methodist women influenced federal policies with letter-writing campaigns that lobbied congressional representatives to vote for federal aid to education distributed with the condition that funds be withheld from schools that refused to admit minority students.

In 1959, school closures made mockery of the system of free public education. Entire city school systems closed and private schools for fee-paying students opened to circumvent forced school integration. The Woman's Division reminded Methodist women that parents who supported closure of school systems surrendered to others their voice in the free public education of their community's children. The Department of Christian Social Relations appealed to parents and citizens to support the basic right of children to education so that the public school system could be saved.[21]

In 1953 when the possibility of federal requirements for the integration of public schools drew near, people reconsidered the implications of where they lived. If public schools were integrated, children would be sent to the nearest school. Suddenly the new way to avoid integration was clear: towns could be delineated so that blacks would live in some areas and whites would live in other areas. Public schools would be open to all races, but if they were also neighborhood schools, only students from that area would attend that school, and school boundaries could be drawn to follow the color line. What had existed before in a general way as "black neighborhoods" and "white neighborhoods" became more clearly defined and more rigidly entrenched with social threats attendant on anyone who dared to defy the new convention.

Methodist women launched their campaign for open housing in 1957. They lobbied for an end to discrimination in federal housing policies, loan policies, urban renewal programs, and restrictive housing covenants.[22] During a national housing shortage they advocated federal programs to provide low and middle-income housing and berated the fact that discrimination in jobs and housing forced blacks to live in some of the nation's worst slums.[23] The Woman's Division set as its goal for the nation "a decent home and suitable living environment" for every family, regardless of color, race, national origin, or religion, to the end that segregation would exist neither by law nor by custom.[24] The Department of Christian Social Relations asserted the priority of housing:

> Housing is, in the opinion of many who have studied the subject, the keystone on which the foundation of the future community pattern will be built. If our housing pattern follows the trends now indicated, the result may well be a complex of ghettoes . . . where each racial or cultural group of citizens will live in more or less self-contained communities with great tensions appearing every time expanding population concentration brings their established borders into conflict.[25]

School integration could not be fully completed or successful without a commitment to open and integrated housing. Methodist women found it easier to approach discrimination in housing by supporting changes in federal laws than by taking specific steps to integrate local neighborhoods. Although they sponsored integrated consultations to deal with tensions over school integration and housing, and recognized the inseparability of the two issues, their willingness to make a commitment to integrate local public schools exceeded their commitment to integrate local housing and foreshadowed a divergence in national emphasis on these two significant steps in the advancement of human rights.

NOTES

1. *Annual Report of the Woman's Division of Christian Service of the Board of Missions of The Methodist Church*, January 19, 1953, pp. 31-32.
2. *Annual Report*, January 16, 1954, p. 54.
3. Murial Day claimed that Scarritt College in Nashville and the National College for Christian Workers in Kansas City had found ways to have interracial student bodies before the law was interpreted that way. Murial Day, "Learning to Live Together . . . another article on the home mission theme for 1957-1958 'Christ, the Church, and Race,' " *The Methodist Woman* (April 1957): 13.
4. Thelma Stevens and Margaret R. Bender, "Information and Action." *The Methodist Woman* (January, 1954): 25.
5. *Annual Report*, January 16, 1954, p. 54.
6. Southern Regional Council, "The Schools and the Courts," cited in " 'Brotherhood' Is a Local Responsibility," *The Methodist Woman* (February, 1954): 23.
7. The resolution read: "We affirm anew our determination to work with greater urgency to eliminate segregation from every part of our community and national life and from the organization and practice of our own church and its agencies and programs. We rejoice that the highest tribunal of justice in this

land, the Supreme Court of the United States, proclaimed on May 17, 1954, that segregation in public education anywhere is an infringement of the Constitution and a violation of the Fourteenth Amendment. We accept our full Christian responsibility to work through church and community channels to speed the process of transition from segregated schools to a new pattern of justice and freedom." "Affirmations of the Assembly," *The Methodist Woman* (July-August, 1954): 43.

8. Alice Knotts, ed., "Thelma Stevens' 'Thorns that Fester': An Oral Biography and Interview," December 5-7, 1983, pp. 127-28. A transcript of this interview is located at the Women's Division of the General Board of Global Ministries of The United Methodist Church, New York City.

9. Executive Committee Meeting, *Annual Report*, April 26, 1955, pp. 16-17.

10. Executive Committee Meeting, *Annual Report*, September, 1954, pp. 76-77.

11. "Progress in Interracial Practices," *The Methodist Woman* (November, 1954): 14.

12. Day, "Learning to Live Together," p. 13.

13. Executive Committee Meeting, *Annual Report*, September, 1955, p. 29.

14. "Five Years' Progress in Meeting the Needs of Children and Youth," *The Methodist Woman* (November, 1955): 27, citing *Southern School News*, Southern Education Reporting Service.

15. [Thelma Stevens], "Everyone Has the Right," *The Methodist Woman* (February, 1957): 28-29.

16. "Five Years' Progress," p. 28.

17. Mrs. Robert L. Wilcox, "Progress in School Integration As Seen by Four Jurisdiction Secretaries, Southeastern Jurisdiction," *The Methodist Woman* (February, 1958): 28.

18. Ibid., p. 29.

19. Alice Knotts, "Race Relations in the 1920s: A Challenge to Southern Methodist Women," *Methodist History* (July, 1988): 199-212.

20. Wilcox, "Progress in School Integration," p. 28.

21. "After the Tenth Anniversary," *The Methodist Woman* (February, 1959): 27.

22. *The Methodist Woman* (November, 1957): 24; Journal, *Annual Report*, January, 1958, p. 71; Executive Committee Meeting, September 1958, pp. 50-51.

23. "Housing for the Nation's Families," *The Methodist Woman* (May, 1958): 45, citing the Report of the Governor of Pennsylvania's Committee on Housing.

24. Journal, *Annual Report*, January 1959, p. 93.

25. "Guide for a Workshop on Housing," *The Methodist Woman* (April, 1959): 29.

"And the Pressure Never Let Up": Black Women, White Women, and the Boston YWCA, 1918-1948

SHARLENE VOOGD COCHRANE

The Boston YWCA, the first in the United States, was founded in 1866. As the organization celebrated its seventy-fifth anniversary in 1941, Lucy Miller Mitchell became the first black woman elected to the Board of Directors. Serving on the board for seven years, Mitchell was a trailblazer in the efforts of both black and white women to diversify the YWCA, making its practices consistent with its stated philosophy and policies.

Recent research in the Boston YWCA archives, completed as part of the development of the YWCA's 120th anniversary exhibit, "Empowering Women," has uncovered descriptions of Boston women working to diversify the organization. The information includes reports of the Student YWCA Interrace Committee from 1924 to 1944, and a 1944 report of the Boston YWCA summarizing interracial practices since 1920.

These archival discoveries suggest that the Boston YWCA moved toward ethnic and racial diversity. Although steady, this movement proceeded slowly and needed constant prodding, goals taking years to implement. Prodding and pressure came from both black and white women at every level of the

YWCA—the National Office, the students, and women within and outside of the Boston organization. Through these women, "the pressure never let up"—that is, they kept issues alive, raised points at every opportunity, and set a context for and educated others to see the connections or disparity among YWCA rhetoric, ideals and practices.[1]

When Lucy Miller Mitchell moved to Boston in the 1920s, the black community made up two percent of the city's population, as it had consistently for several decades. During the nineteenth century, blacks had clustered on the north slope of Beacon Hill, near the African Meeting House, built in 1806. Overcrowding and the construction of tenements for Italian and Jewish immigrants led blacks to move out, first to the South End and then to Roxbury. By 1920, a steady stream of blacks from the South and the West Indies arrived. Communities established organizations serving residents' needs, including churches of several denominations and settlement houses, such as the Robert Gould Shaw House in Roxbury and the Harriet Tubman House in the South End.

In 1920, only a few black women participated in YWCA programs or activities. The first YWCA had been organized by upper-class women to guide and guard New England's single, rural women coming to the city to work in the years immediately following the Civil War. The YWCA provided a safe, inexpensive place to live, as well as assistance in finding work, for primarily Protestant, white women. The founders expected residents to worship daily, exhibit upright moral character, and follow the rules of their new "home." The first housemother clearly stated her expectations: "The Superintendent would be grateful to the ladies connected with the Association if they would discourage as much as possible the attempt made by Irish Roman Catholic girls to frequent the rooms in search of employment—the object of this organization being to benefit principally our New England girls over whom we can exert a lasting influence."[2]

Black women were served even less than the Irish within the YWCA. Occasionally a black woman would be allowed to stay for a day or two at the residence, until "more appropriate" lodging could be found with a black family. A few black women took part in clubs or training programs. Anna Wade Richardson, for example, was part of the Bible Study group at the Berkeley residence in the 1880s. She left Boston to start a school in Marshallville, Georgia, which was partially funded for over a decade by her friends at the Boston YWCA. Such events and individuals, however, were rare.[3]

By the 1920s, the YWCA had changed considerably. It had become a membership organization, shifting its focus from upper-class directors helping young working women to a broader spectrum of women designing and carrying out programs for themselves. A growing outreach effort accompanied this shift, expanding membership to younger girls, mothers, older women, and immigrants. The Boston YWCA joined the National YWCA in 1912, which led to a broader interpretation of its policies. New leadership began to come from the women using and working within the YWCA, while national conventions and personnel brought a wider view to the local organization.

Lucy Miller grew up in Florida, attending Mary McLeod Bethune's school in Daytona Beach. Her family first came to Boston in 1916, when her brothers attended Northeastern University. She lived one block from the Harriet Tubman House in the South End, where most of the black families in that area of brownstone townhouses rented out part of their home to black students, who were not allowed in any of Boston's college dormitories. Miller returned South to school, influenced by her first National YWCA conference, which she attended as a high school graduate. Juliet Derricott, a national secretary at the conference for black women convened in Atlanta, Georgia, convinced Miller to attend her own alma mater, Talladega College in Alabama. After graduating from college and returning to Bethune's school to teach for one year, newly married Lucy Miller Mitchell moved to Boston in 1924.

Mitchell raised two children, giving many talks during these years at churches, urging support for black church-related colleges, such as Talladega. After volunteering at her own children's schools, she studied education at Abigail Eliot's school and received a Master's Degree in the new field of early childhood education from Boston University in 1935. She then developed the model nursery school at Robert Gould Shaw House and became a respected professional educator. Mitchell later led efforts to improve and license day care and consulted for the national Head Start program.

While Mitchell was settling into her life in Boston, the YWCA faced two important issues: whether to support the development of a black branch of the organization, and establishing clear and fair policies for the YWCA in housing and facilities use.

The name most associated with efforts in the 1920s to encourage racial diversity within the YWCA was Mrs. Everett O. Fisk. Fisk lived in the wealthy suburb of Brookline, and served as education chair and vice president throughout the decade. Little information is available about her, although her efforts to raise issues are well-documented. In 1921, she brought a member of the Urban League to the board to speak about "the colored girl problem." The representative, Mrs. Barney, urged the board to make specific its position regarding black women living in the YWCA residence. Fisk met with other members of the Urban League and pushed the Council of Social Agencies to call a meeting of the various social institutions in the city. She chaired a conference of the association for all social agencies to consider the welfare of young black women. Her committee continued to meet, again reporting that many people in the community wanted a more open housing policy.[4]

The YWCA board failed to make its own residential policy clear and welcoming. It also did not support an effort to establish a residence specifically for black women. In 1925, Victoria Saunders, a black social worker, approached the board seeking support to use a building in the South End for club rooms and overnight lodging, with the hope of becoming a branch of the YWCA. The YWCA leadership discussed this request with Eva D. Bowles, a black member of the national staff serving as Administrator of Colored Work in Cities. By this time, Saunders hoped to establish a day nursery, rooms for twenty-five young women, club rooms, and a food service. She tried to purchase furniture from the YWCA residence to help get it started. A letter from Bowles suggests that she was not supportive of the project, saying that groups wishing to duplicate YWCA programs and services seldom realized the effort and financial processes involved. She suggested to the Boston group that their YWCA should be interracial, admitting any girl to any program on her merits, not developing programs according to race. She added that the time might not be right to give this project the time and energy necessary to be of the highest quality, since the YWCA was in the midst of a major building campaign. Shortly after receiving this letter, the Boston board declined to assist in establishing this residence.[5]

Saunders went ahead anyway, moving into 511 Columbus Avenue, a five-story building with a cafeteria in the basement, club space, and rooms for girls. The project was not mentioned again in the YWCA reports, and apparently it did not exist for very long. Mitchell reported at the time of the 1944 report that Victoria Saunders never had much of a following among the black community and the project "might not have prospered even if we had given her the aid she requested." Mitchell saw this episode as important not because of the end of the request, but because it is characteristic of the Association's ambivalent attitudes during those years toward efforts of blacks to work with the YWCA.[6]

It is worth noting that at exactly this time, the black community was facing another issue around the question of supporting segregated institutions or working to integrate predominantly white ones. In this case, a black hospital wishing to expand was fought very hard by radical black newspaper publisher William Monroe Trotter, in a controversial effort that led to the closing of the hospital and the eventual integration of Boston City Hospital. This was also the time during which Trotter and the student YWCA (there is no indication in the records that they were working together) both tried to move Boston hospitals to allow black women to train as nurses.[7]

In 1929, the Boston YWCA opened its new facility, a large modern complex still in use today, on Clarendon Street at the edge of the South End, about half a mile from the center of the black community. When the new building was about to open, the student YWCA, which planned to use meeting rooms there, met with city YWCA representatives to assist in "promoting right race relations" through the use of its facilities. Chairpersons and secretaries of the city departments and the president and executive secretary of the Student Board met to establish policies. The group confirmed a general policy conforming to the national policy—absolutely no discrimination in the use of dining room, cafeteria, Pioneer residence, and other facilities and programs. A committee of black and white members would consider together any cases of discrimination arising outside this general statement.[8]

One of the most dramatic elements of the new structure was a swimming pool built in an innovative technique of suspending the pool from the fifth-story floor. The pool was an immediate success, used by the many clubs within the YWCA and open to the community. The swimming pool was an exception to the "no discrimination" agreement, and the planning group decided policy regarding its use would be made later. Apparently even this well-meaning group could not decide on a suitable policy. For some years the pool was available to black women as members of specific clubs and groups within the YWCA programs. But it was not open to black women during open swim times, and black groups from outside the YWCA, such as clubs from Robert Gould Shaw, had to have special permission to use the pool.

Throughout the 1920s and 30s, as the City YWCA slowly confronted its own racism and clarified its policies, the Student YWCA was taking much stronger action to diversify itself and affect Boston-area colleges' racial practices. With more than a dozen institutions of higher learning in and around Boston, the potential existed for a student organization to affect large numbers of people. Women at several schools were involved: Simmons, the Practical Arts and Letters College and the College of Liberal Arts of Boston University, and Sargent College. Following the national student convention in 1923, several women decided to find a way of better understanding one another and racial issues in Boston. Their efforts included regular discussions, research about racial practices and attitudes on campuses and in the city, and organized action.

The group initially received help from Constance Ridley, a secretary at Robert Gould Shaw House. She assisted the women in organizing a first meeting of black and white students. "In the first discussions there was considerable groping about in an endeavor to become familiar with the general aspects of the problem, but by autumn the group seemed eager to concentrate upon a definite line of study for the year and to give honest thought and preparation to the meetings."[9]

By the fall of 1925, with growing talk and trust, the group expanded to twelve black and twelve white members, with a program of monthly meetings. Each meeting included discussion, often based on readings, and a program "revealing the cultural contributions of the modern Negro." The group received a boost the following year when two members of the National Conference of Settlements at Cleveland, Ohio, said that "the Boston Discussion Group had made the greatest advance of any in the country in promoting right race relations."[10]

The group grew in membership and developed more activist tactics. Monthly open meetings were held, in which speakers and performers were invited to share information and cultural experiences. Their initial research efforts focused on finding out about racial practices on their own campuses and trying to bring black and white students together in small group discussions.

Three research committees studied racial problems and issues throughout the city and attempted to influence their resolution. The Education Committee assembled black and white representatives from fourteen local schools and colleges, who collected information, made reports, and organized discussion groups of white and black students on their respective campuses.

At the time there were no nursing schools or hospitals accepting black women for nurses' training. The Interrace Committee set about to change this policy, and met, quietly and without publicity, with doctors, hospital superintendents and trustees. In 1929, after much effort, two young women were admitted to the Nurses Training Course at Boston City Hospital.

Two committees researched conditions in industry and business. The Industry Initiative collaborated with efforts of the Boston Urban League to analyze and publicize the job situation for black men and women. The Urban League placed about one thousand of five thousand applicants for jobs, mostly in domestic service. Documentation was collected on the difficulties of blacks in obtaining work in clerical positions and the Boston Elevated, as well as the wage discrimination for black women once they received positions. Students teamed up to study businesses' racial practices. Black women would attempt to eat at certain lunch counters or use facilities at a store. Their experiences were reported to the study group, and white members would interview business leaders. Records were kept of ways the practices did not match the spoken policies: "The report of practices was seldom wholly praiseworthy."[11]

The Student YWCA Interrace Committee continued its work until 1944, settling into a routine of monthly meetings with speakers, widening their focus to consider all races and minority concerns. The large group continued to support smaller discussion groups on Boston area campuses. Its greatest impact appears to have been between 1925 and 1930, however. According to the 1944 report, its biggest problem was the short life span of each college generation. Just when members of the group were educated and ready to make an impact, they would graduate and the process would have to begin again. A further difficulty was evaluating their work, since the committee's influence on students in their later years was not known.

Despite these problems, members of the early Interrace Committee were real pioneers, stepping into untried territory by talking and working together. Two women were most involved in this student committee's work. Constance Ridley Heslip, a black woman who helped the committee to get organized, continued to support the group through Robert Gould Shaw House and the National Conference of Settlement Workers. Helen Morton, a long-time volunteer and secretary of the Interrace Committee, went on to become executive secretary of the Cambridge, Massachusetts, YWCA. The Student YWCA began its efforts not only to diversify, but also actively to seek better relations throughout Boston's colleges and the larger community.

Slowly, more black women became involved in YWCA programs and activities. Through "eternal vigilance and . . . never letting any situation reach a crisis," discriminatory actions were discouraged and dealt with (outside of the pool policy), and gradually a small number of blacks became more involved in programs. However, some black women who were very active in the black community did not support the YWCA because their experience found the association "prejudiced and discriminatory."[12]

By 1937, this lack of service to the black community was of increasing concern and the board requested that the Program Committee make a study of blacks and the YWCA. The study was the most thorough ever undertaken by the Boston Association. It included investigation of every group connected with the YWCA, an inquiry into recreational facilities in the community, and a week-long visit by Isobel Lawson, a black woman serving as secretary of the National Services Division. She interviewed key persons in the city and held meetings with various groups within the local YWCA. The Program Committee made its report in 1939. It showed that sixty-four black women participated in programs, half under the age of seventeen and half between ages seventeen and thirty-five. Nearly all the women were in clubs, all were single, and all lived in Boston or Roxbury. The recommendations were clear: the YWCA was still seen as discriminatory, and more active messages had to get out to the community. Specific measures were encouraged, such as having black women from the community serve on the board and inviting black volunteers to come to club meetings to talk about subjects other than race. As part of the recommendations from this report, the pool was finally declared open to all women. While the report sounded far-reaching, in fact its recommendations were not publicized, and no clear messages were immediately sent to the nearby black community.[13]

In 1940, however, Sara Conyers, a black member of one of the Industrial Clubs, was appointed to the board for a short period, representing that group of working women members. The following year, the board invited a black community leader, Lucy Miller Mitchell, to run for board office. Mitchell was by then directing the nursery program at the Robert Gould Shaw House and was a respected professional in the developing area of nursery and day care education. Following her election to the YWCA board, she served for seven years, chairing the Public Affairs Committee.

Mitchell recalls that even though policies in general had been agreed on by the board to welcome blacks to all the programs, a huge job remained to encourage racial mixing of club groups, craft groups, and gym programs. The process of changing these practices and of making the pool truly available to blacks involved constant work, the process being "slow but steady, and the pressure never let up." Mitchell was constantly involved with interpreting the YWCA to the community, through the work of the Public Affairs Committee. She is understated about her achievements during this time, saying her activities were "not spectacular, and received no publicity, but were meaningful and had impact on community attitudes and practices." The accomplishment she values most is that the pool was completely integrated by the time she left office in 1948.[14]

Two factors played a role in this change. First, the national organization, in pushing the local YWCAs to become more inclusive, constantly provided support and justification to those in the local association who wished to move in that direction. They could use the national policy to bolster their arguments. Both the student and city YWCAs responded to stimulation from the national leadership. Conventions and visits by national secretaries constantly pushed the local organizations for response. In 1923, the student group organized the first black-white study group in Boston, following a national convention attended by several Boston Student YWCA representatives. Visits from the national leadership urged the city group along throughout the 1920s and 30s, and the National Convention of 1940, urging local groups to study their own interracial practices, led the Boston YWCA finally to clarify and expand their local policies and compile a report documenting their struggles. Movement on the local level appears to be closely related to activities of the National Association.

The second force was the moral power of the argument that the YWCA was a Christian organization, and that Christian principles of equality, love for all, the oneness of all under Christ were compelling reasons for action. As Mitchell said, "As one of the most influential Christian bodies in the country, both at the student and community level, there wouldn't be any other stand that the organization could take other than to be in the forefront of eradicating racism in this country." While this might be true, the argument needed to be made constantly and coherently throughout the board and membership meetings, and women within the YWCA, through their constant talk, continued to build the context for understanding this moral argument.[15]

The strategy that seemed to propel the YWCA toward the inclusive policy finally accepted was the application of constant pressure. When asked how pressure was applied during this period to change the YWCA, Mitchell smiled. "We just kept talking," she says. "At every meeting we would raise issues, we kept bringing them up, and presenting the rationale and reasonableness and moral power of our arguments. Eventually our position prevailed."[16]

By 1948, the Boston YWCA was a fully integrated organization, both on paper and in its actual policies, offering services to all Boston women. This inclusiveness came about in a slow, steady way from its founding in 1866, with the most visible changes occurring after 1918. Women who brought about these changes worked on both the national and local levels, as students, working women, YWCA members, staff and administrators. The pioneering student leaders, like Constance Ridley Heslip and Helen Morton, worked to understand and educate others within Boston's colleges. Fisk kept the issues alive in the city YWCA in the 1920s, and Lucy Miller Mitchell kept talking and putting on the pressure in the 1940s. Each of these women faced a difficult challenge, each of them kept talking, setting every decision within a moral context, making connections between the policies and practices of the YWCA, confronting the disparities, educating the organization's leaders and members, and keeping the pressure on for a diverse, welcoming, and just YWCA.

NOTES

1. Lucy Miller Mitchell, *Black Women Oral History Project*, Radcliffe College, Schlesinger Library, 1987, p. 49.
2. YWCA, *Board Records*, 1867. Thousands of Irish immigrants came to Boston after 1845 and young Irish women needed the kinds of residential and employment support offered by the YWCA. While many native Bostonians agreed with the superintendent, many Irish leaders discouraged their young women from the organization because of its requirement that the women follow daily Protestant worship.
3. YWCA, *Annual Report*, 1880-90.
4. "Chronological History of Interracial Practices, Boston Young Women's Christian Association, 1918-1944," pp. 2-4.
5. *Ibid.*, pp. 4-6.
6. *Ibid.*, p. 4.
7. "William Monroe Trotter, One-Man Protester," slide-tape, Institute for Boston Studies, 1985.
8. "The History of the Interrace Committee which was Sponsored by the Student Y.W.C.A., Boston, Massachusetts, 1924-1944," p. 3.
9. *Ibid.*, p. 1.
10. *Ibid.*

11. *Ibid.*, pp. 2-3.

12. Melnea Cass, *Black Women Oral History Project*, p. 87. Cass returned to the YWCA as an older woman, and the Clarendon Street building now bears her name. The 1944 history supported Cass's view: "The YWCA from 1920 made slow but steady progress in race relations . . . the negroes have at times had just cause to doubt our sincerity . . . experiences did not add to their confidence in us as a Christian organization." "Summary of Chronological History," p. 9.

13. "Summary of Chronological History," pp. 5-6.

14. Mitchell, *Black Women Oral History Project*, pp. 48-52; personal interview, August 1988.

15. Mitchell, *Black Women Oral History Project*, pp. 48-52.

16. Mitchell, interview.

The Contributors

Allida M. Black is a doctoral candidate in American History at The George Washington University and an adjunct instructor of history and government at Dutchess Community College. She is the author of "Championing a Champion: Eleanor Roosevelt and the Marion Anderson Freedom Concert," (*Presidential Studies*, August 1990). Her dissertation examines Eleanor Roosevelt's role in shaping the civil rights and civil liberties stance of the liberal wing of the national Democratic party.

Annette K. Brock is Head of the Department of Social and Behavioral Sciences at Savannah State College, Savannah Georgia. She received her Ph.D. from the University of South Carolina, her M. Ed. from Duke and her M.S. from Savannah State College and has also studied at the University of North Carolina at Chapel Hill and Harvard. She has done research in Afro-American culture in the Low country of Georgia and South Carolina.

Mary Fair Burks received her B.A. from Alabama State University, her M.A. from the University of Michigan, and her Ed.D. from Columbia University. She has also studied at the Sorbonne, Oxford University, Harvard University, Yale University and the University of Indiana. Her dissertation was entitled *A Survey of Black Literary Magazines in the United States, 1859-1940* and she has published widely in such journals as *The Western Journal of Black Studies* and *Black Literature Forum*. Her most recent teaching position was at the University of Maryland at Princess Anne.

Broadus N. Butler has served in a range of administrative, scholarly, and civic positions, including Graduate Administrator of Wayne State University College of Liberal Arts, Assistant to the United States Commissioner of Education, President of Dillard University, Director of Leadership Development in Higher Education of the American Council of Education, President of the Robert R. Moton Center for Independent Studies and Chairman of the International Affairs Committee of the National Board of the NAACP. Most recently he was an Ely Lilly Foundation Visiting Scholar, a John D. and Catherine T. MacArthur Foundation United Negro College Fund Distinguished Scholar-at-Large and a Director of Archives of the Martin Luther King, Jr., Center for Nonviolent Social Change.

Sharlene Voogd Cochrane received her B.A. from Hastings College, her M.A. in American Studies from New York University and her Ph.D. in American History from Boston College. She teaches history and American Studies at Lesley College in programs for adults. She is the editor of *Boston's History: A Resource Book*. Her research focuses on the relationships between individuals and institutions in American culture.

Vicki L. Crawford, an Assistant Professor in the Department of English at Morehouse College, is currently participating in a post-doctoral fellowship program at the University of North Carolina. She is completing a book on rural black women in the Mississippi civil rights movement.

Marymal Dryden is Unit Head for Public Service, Division of Continuing Education, Georgia State University. She was the director of the conference at which these papers were presented. A former Associate Professor of Social Work at the Atlanta University School of Social Work, she received her B.A. from Spelman College and her M.S.W. from Atlanta University.

Dr. Jacqueline Grant is an Associate Professor of Systematic Theology at the Interdenominational Theological Center in Atlanta. She is the author of *White Women's Christ and Black Women's Jesus* (Scholars Press, 1989). Her articles include "Black Theology and the Black Woman," "Black Theological Education: Dilemma and Deliverance," and "Womanist Theology: Black Women's Religious Experience As a Source for Doing Theology."

Alice G. Knotts is Program Coordinator for the Institute for Interfaith Studies of the Center for Judaic Studies at the University of Denver. She holds a B.A. degree from the University of Puget Sound, a B. Div. from Drew Theological School, a M.S. from the University of Oregon, and a Ph.D. from The Iliff School of Theology and the University of Denver. Her dissertation is entitled *Bound by the Spirit, Found on the Journey: The*

Methodist Women's Campaign for Southern Civil Rights, 1940-1968. She is national co-president of the Methodist Federation for Social Action.

Donna Langston is an Assistant Professor of Women's Studies at Mankato State University in Mankato, Minnesota. She received her B.A. and M.A. from Western Washington College and her Ph.D. from the University of Washington. Her dissertation was entitled *Philosophies of Feminism.* She has published a number of articles in such periodicals as *Northwest Passage* and *Nature, Society and Thought.* Her poetry has appeared in several anthologies and numerous magazines.

Mamie E. Locke is an Associate Professor of Political Science at Hampton College. She received her B.A. from Tougaloo College, and her M.A. and Ph.D. from Atlanta University. She was a delegate to the Virginia State Democratic Convention in 1984 and her publications include "Outsiders in Insider Politics: Black Women and the American Political System," in *An American Government Reader* (Kendall Hunt Publishers, 1987).

Grace Jordan McFadden is an Associate Professor of History at the University of South Carolina where she is director of Afro-American Studies. She received her B.A. from California State University at Sacramento, her M.A. from the Catholic University of America and her Ph.D. from Union Graduate School in African-American History. She is the author and executive producer of "Quest for Human Rights: The Oral Recollections of Black South Carolinians."

Carol Mueller is an Assistant Professor at Arizona State University-West in Phoenix. She received her B.A. from the University of California, Berkeley, her M.A. from Rutgers University, and her Ph.D. in Sociology from Cornell University. She is the co-editor of *The Women's Movements in the United States and Western Europe: Feminist Consciousness, Political Opportunity and Public Policy* (Temple University Press) and editor of *The Politics of the Gender Gap: The Social Construction of Political Influence* (Sage). Her articles have been published in such journals as *Public Opinion Quarterly, Social Forces,* and *Women and Politics.*

Clarissa Myrick-Harris is an Assistant Professor in the School of Journalism at the University of Georgia. She received her B.A. from Moris Brown

College, her M.A. from The Ohio State University, and her Ph.D. from Emory University. Her dissertation is entitled *Mirror of the Movement: The History of the Free Southern Theater as a Microcosm of the Civil Rights and Black Power Movements, 1963-1978.* She directed Emory University's Colloquium "Black World People: Understanding Each Other Through Literature" (March 1983).

Sandra B. Oldendorf holds a doctorate in curriculum and instruction from the University of Kentucky. She has taught in the Illinois Public School, at Berea College and at Western Carolina University. Beginning in August 1990, she will be an Assistant Professor of Education at Western Montana College at Dillon.

Charles Payne an is Associate Professor of African-American studies, sociology and urban affairs at Northwestern University. Primarily interested in social change, social inequality and Afro-American culture, he is the author of a book on urban schooling *Getting What We Ask For* (Greenwood, 1984) and is currently completing a book on local participation in the civil rights movement in Mississippi.

Bernice Johnson Reagon, Ph.D., is a curator in the Division of Community Life at the Smithsonian Institution, National Museum of American History and is the recipient of a MacArthur Fellowship (1989-1994). She is a specialist in African-American oral, performance and protest traditions and has been in the forefront of efforts to advance the study and understanding of African-American culture and legacy. She was a member of the original SNCC Freedom Singers and is founder and artistic director of Sweet Honey in the Rock, an internationally acclaimed vocal ensemble of African-American women singers. In addition to numerous articles, her publications include, *Voices of the Civil Rights Movement: Black American Freedom Songs, 1960-1965* (a three-record collection), *Black People and Their Culture: Selected Writings from the African Diaspora* (1976), and *Compositions One: The Original Compositions and Arrangements of Bernice Johnson Reagon* (1986).

Jacqueline Anne Rouse is an Associate Professor at Morehouse College and an Assistant Editor of the *Journal of Negro History*. She is the author of *Lugenia Burns Hope: Black Southern Reformer* (University of Georgia Press, 1989).

Anne Standley is a Ph.D. candidate in history at Yale University.

Melissa Walker is chairperson and Associate Professor of English at Mercer University, Atlanta, where she teaches African-American literature, women's studies, and contemporary fiction. She is the author of *Writing Research Papers: A Norton Guide* (3rd edition, forthcoming 1991) and *Down from the Mountaintop: African-American Women's Novels in the Wake of the Civil Rights Movement* to be published by Yale University Press in the Spring of 1991.

Barbara A. Woods is an Assistant Professor at Southern College of Technology and is presently a post-doctoral fellow at the Duke/University of North Carolina, Chapel Hill Center for Research on Women. Her articles include one on the origins of the South Carolina Conference of the NAACP. She is completing a major book on Modjeska Simkins.

Index